The Seven Fatal Management SINS

Understanding and Avoiding Managerial Malpractice

The Seven Fatal Management SINS

Understanding and Avoiding Managerial Malpractice

John W. Collis, M.B.A., J.D., Ph.D.

S_L^t

St. Lucie Press
Boca Raton, Florida

Library of Congress Cataloging-in-Publication Data

Catalog information may be obtained from the Library of Congress

© 1998 by CRC Press LLC
St. Lucie Press is an imprint of CRC Press LLC

No claim to original U.S. Government works
International Standard Book Number 1-57444-015-2
Printed in the United States of America 1 2 3 4 5 6 7 8 9 0
Printed on acid-free paper

*Dedicated to
my wife, Helen*

Farcus

by David Waisglass
Gordon Coulthart

"Forgive me, Father, for I have mismanaged."

Table of Contents

IV. THE ROAD TO GREATNESS:
A SUMMATION, NOT A CLOSING ARGUMENT

Preface

Much has been written about organizations in general; however, when one searches for current collective information concerning the *performance* of those who manage them, very little research is available. Even though it may be common knowledge that managers influence all phases of our modern organizations and attempt to guide them toward accomplishing their goals, we still lack answers to important questions regarding the makeup of managers—in particular about managerial competency. How do they *perform* in their role as managers? How well are they doing their jobs? Are our organizations being managed by the best and the brightest? Who rises to the top and how do they get there? Is the word to describe the norm regarding organizational performance "excellence," or is it "mediocrity"? Has there been a failure by managers to manage? What are the obstacles to effective management? Can they be eliminated?

Are today's managers more interested in managing their careers or in managing their organizations? Are they using the "team player" approach to get to the top? Are they preparing their organizations to meet the challenges of the future, or are they too preoccupied in keeping up with the problems at hand? Are many corporations today in trouble because of mismanagement? Are managers properly prepared for their jobs? Is there such a thing as the "right" training for managers? How important is formal education in preparing managers to manage organizations? What makes managers tick? Why are there poor managers—what managerial sins do managers commit? Which ones are fatal?

Do managers have clear or fuzzy visions of their organizations' goals? Do they see the entire spectrum, or are they myopically focused? Do they believe that the bottom line is the "real" and only measure of successful performance? How do they define success? Are they committed to the status quo? Are they inclined to use the quick and/or the simplistic fix to solve organizational problems? Are they just shuffling people or building stable organizations? Is the organizational norm to "look good" at any expense? Do managers view employees as people or as machines to be utilized? Do they regard employees' salaries as expenses or as investments? Is corporate restructuring vision led or problem driven? Do managers really understand the difference between downsizing and rightsizing? Are they truly embracing the concept of total quality management?

Do they distribute corporate profits equitably? Are managerial compensation packages in line with those for the rest of the organization's stakeholders? Is there something wrong with the principle that the wealth of the organization should be proportionately shared and enjoyed by those who have helped make it happen? Do managerial decisions come from the head, the heart, or both? What word can be used to describe how organizations are generally being managed today—excellent, good, poor, or negligent? To whom are managers accountable? Who "really" monitors the managers? Should managers be required to hold press conferences? Should corporations be required to have a public director on their boards? Where applicable, should the president of the union be a member of the board of directors? Should a manager's term in office be limited and replaced by a revolving contract?

The purpose of this book is to examine these and a number of other delicate, sensitive, complex, and important issues. Through extensive interviews and the use of a nationwide comprehensive survey involving thousands of individuals knowledgeable about the business community, coupled with in-depth research of the subject matter and knowledge drawn from the author's expertise in this area, the book provides valuable and insightful information regarding this important yet much neglected area. The survey was carefully structured to help gather the necessary information to accurately assess managerial competency—managerial performance—from various aspects. The survey was sent to:

- Presidents and/or CEOs of Fortune 500 companies
- Presidents and/or CEOs and senior managers picked randomly from companies other than the Fortune 500
- Directors of various corporate boards
- Union presidents
- Business news editors representing the media
- College and university business school deans (hereinafter referred to as university business deans)

- College and university business professors teaching business policy courses at either/or the graduate and undergraduate levels (hereinafter referred to as university business professors)

The responses have been tabulated and are reported, along with an analysis. The results are both interesting and informative in understanding the makeup of managers.

The book provides an assessment of the *performance* of current managers. It reports on the managers who lead or have led U.S. organizations—the privately held and the publicly owned, the small and the large, the for-profit and not-for-profit, those that manufacture goods and those that provide services. It includes managers from many organizations, such as IBM, Westinghouse, American Express, Tenneco, Goodyear, Digital Equipment, General Motors, K-Mart, Time Warner, Eastman Kodak, Sears, Computer Land, Lincoln Electric, Wal-Mart, General Electric, John Deere, Caterpillar, Chrysler, Ford, Motorola, Coca-Cola, Pepsi, Coors, Nike, Exxon, Microsoft, Apple Computer, and Disney.

The purpose of the book is to both evaluate the manager's ability to manage and to help readers understand and avoid the seven fatal managerial sins. The recent forced resignations and firings of executives sent a message to the business community that all is not well in our corporations. The book also serves as a "wake-up call." The collapse of many businesses and the removal of well-known managers have caused people to question the competency and performance of managers and to scrutinize their corporate responsibility and corporate accountability. They ask, "Who is minding the store?"

The criticism lodged against many managers is not just for bad business judgments or for accidental or gross negligent acts, resulting in organizational damage; it is also for deliberate and intentional acts. They are accused of malfeasance and/or misfeasance. The question is posed: "If the activities of other professionals (doctors, lawyers, educators, and accountants) are carefully monitored, shouldn't the activities of managers also be monitored?"

The intent of the book is to report and inform, not to confuse or destroy. An informed society is a better society. The manager's presence is needed more in the boardroom than in the courtroom. It is hoped that the book will help bridge any gaps and correct misunderstandings that exist among managers, employees, the business community, and society. If the bridge between managers and the other corporate stakeholders is in any way weak or shaky, it must and can be made strong and steady. Managers must take the initiative and time now to analyze any existing or potential problems, whether real or imagined, and try to solve them while they are able to do so under non-adversarial conditions—for if they don't, they may find their problems being solved under adversarial conditions. Other professions found that to be the case and can so testify. Some would argue that management is not a profession and that there are no standards for managers. If management is not a profession, it ought to be, and those who lead organizations must be professionals. Nothing less should be acceptable. Many depend on managers' judgments. They are employed to achieve quality—high quality—and excellence, not mediocrity, should be their goal.

While the book reports and analyzes the findings of the aforementioned nationwide survey, as well as interviews regarding the status of managerial competency, needed improvements to correct any deficiencies that may exist are suggested. In summary, the purpose of the book is, to borrow a quote from Professor Fred Friendly, "not to make up anyone's mind but to open minds, and to make the agony of decision making so intense one can escape only by thinking."

So far, very little has been published regarding the performance of U.S. managers as a group. This is a very important area in the field of management, and much interest exists for good scholarly research, yet very little has been done. The importance of this book derives from both its timing and its content. The business community, as well as academia, thirsts for good books on management. *The Seven Fatal Management Sins* fills a true need.

It is important to note that, despite the tone of some of the comments in the preface, this is an optimistic book. The good news is that there are many outstanding managers leading some of our organizations. The last chapters in the book focus on them. The last chapters also suggest the necessary steps to be taken by those who have committed the fatal managerial sins in order to get back on the road to "goodness."

No book is the work of a single person, and this one is no exception. I would like to express my sincere appreciation to all who assisted me in the development of this project. So many people have contributed directly and indirectly that I cannot possibly even name most of them.

I am greatly indebted to the various authors who either wrote or spoke in the area of my research and whose works are reflected herein. Over the years, many people with whom I have been associated, especially colleagues and students, have been helpful in shaping my views and thus have contributed to this book. The absence of a long list of names, however, in no way reflects a lack of appreciation on my part. I am indeed grateful to all.

I gained insight during the development of this project from various people who were willing to share their experience, ideas, and expertise with me by responding to phone calls, questionnaires, and interviews. I am most appreciative of their time and thoughts. Each of them gave of their time freely and willingly. Furthermore, I gratefully acknowledge the courtesy of holders of copyrighted material who generously granted permission to quote their material. Specific recognition is given at the appropriate places in the text.

I extend my thanks to Shauna Smith, Theresa Linkletter, Lauren White, Connie Worrell, and Jerry Allison, graduate research assistants, for their help with various segments of this work. Sincere appreciation is extended to Tonita Wamsley and Judith Noel for their careful preparation of the manuscript. They were tireless in their efforts to meet deadlines. I also want to thank Irene Kremer and Terri McMaster and all the staff at the St. Ambrose University MBA office for their support and help in completing this work. Their professionalism, good nature, enthusiasm, and positive attitude made the task much more enjoyable. Thanks also to my colleague and friend Dr. Floyd Begin for the advice, encouragement, and interest he expressed in this work.

I want to thank the people at CRC Press LLC who provided assistance and support whenever needed. They consistently strive to produce quality products. In particular, I want to express my thanks to my editor, Sandy Pearlman, for her professional expertise, creativity, enthusiasm, and commitment to the book. Her editorial talents have been invaluable. She played a critical role in the development of the book. It was a pleasure working with her.

I would like to pay special tribute to my parents as well as to my wife's parents—leaders who taught me, by example, the meaning of love, heart, caring, compassion, and service.

Mostly, I am grateful to my wife, Helen, not only for her "editorial" comments and her insightful and creative suggestions, which helped make the book more readable, but also for her unending support, encouragement, faith, and love, which have made any obstacle conquerable.

Finally, the list would be incomplete if mention were not made of Penelope, our cat, who during those long and lonely "wee" hours of the morning, while I was trying to complete one more page, consistently and faithfully kept me company and made sure I stayed awake and that the papers on my desk were warm and "properly" scattered!

About the Author

Dr. John Collis is Dean of the College of Business, Director of the H.L. McLaughlin Master of Business Administration (M.B.A.) Program, and Professor of Economics and Business Administration at St. Ambrose University. As Dean of the College, he manages a number of departments and programs. One of the programs, the H.L. McLaughlin M.B.A. Program, grew under his leadership to a record high of over 680 students. It is the largest in the state of Iowa and in the top 25% nationwide. It has been nationally recognized for its high quality.

As Professor of Economics and Business Administration, Dr. Collis teaches a number of courses in the M.B.A. Program, including Capstone Seminar (Policy Formation and Implementation); Organizational Theory, Behavior and Communication; Legal and Social Environment of Business; and Business Ethics. In all, he has taught more than 35 different courses, at both the graduate and undergraduate levels.

Trained in business, law, education, and administration (he received his B.S., M.B.A., and J.D. from the University of Kentucky and his Ph.D. from the University of Iowa), he also served as Chairman of the Division of Business Administration, Accounting, and Economics at Iowa Wesleyan College.

Dr. Collis has held many appointed and elected positions in professional organizations and has served on numerous professional and academic committees, including appointment as program evaluator for baccalaureate and graduate degree institutions by the Association of Collegiate Business Schools and Programs and as a director on the Midwest Deans Association's Executive Committee. He has conducted numerous seminars, served on panels, served as a consultant, and spoken to many groups on various business-related topics, as well as law and ethics.

Dr. Collis has received a number of academic honors, including the Perry Eugene McClenehan Award for the outstanding candidate for an advanced degree in educational administration at the University of Iowa and the J. Raymond Chadwick Award for the Outstanding Teacher of the Year at Iowa Wesleyan College. The award is given in recognition of superior teaching, academic, and professional excellence; contribution to scholarship; development of effective programs of high quality; contributions to the college community; and positive interpersonal relationship with students and colleagues.

He is the author of *Educational Malpractice: Liability of Educators, School Administrators and School Officials* (Charlottesville, Virginia: The Michie Company, 1990), the first book published in this subject area. He has reviewed various books in law, marketing, and management for several publishing companies. His research interests are in business ethics, business policy, education law, and organizational behavior.

PART I

Setting the Stage to Tackle the Issue: Managers and Managing in America

CHAPTER 1

Managing Climate in the United States

> Anyone can hold the helm when the sea is calm.
> —Publilius Syrus

> The highest and most lofty trees have the most reason to
> dread the thunder.
> —Charles Rollin

Managerial Performance: An Overview

With the manager's influence entering into almost every aspect of life, the competency of managers is of great interest to businesspeople, government officials, and educators around the world. Recent developments have caused the public to examine and scrutinize managers more than ever before. People want a closer look at those who are "minding the store"—those at the top of organizations, the presidents and the chief executive officers.

Except for, perhaps, a small number of chief executives (the Jack Welchs, the Lee Iacoccas, the Sam Waltons, the Ted Turners, and the Donald Trumps of the world), by far the biggest majority of the "chieftains" remain relatively obscure to the public. For example, how many Americans know the names of the chief executive officers of the Fortune 500 companies? Who are these people who lead the organizations that impact our daily lives? If one were to ask a sophisticated MBA class to name the CEOs of even the largest organizations, the response certainly would not be overwhelming. Some employees cannot name the CEO of their own company. Furthermore, their obscurity continues after their retirement. While many of these CEOs are little "monarchs" at their companies during their six or seven years of tenure, enjoying all the rights and privileges of the office, several days after retirement they become "has-beens," even in the companies from which they just retired. As Walter B. Wriston, former chairman of Citibank Corp., puts it, "When you retire...you go from who's who to who's that..."

3

Despite the influence they have on our lives, they remain one of the most underreported groups. Journalists, for example, keep the public abreast of what is happening around the country, yet when it comes to "happenings" inside corporate boardrooms, these same journalists haven't really been able to mirror the occurrences. This is not to say that is bad but rather to make the point that very little is known about these "power elite" who call the shots and impact our lives for better or worse. Generally, unless something occurs during these CEOs' tenure that has a significant and negative impact, they serve their time as chiefs and depart "unnoticed" by the general public. When it comes to the degree of respect and admiration that the employees have for the CEO, scores range from a minus to a perfect ten. For example, one former chief executive writes that "not all of these corporate celebrities are objects of admiration. Some are envied for their opulent life-styles and the prodigious rewards that make these possible. Indeed, the early 1990s have brought a tidal wave of anger at what many people regard as utter excess."[1]

With the exception of perhaps some earlier research by institutions such as the American Management Association, which operated a competency development laboratory as part of its Institute for Managerial Competency for about ten years ending in the late 1980s, and the work of such scholars as Richard E. Boyatzis, who conducted research in this area in the late 1970s and early 1980s and reported in his book *The Competent Manager, A Model for Effective Performance*,[2] and some general discussion in William Whyte's book *The Organization Man* (1956)[3] and Michael Maccoby's book *The Gamesmen*,[4] published in 1976, there hasn't been extensive research (and practically none in the late 1980s and 1990s) focusing on managerial competency.[5] Competency is closely related to quality, and, of course, quality matters, according to W. Edwards Deming; it starts not at the factory floor but at the very top.

A close look at how these senior managers perform is of utmost importance, not only to top executives of corporations and others with leadership roles in organizations, but also to those who teach and those who are being taught the profession of management. It is also of significant importance to the general public, whose lives are affected by these managers' performance. A lot of money is invested in this "intellectual capital," which is a very valuable corporate asset. There is a strong need for organizations to develop leaders at all levels. Yet, it is clear that many senior executives are sacrificing the future of their organizations due to their incompetency—their mismanagement. We can blame company failures on a number of factors, such as economic conditions, but in the end it generally adds up to one word—incompetence. We have to be careful not to confuse bad management with destiny.

The Past, The Present

In the last several years, we have seen great efforts by corporations to "retool their workers," to increase their educational base. The results in some cases have been good and even great, but in other cases, concerns regarding sincerity and effectiveness are legitimate issues. So, is corporate America heading in the right direction? Are corporate actions well thought out, or are such actions just short-term appeasements? Today's CEOs, in general, have more "formal" education than those of the past. They have more information regarding their organization, their industry, their customers, and their competitors. The jury, however, is still out as to whether all of that enables these managers to make better qualitative and sound decisions. On the educational side, we have seen a shift in the type of students who are attracted to business schools. Universities are more serious in teaching management—as though it is a science.

Managers today do not have the safety net of the 1960s, when loyal employees did not think selfishly of personal gain but rather focused on what they could do to better their organization. Even though the organization did not reciprocate in kind, in appearance at least if not in reality, the employees were at home, and the paternalistic company was there to protect them. Many employees felt that criticism against the company was criticism against themselves.

In the late 1970s, management tended to be more arrogant; little recognition was given to global competitiveness. Labor was still regarded as the enemy and less emphasis was given to participative management. Today, greater emphasis is placed on empowerment of employees and on modern management information systems. The thought is that for organizations to remain competitive, they need to be lean, they need a greater emphasis on quality, and they need to shift toward a more professional form of management. Because of technology, as well as other factors, managers today have to be more focused and quick to respond. The organizations that will remain successful will be those that have positioned themselves for change and are able to adapt quickly and effectively. Consequently, an important duty of the CEO is to properly position the company for the future. This must be accomplished through the necessary restructuring, and it must be vision led, not problem driven. A comment by Howard Coonley, an author, is very relevant here: "The executive of the future will be rated by his ability to anticipate his problems rather than to meet them as they come." Some would argue that restructuring that is problem driven rather than vision led is like "shoot, aim, ready."

Positioning the organization for the future requires the "best and the brightest" at the top. In the book *The American Challenge* by Servan-Schreiber,[6] written in 1967, the French journalist warned European managers to get on the ball or those super-managers from the United States would sweep them away. By the 1980s, American managers didn't look like super-managers anymore.[7] American management has been on a roller coaster. It is no longer a matter of people working harder. An organization that does not have a work force that works smart and effectively does not have a bright future. To better understand the work force, we need to start at the top of the organization. We need answers to a number of questions: What are the prerequisites to manage effectively? To manage responsibly? To lead effectively? To lead responsibly? Can they be easily identified? How do we identify the people who can handle complex tasks, who will voluntarily shoulder themselves with new responsibilities, who can foresee problems, who can make independent decisions, who can respond quickly, and who can find ways to add value?

For organizations to survive in the future, they must not only be convinced that being led by the best and brightest helps the organization, but that without the best and the brightest at the helm, the chance for survival is nil at best. The organizations that will be the survivors in the future will be smarter, faster, and more innovative, and they will need people at the top who think that way. But thinking alone is not enough. It will take know-how and courage to implement and to carry on their convictions—their plans. It will take more than knowing the prerequisites to effective management and leadership. CEOs must identify and eliminate the obstacles to effective management and leadership. In the chapters ahead, we will identify these obstacles and strategize ways to eliminate them.

Turbulence in the Ranks

In the past, employees looked for a permanent home in the organizations where they worked, but today's best young executives neither expect nor want a lifelong career at a single company. Many of them don't want to be part of a large corporation; rather, they want to carve out a niche of their own. Many of the Fortune 500 companies have lost their luster as places to work. In a recent study of career preferences conducted by Opinion Research Corp., only 1% of the 1,000 respondents said they would freely choose to be corporate managers.[8] "To succeed in a large organization," says one executive, "you've got to put on a mask and tuck part of your true self away. I'm not willing to do that."[9] Another executive asks why people would want to manage organizations that view them as an expense and can eliminate them overnight. Many feel that the statement "if I work hard, the company will take care of me" is no longer true. That philosophy no longer prevails in many of today's organizations.

The top people in this business generation are also often unwilling to subjugate their personal lives to corporate demands. The new generation resents the idea that the best bureaucrats, as opposed to the best performers, are more likely to get ahead. The rewards go to the best politicians, who are not necessarily the most able executives. "People are not encouraged to be creative. They really want you to wear the same hat and the same coat as everybody else."[10] It's too easy to get pigeonholed or stuck in a dead-end job with no way out. Top managers say they want risk takers, but they don't.[11] "I have no interest in a blue-suit and traditional corporate life," says one executive. "I have much more progressive views about what a job should be."[12] They don't want to spend their careers putting out fires while someone else receives the recognition.

The recent forced resignations and firings of executives sends a message to the business community that all is not well in U.S. corporations. The collapse of many businesses, the removal of well-known managers, the mounting fines lodged against many organizations, and the numerous indictments brought against managers have caused many to question both the competency and the performance of U.S. managers and to scrutinize their corporate responsibility and accountability. The question being asked across the nation is: Do managers really know what they are doing?

Last year we read how Congress and the president couldn't agree on how to balance the budget, and so a partial government shut-down occurred— not just once, but many times! Does this demonstrate responsible and effective leadership? We read about the baseball strike. Does anyone want to classify that as being management at its best? How should we describe such leadership? How were these two situations handled from a management perspective? Were sound management principles applied? What has really happened to so many organizations that were sound and healthy not too long ago but are now in trouble or no longer with us? What about some of our so-called leaders who have vanished before their time—why are they no longer "navigating" their organizations? We need answers to these questions. However, to arrive at the right answers, we need proper analysis. You will have the opportunity to examine the data and to visit with present and past leaders in the following chapters.

Corporate America needs leadership—sound leadership—to manage its organizations. After all, America is the hub of capitalism, and anything short of having the best and the brightest at the helm should be unacceptable. That doesn't necessarily mean leaders who can part the waters, but rather leaders who can lead effectively. Let's try to guide those who are not already there so they can join the "giants" of successful organizations. As Winston Churchill said, "It is no use saying, 'we are doing our best.' You have got to succeed in doing what is necessary."

Notes

1. Thomas R. Horton, *The C.E.O. Paradox: The Privilege and Accountability of Leadership* (New York: AMACOM, American Management Association, 1992), p. xiii.
2. Richard E. Boyatzis, *The Competent Manager: A Model for Effective Performance* (New York: John Wiley & Sons, 1982).
3. William H. Whyte, *The Organization Man* (New York: Simon and Schuster, 1956).
4. Michael Maccoby, *The Gamesmen, The New Corporate Leaders* (New York: Simon and Schuster, 1976) Bantam edition, 1977.
5. Some of the work of other institutions and scholars studying the general field of managerial competency and isolating and testing specific managerial competencies is described in Thomas A. Horton's book, *What Works for Me: 16 C.E.O.s Talk About Their Careers and Commitments* (New York: Random House, 1986).
6. Jean Servan-Schreiber, *The American Challenge* [translated from the French by Ronald Steel] (New York: Antheneum, 1968).
7. Harold J. Leavitt, *Corporate Pathfinders* (Homewood, IL: Dow Jones-Irwin, 1986), p. v.
8. Kenneth Labich, "Kissing Off Corporate America," *Fortune*, February 20, 1995, p. 44.
9. Ibid., p. 47.
10. Ibid., p. 50.
11. Ibid.
12. Ibid., p. 52.

CHAPTER 2

Managerial Malpractice—Myth or Reality?

It is the duty of the law to remedy wrongs that deserve it—for every man that is injured ought to have his recompense.
—William L. Prosser[1]

Whatever you do, you should want to be the best at it. Every time you approach a task, you should be aiming to do the best job that's ever been done at it and not stop until you've done it. Anyone who does that will be successful—and rich.
—David Ogilvy

In the words of the ancient Romans: "Fiat justitia, ruat coelum" (let justice be done, though the heavens fall).

It is hard to argue against accountability.

A profession is better off if it can govern itself than if it has to be governed by others.

Many of us are familiar with the terms "medical malpractice" and "legal malpractice." Malpractice occurs when professionals do something "unprofessional." While many agree with malpractice as a legal remedy which is designed to correct alleged wrongs, there are those who not only oppose such a remedy, but are vehemently against it. Malpractice as a cause of action has been extended to a number of professions including psychiatry, accountancy, architecture, engineering, and dentistry. Recently, it was extended to clergy and is now moving to education.[2]

Consequently, suits for professional malpractice are not an imagined threat to professions but a real cause of action which poses a serious concern for many of them. It is a cause of action that is not new, but rather one that has been recognized by law for many years. In struggling with it, courts have

9

defined, and in some cases redefined, the basic elements of malpractice. Courts have enumerated what needs to be alleged and proven in professional malpractice cases. They have also established possible defenses that may be available to the professional who is being sued.

That background, coupled with the dissatisfaction and criticism lodged by many stakeholders against some of our corporate leaders, has given rise to the question: Should the courts entertain a new cause of action against corporate leaders—"managerial malpractice"? Because of its importance and significant implications, we will briefly deal with this issue at the outset.

Is There Evidence of Corporate Mismanagement?

The criticism lodged against many managers is not only for bad business judgments or for accidental or gross negligent acts resulting in organizational damage, but also for deliberate and intentional acts. Managers are accused of malfeasance and/or misfeasance. Thus, the question that is being asked is: If the acts of other professionals (i.e., doctors, lawyers, and educators) are being carefully monitored, shouldn't the acts of managers also be monitored?

The Code of Hammurabi was the first set of codified laws to deal with social rules. It included some specific regulations about the practice of medicine. The Code was assembled and inscribed in stone about 4,000 years ago. The Code described the payment due a physician for various services and the penalty for certain acts that we now term malpractice. It provided as follows:

> If a doctor has treated a Free Man with a metal knife for severe wound, and has cured the Free Man...then he shall receive ten shekels of silver.
>
> If a doctor has treated a man with a metal knife for a severe wound, and has caused the man to die...his hand shall be cut off.[3]

In 1514, one Fitzherbert is quoted as having said, "it is the duty of every artificer to exercise his art rightly and truly as he ought."[4]

It seems exceedingly clear that an alarm bell has been sounding for a good while now. The Reagan years, in particular, were a period of greed and excesses on the part of many corporate managers. Acquisitions and CEOs' perks were extolled on the pages of the *Wall Street Journal*. *Barbarians at the Gate* told the story of greed in corporate America. We read about numerous businesses that failed. The question that has been asked over and over is why these so-called powerful businesses of not too long ago are in such a mess. Was it due to the economy? Was it because of the products they sold? Was it competition that brought them down? Was it timing? Whatever the cause or causes might have been, unquestionably, a lot of the blame is and should be attributed to the "chieftains" who guided them.

It is a somewhat elementary management theory that the success or failure of a company reflects the success or failure of the CEO. He or she must anticipate what is going to happen in the organization. The CEO must have the vision to see not only down the block, but also around the corner. In view of this, we need to ask: If the organization fails to accomplish its mission, does that mean the CEO failed in his or her duties to the organization? If the answer is "yes," should the person in charge of the organization have to pay the consequences? If, on the other hand, the answer is "no," are we saying that managers are not accountable for their actions? How do they justify taking the credit if the organization succeeds? Furthermore, when that happens, some CEOs demand additional compensation. Are we to assume that it is easier to identify success than failure?

It is hard to deny or justify the fact that some present-day CEOs have failed their organizations. Many failures occurred because of negligence, because of gross negligence, and, in some cases, because of CEOs' intentional wrongdoing. Many of these misdoings were overlooked, others were "rewarded," and still other wrongs resulted in the dismissal of the CEOs. To err is human, and professionals are human. Therefore, it should come as no surprise to learn that professionals do not always accomplish what they set out to do in their work. Many times, when they fail in their missions, nothing happens to them, even though someone was harmed; however, occasionally that someone who has been harmed, or thinks that he or she has been harmed, turns to the courts for help. Unfortunately, according to some critics, wrongs that should occur occasionally now occur much too frequently—as has been witnessed in the last two decades.

Suing someone is easy—some would say too easy! Winning a suit is much more difficult. Complaints must be properly drafted and brought under a specific legal theory. A number of legal theories have been used to bring suits against professionals, but professionals have not been left defenseless. Professionals may assert a number of recognized defenses to protect themselves. Consequently, these theories must be tested and balanced against applicable legal defenses available to professionals.

Courts have been called to rule on many of these theories and defenses in a number of professions. There are, therefore, many cases which may be used as persuasive authority by the courts, if and when they are called, to decide cases dealing with managerial malpractice. These professional malpractice cases will serve as a guide and as a standard to compare and to test the various arguments advanced for and against the recognition of managerial malpractice as a cause of action.

Before discussing managerial malpractice, we need to define the term "malpractice." In the first edition of *Black's Dictionary of Law* (1891), under the term "malpractice" the reader is referred to "mala proxis," which is defined as "Malpractice; unskillful management or treatment....[5] In the fifth edition, the term "malpractice" is defined as:

> Professional misconduct or unreasonable lack of skill. This term is usually applied to such conduct by doctors, lawyers and accountants. Failure of one rendering professional services to exercise that degree of skill and learning commonly applied under all the circumstances in the community by the average prudent, reputable member of the profession with the result of injury, loss or damage to the recipient of those services or to those entitled to rely upon them. It is any professional misconduct, unreasonable lack of skill or fidelity in professional or fiduciary duties, evil practices, or illegal or immoral conduct....[6]

Reaction to the Term "Managerial Malpractice": Friend or Foe?

Charles Smith begins his book *Products Liability* as follows:

> Products Liability! How do you react—apprehensive, enraged, calm, stunned, understanding, alarmed, disturbed, inept, frightened, dismayed, agitated, worried, harassed, terrified, confident, appalled, ignorant, knowledgeable, outraged, or...?[7]

How do you react when the words "product liability" in the above quote are replaced with "managerial malpractice"? The validity of the criticism lodged against our top leaders for managerial performance can be debated. Arguments abound on both sides of the issue. This book is not a place to air these arguments. Even though people may have difficulty defining or understanding the meaning of these terms, they know when managerial incompetence occurs. It's like a U.S. Supreme Court Justice's famous statement about obscenity: "I can't define it," he said, "but I know when I see it."

In a recent nationwide survey of deans of colleges of business (see Appendix 1) conducted by the author, the following statement was posed: "There are instances in organizations where managerial malpractice may be a proper legal remedy/cause." Responses indicated that 54% of the deans either agreed or strongly agreed with the statement while only 18% disagreed or strongly disagreed. The remaining 28% neither agreed nor disagreed. When the same statement was posed to university business professors teaching strategic management, 49% of those responding either agreed or strongly agreed with the statement, 25% disagreed or strongly disagreed, and 26% neither agreed nor disagreed.

While 50% of the CEOs who responded either disagreed or strongly disagreed with the statement, only 6% agreed with it. When it came to union presidents, 50% agreed or strongly agreed, while 25% disagreed or strongly disagreed. Interestingly, 45% of the business news editors, who analyze and report on U.S. business, either agreed or strongly agreed, while 22% disagreed.

In order to gain further insight into how various informed groups view the concept of "managerial malpractice," the panel was asked: "How do you react to and interpret the term 'managerial malpractice'?" The following is a sample of the responses given by the university business deans:

- Its time has come. The fact that it may be hard to prove should not be used as an excuse.
- Not making a good faith effort to act in the best interest of shareholders, customers and the public in general.
- Happening everywhere, difficult to codify.
- Irresponsible decisions that hurt others.
- Willful wrong that affects stakeholders.
- Incompetence.
- Unethical.
- Useless concept.
- Manager consistently doing the wrong things.
- Actions by management that threaten their organizations' viability. Business organizations must thrive in order to provide opportunities for future generations. To bungle that responsibility is managerial malpractice.
- Sounds like a legal term. Don't like it.
- Holding management accountable for ineffectiveness.
- Purposeful unethical decisions or lack of decisions.

- Doing things to enhance self and not the employees—not being sincere and trustworthy.
- Managers whose decisions are guided by self-interest over the interest of shareholders and employees.
- Managers who do things differently than most prudent managers would.
- Personal liability for poor outcomes.
- Favorably; surely the failure of so many top-flight firms is inexcusable.
- Why shouldn't CEOs be held accountable for their wrongdoings? Are they above the law?

Responses by university business professors included:

- It suggests accountability to me.
- I am very comfortable with it. It does, however, need to be sensitively treated.
- Situations where managers knowingly violate legal or ethical principles.
- Making mistakes that can do damage to the organization, not just financially, but also in terms of ethical behavior.
- Deliberate or poor performance.
- I think it's a ridiculous term because there is no right answer and unlike medicine, there is not ultimate measure of performance. Management is trade-offs!
- Doing things for personal reasons and not for the good of the organization.
- Lining their own pockets at the expense of the firm.
- There may be limited situations where managers overstep the boundaries of their position.
- They are open for suit as are doctors and lawyers for actions performed on the job.
- Practices which violate the law and ethics.
- Operating in my best interest instead of the stockholders' best interest.
- If we don't hold them accountable for wrongdoing, are we prepared to sweep their wrongs under the rug?

Comments by CEOs and chairmen of boards included:

- Failure to act as a reasonable person (manager) is expected.
- Abuse of power.

- Dishonesty, self-serving.
- Offensive and pejorative.
- There will always be some incompetent and dishonest managers to whom the term would apply.

Union presidents reacted as follows:

- Not performing duties.
- Assume it to be a charge against an incompetent manager who violates ethics/standards of managerial practice.
- Decisions based on self-interest.
- Not conducting themselves toward betterment of organization.
- Immoral, illegal actions.

The comments of the business news editors are along the same line:

- Poor judgment.
- Another opportunity for lawsuit abuse.
- Gross negligence; deliberate malfeasance.
- Deliberately disregarding rules of the company.
- It is real. Some managers inflict fatal wounds to their organization by their unsound/illegal acts.
- Management action or inaction that hurts the company and inevitably employees.
- Incompetent management.
- Not getting the manager you've paid a salary to/for.
- Failure to manage employees for the best interest of the organization and the employees.

Surprised? These comments are reported here to inform—not to confuse or destroy. They are discussed here to prevent rather than encourage litigation. Unquestionably, an informed profession is a better profession. Our aim is to keep the CEO out of trouble and away from the courtroom. The CEO's presence is needed more in the boardroom than in the courtroom.

In an attempt to get the reaction of others (besides the panel) regarding the term "managerial malpractice," the Internet was used to ask the following question: "Do you think it is time that courts recognize a new cause of action by stakeholders against managers who are negligent or grossly negligent in the performance of their duties? The theory would be managerial malpractice!" Judging from the numerous responses, there is considerable interest in this area. One person responded as follows:

We assume that managers have a social, ethical and moral responsibility to the employees that work for them. However, in a capitalist marketplace, their only allegiance is to the owners or shareholders. If they are doing what is in the best interest of either of these two groups (depending on whether the company is private or public) then they are doing what they get paid to do (make money and make more money).

I work as an HR professional where there is a common misconception that I am representing the best interest of the employees. This is false. My only obligation is to the owners with respect that I: 1) attract and retain the best employees that meet the needs of the company; and 2) keep their butts out of court with respect to labor laws.

That's it. While it may seem cruel, I have no allegiance to the employees and fully understand my role as an employee. I expect nothing more than a paycheck for the exchange of my services; loyalty and mis-management are things of the past, or rather were tools used by owners/managers to attract and retain employees in the past. While they were admirable things, they should not become actionable. In fact, from an HR perspective, there are perhaps way too many laws that protect the employee and put business at a competitive disadvantage already. If you feel that you have been a victim of mis-management, market your skills to somebody else. You have kept yourself marketable, haven't you???

Another person stated:

What about the case where "managerial malpractice" puts a major enterprise in danger of going under—leaving thousands of people out of work and a whole town in trouble?

This is no idle question. It happens. Often. The textbooks (and the newspapers) are full of examples.

An MBA student said: "I have experienced 'managerial malpractice' first hand and I believe it should be actionable!!!" Additional responses included:

▪ It is actionable. It's called going out and getting another job. Does everything that doesn't go someone's way have to be the subject of a lawsuit these days? It seems quite immature to me. Just because we are taught, as children, that, if you work hard, you will gain success, doesn't mean it really happens that way.

■ I have found from personal experience that an employee cannot rely on what is written in the employee handbook (management reserves the right to change and interpret at will)—where does that leave us? It leaves us with the ability to raise the issue through the management chain, to get outside advice on the specific case, or to resign.

■ Sue, if you also have "Employee Malpractice." Seriously though, the cynic in me wonders if we need the courts to help us any-more with internal corporate affairs. (Speaking of affairs, they have everybody so jittery about sexual harassment that some people aren't sure where the dating/sexual harassment line is.) Unless the corporation is dysfunctional, malpractice results in being fired. Help from courts: thanks, but no thanks.

■ When are folks going to wake up to the simple fact you only get hired to do work someone else wants to avoid. By definition, most managers are employees. And business owners can't com-mit malpractice even if they pull off another Howard Johnson's "own the work and give it up" move...they own the place. Nobody forces people to take or keep jobs. Most who stay tend to not look for excuses.

■ Why shouldn't they be held accountable. How can one logi-cally argue for medical malpractice and be against managerial malpractice? How can we be in favor of suing a neurosurgeon who in a very delicate operation made a mistake resulting in damage to the patient, yet be against suing a manager who, in fact, premeditated the demise of his organization or who wrong-fully and intentionally kept an employee from getting to his deserved place in the organization? Accountability should be a must in all professions!

A Wake-Up Call or a Call for Action?

It is hard to argue against accountability—accountability of doctors, lawyers, accountants, teachers, top-level managers, or anyone else. Professionals need to perform their work professionally. That is the agreement they make, ex-pressly or implied, with those who hire them and who pay them. That is also the expectation of those whom they guide and those with whom they inter-act. Anything short of that is not acceptable—it cannot and should not be tolerated. If they don't meet that standard, they must be held accountable. Of course, that may mean paying for the consequences—their wrongdoings. It may mean a managerial malpractice suit. Whether or not such cause of action is termed "managerial malpractice" is not the issue. The issue is whether the "unprofessional conduct" of CEOs and top-level managers should be swept under the rug and, further, whether the executives should be held accountable for their actions.

Undeniably, there are a number of problems associated with recognizing a new cause of action such as "managerial malpractice"; however, these problems are not insurmountable but solvable. For example, it can be argued that this is a new and novel issue and therefore should not be recognized, but it would appear that history and logic would dictate otherwise. Should the test to determine if a court should hear a case be whether the cause is a new one or, rather, whether the claim has merit? If new causes of action are not entertained by courts merely on the grounds that they raise "new" and "novel" issues, then, are the courts not static and incapable of evolving to adapt to the changing needs and circumstances of modern society? To use Dean Prosser's words, "The progress of the common law is marked by many cases of first impression, in which the court has struck out boldly to create a new cause of action, where none had been recognized before."[8] New torts, such as managerial malpractice, develop in response to society's demand that a court should aid a claimant who has suffered injury through a defendant's wrongdoing. There is evolution of tort law to meet the needs of a changing society. The courts do not, and should not, operate in a vacuum, and public demand for change is one of the factors influencing the courts to recognize new causes of action.[9]

Absence of precedent for recognizing a legal duty should not be fatal to a plaintiff's claim. Judge Crane wrote that the common law "does expand with reason. The common law is not a compendium of mechanical rules written in fixed and indelible characters, but a living organism which grows and moves in response to the larger and fuller development of the nation."[10] It thus follows that courts must examine judicial and legislative trends to discern if public policy compels them to recognize the new theory. "Law is not merely a body of static rules to be obeyed by all citizens who are subject to its sanctions. It is a dynamic process by which rules are constantly being adopted and changed to the complex situations of a developing society."[11]

Justice Oliver Wendell Holmes wrote: "The life of the law has not been logic; it has been experience." Another scholar's version concerning the life of the law is:

The life of the law has been logic; it has been experience. The felt
necessities of the time, the prevalent moral and political theories,
intuitions of public policy, avowed or unconscious, even the prejudices which judges share with their fellow men, have had a good
deal more to do than syllogism in determining the rules by which
men should be governed.[12]

Thus it becomes evident when one examines the law that courts are not
precluded, nor have they abstained, from creating a new cause where none has
previously existed. For example, courts have allowed claims previously unrec-
ognized in tort law, such as claims for loss of consortium resulting from
physical injuries to the plaintiff's spouse,[13] intentional infliction of mental
distress resulting from extreme and outrageous conduct,[14] negligent infliction
of emotional distress,[15] invasion of privacy,[16] injuries caused by defective
products,[17] and other injuries which do not fit into traditional tort categories.[18]

In view of this judicial trend, if courts were to recognize managerial
malpractice as a cause of action, they would only be expanding somewhat
the existing trend. Yet, it is important to remember that courts must proceed
cautiously. Prosser, a legal scholar, notes:

It does not lie within the power of any judicial system to remedy
all human wrongs. The obvious limitations upon the time of the
courts, the difficulty in many cases of ascertaining the real facts or
of providing any effective remedy, have meant that there must be
some selection of those more serious injuries which have the prior
claim to redress and are dealt with most easily. Trivialities must be
left to other means of settlement, and many wrongs which in themselves are flagrant—ingratitude, avarice, broken faith, brutal words,
and heartless disregard of the feelings of others—are beyond any
effective legal remedy, and any practical administration of the law.[19]

To that end, however, it must be noted, as Prosser points out, that "it is the
business of the law to remedy wrongs that deserve it—for every man that is
injured ought to have his recompense.[20]

It would appear that the arguments advanced herein demonstrate that to
deny a cause of action for managerial malpractice on the basis that it is new
or novel is very weak at best. Precedent in other areas, as well as logic,
dictate otherwise. The question that needs to be asked is: Can sufficient
facts be alleged to give rise to a justifiable managerial malpractice cause
of action?

In addition to the "novel" issue argument, there are a number of other arguments for refusing to endorse the concept of malpractice. Consider, for example, (1) flood of litigation and (2) financial burden. It has been argued that once the door opens, an avalanche of (managerial malpractice) litigation will probably ensue, with founded as well as unfounded actions. If every employee who is unhappy should bring suit against his or her employer for managerial malpractice, the country's courtrooms would be immediately overwhelmed. Even if it can be assumed, at least at the outset, that this would happen, should the courts deny a claimant who has a "founded" action his day in court because of fear that those with "unfounded" claims will rush to the courts? It would appear justice dictates otherwise. After all, the system has built-in penalties for those "unfounded" claims. If the penalties are inadequate, more should be imposed. It would be more equitable and proper to consider more built-in penalties for the "unmeritorious" claims than to deny the meritorious ones. Should a court deny a meritorious claim because it does not know how to handle it or because the meritorious claim may open the door to other meritorious claims? Would such a denial be consistent with our legal system?

Professor Prosser writes:

> It is the business of the law to remedy wrongs that deserve it, even at the expense of a "flood of litigation," and it is a pitiful confession of incompetence on the part of any court of justice to deny relief on such grounds....And it is no objection to say, that it will occasion multiplicity of actions; for if men will multiply injuries, actions must be multiplied; for every man that is injured ought to have his recompense...So far as distinguishing true claims from false ones is concerned, what is required is rather a careful scrutiny of the evidence supporting the claim; and the elimination of trivialities calls for nothing more than the same common sense which has distinguished serious from trifling injuries in other fields of the law [citations omitted].[21]

So the argument given by some in opposition to malpractice claims, that it would bring about countless numbers of real or imagined claims, has to be viewed from all perspectives. For example, even if that were the case, aren't we looking for justice? Couldn't physicians and hospitals make the same argument? Is such an argument proper and consistent with our legal system and what and whose interests are served if the argument is followed? Is our system so weak that it would allow all those who sue to win, regardless of the merits of their claim? A careful study of our system would indicate otherwise. Certainly, every patient who does not get well following an injury or illness is not awarded monetary damages against his or her doctor. Nor does every client who loses a case recover from his or her lawyer.

The determining factor should be whether a wrong resulting in an injury has been committed. Is there a legitimate claim? Commenting on this issue, the Pennsylvania Supreme Court stated:

> Throughout the entire history of law, legal Jeremiahs have moaned that if financial responsibility were imposed in the accomplishment of certain enterprises, the ensuing litigation would be great, chaos would reign and civilization would stand still. It was argued that if railroads had to be responsible for their acts of negligence, no company could possibly run trains; if turnpike companies had to pay for harm done through negligence, no roads would be built; if municipalities were to be financially liable for damage done by their motor vehicles, their treasuries would be depleted. Nevertheless, liability has been imposed in accordance with elementary rules of justice and the moral code, and civilization in consequence, has not been bankrupted, nor have the courts been inundated with confusion.[22]

Courts may argue that recognizing managerial malpractice as a cause of action will spur an enormous amount of litigation and/or that it will cost too much. Consequently, many may suffer a wrong that will not be "righted." Such an argument is too superficial, too vague, and inconsistent with sound legal and logical principles. Our legal system and our moral code demand more than that as a justification for not recognizing managerial malpractice as a cause of action. If we accept those arguments as a justification, are we prepared to apply them to other professions (i.e., medicine)? Is not medical malpractice a financial burden on the medical profession? It is true that more medical malpractice suits raise medical insurance costs for physicians and for hospitals, and, consequently, doctors and hospitals may raise their fees—to the detriment of the patients. If that is not acceptable, what is the alternative? The question that will finally have to be answered is: How can the interests of all parties best be balanced?

It is interesting to note that companies are "forcing" workers to sign "employment-at-will" contracts. A clause in the contract that employees are asked to sign provides that their jobs and pay may be terminated at any time, with or without cause, at the sole discretion and option of the company. What message does such a clause convey? What has happened to loyalty and trust?

Does the clause foster trust and loyalty? Are both parties on equal footing? Is this just open and honest communication? Where does this leave the worker? If we don't change direction, we are likely to end up where we are headed. The question is whether we want to go there.

So, let's again pose the question: Is there such a thing as managerial malpractice? Can one envision sufficient facts or conduct that will bring managerial malpractice to the forefront? Frank Lloyd Wright said, "A doctor can bury his mistakes, but an architect can only advise his client to plant vines." What can the organization do? What can the employees do? What about those great big executive compensation packages suggested by some of the executives themselves and approved by their buddies on the board? Are they part of what executives are expected to do and should be doing? What about a severance package of over $90 million to a president who has been with the company for only a very short time? Is it fair to the shareholders? Is it fair to the employees? Is there reason for concern? Who should review such an action? The board? What if the board is primarily made up of supporters (friends) of the CEO— what then? After all, who benefits from such action—the organization or the CEO? Whose interest is being advanced?

What about those employees who are hired and then forgotten? Does the company owe them any obligation? Do they have the right to expect that their supervisors owe them the responsibility to at least promote them and help them reach their potential? What about the executive's obligation to add value to the corporation? What if the executive doesn't meet that obligation, not because he or she can't, but doesn't, due to intentional or negligent conduct or selfish interests? Will it be open season on managers who don't add value? When a CEO is "enthroned," what responsibilities and obligations go along with that title? Sure, the CEO takes a big risk, but what does he or she owe the organization?

Are there truly significant reasons to differentiate between managerial malpractice and other forms of malpractice litigation which currently congest the courts? Could it be argued that under no conceivable set of circumstances could a CEO be liable for the negligent or intentional infliction of damages? Negligence is negligence, whether it is called negligence or malpractice. Perhaps the problem is that some people are troubled by the word "malpractice."

It would appear that reason, justice, and the law demand negative answers to the following questions: Should CEOs be above the law? Should they be protected from their negligent acts? Can society afford to give CEOs complete freedom to do what they want? Should injured stakeholders be denied access to the courts? Access to the courts is a basic legal right which has been honored in American society from its beginning. Believing that there should be a remedy for every wrong, those who thought they were wronged turned to the courts, when other means failed, to have their wrongs "righted." Consequently, almost every important issue had its day in court. It would appear that reason, justice, and the law demand an affirmative answer to the following questions: Should CEOs be held accountable for their actions or inactions which result in injuries to stakeholders? If a person is injured solely through the negligence or intentional conduct of another, should he or she be compensated for the resulting injuries?

The purpose of this chapter is to help bridge any gaps and misunderstandings that may or do exist among stakeholders, CEOs, and perhaps the courts. If the bridge between the stakeholders and the CEOs is shaky, it can and should be made strong and steady. Both CEOs and stakeholders must try to understand the problems and concerns of each other. Cooperation and understanding are crucial. Stakeholders and CEOs are and must be on the same side, not opposite sides. They must cooperate, not compete. They are not nor should they be adversaries. Good management is too important to the preservation of our business community. We have to solve the problems associated with poor management. They must be solved properly, efficiently, calmly, and, above all, equitably. Anything short of that is not acceptable. Time and effort expended to improve management are well spent.

Executives must take the initiative and the time *now* to analyze any existing or potential problems, whether real or imagined, and try to solve them while they are able to do so under non-adversarial conditions. If they don't, they may find their problems being solved under adversarial conditions in a court of law. Sadly, other professions found that to be the case and can so testify. Executives should use this period of time to correct what is not right before the courts enter the arena. Suits sometimes tend to be epidemic. It may be much easier and much wiser for executives to work under the rules they wrote rather than the rules someone else wrote for them. What the future holds in this area depends almost entirely upon how executives deal with this sensitive and troublesome matter. It is time to face reality. Reality cannot and should not be ignored. The bell has been sounding for some time. It is time to wake up and correct that which is wrong! In the words of Winston Churchill, "The price of greatness is responsibility."

Notes

1. William L. Prosser, *Law of Torts* (St. Paul: West Publishing Company, 1983).
2. John Collis, *Educational Malpractice: Liability of Educators, School Administrators, and School Officials* (Charlottesville, VA: The Michie Company, 1990).
3. Donald J. Flaster, *Malpractice: A Guide to the Legal Rights of Patients and Doctors* (New York: Charles Scribner's Sons, 1983), p. 28.
4. William O. Morris, *Dental Litigation* (Charlottesville, VA: The Michie Company, 1972), p. 4.
5. Henry Campbell Black, *A Dictionary of Law* (St. Paul: West Publishing Company, 1891), pp. 744, 746.
6. Henry Campbell Black, *Black's Law Dictionary,* 5th edition (St. Paul: West Publishing Co., 1979), p. 864.
7. Charles O. Smith, *Products Liability: Are You Vulnerable?* (Upper Saddle River, NJ: Prentice-Hall, 1981), p. ix. He used this phraseology, with the exception that he used the words "Product Liability" in place of "Managerial Malpractice."
8. *Educational Malpractice,* 124 University of Pennsylvania Law Review 755, 805 (1976).
9. Destin Shann Tracy, *Educational Negligence: A Student's Cause of Action for Incompetent Academic Instruction*, 58 North Carolina Law Review 593 (March 1980).
10. David Abel, *Can a Student Sue Schools for Educational Malpractice?* 4 Harvard Educational Review 416, 425 (November 1974).
11. Harold J. Grilliot, *Introduction to Law and the Legal System,* 3rd edition (Boston: Houghton Mifflin, 1983), p. 1.
12. David G. Carter, Sr., "The Educator and the Liability of Law of Professional Malpractice: Historical Analysis," paper for the 1979 AERA Annual Convention, San Francisco, April 8–12, 1979, pp. 2–3.
13. Judith H. Berliner Cohen, *The ABC's of Duty: Educational Malpractice and the Functionally Illiterate Student*, 8 Golden Gate University Law Review 293, 303-4 (1978); citing *Rodriguez v. Bethlehem Steel Corp.,* 12 Cal. 3d 382, 525, 115 Cal. Rptr 765 (1974).
14. Ibid., pp. 303–4; citing *Savage v. Boies,* 77 Ariz. 355, 272 P 2d 349 (1954).
15. Ibid., p. 304; citing *Dillon v. Legg,* 68 Cal. 2nd 898, 5 Cal. Rptr 28 (1960).
16. Ibid., p. 304, citing *Pavesich v. New England Life Ins. Co.,* 122 Ga. 190, 50 S.E. 68 (1905).
17. *Educational Malpractice,* 124 University of Pennsylvania Law Review 755, 761 (1976).
18. Ibid.
19. Prosser (note 1), p. 19.
20. Ibid., p. 51.
21. Ibid.
22. *Doyle v. South Pittsburgh Water Co.,* 414 Pa. 199, 218-19, 199 A.2d 875, 884 (1964); see also *Educational Malpractice*, 124 University of Pennsylvania Law Review 755, 765 (1976). Reprinted with permission of the University of Pennsylvania Law Review.

PART II

How American Organizations Are Being Run: Grading the Managers

CHAPTER 3

Assessing the Performance of Managers

Management is not being brilliant...Management is craftsmanship. Most of the time it is hard to work to get a very few simple things across so that ordinary people can do them.
    —Peter Drucker

Without a shepherd, sheep are not a flock.
    —Russian proverb

The best executive is the one who has sense enough to pick good men to do what he wants done, and the self-restraint to keep from meddling with them while they do it.
    —Theodore Roosevelt

Quality is never an accident; it is always the result of an intelligent effort.
    —John Ruskin

One machine can do the work of 50 ordinary men. No machine can do the work of one extraordinary man.
    —Elbert Hubbard

It has been suggested that at least 80% of all problems that businesses face are directly attributable to poor management. Some consultants put the number somewhere between 70% to close to 100%.[1] How do we achieve good management? What is the secret to successful management? Why does one organization do extraordinarily well while another similar organization wallows in mediocrity?

Performance of U.S. Managers: Is Today's Norm Mediocrity or Excellence?

Theodore Roosevelt was quoted as saying, "People ask the difference between a leader and a boss. The leader leads, the boss drives." Today, it is not unusual to pick up the *Wall Street Journal* and read about some CEO who has been fired, terminated, let go, or who resigned at a point in his or her career when such action would not have occurred unless the CEO was in deep trouble. In introducing an article by Chrysler chairman Robert Eaton, the following comment was made:

> Disparaged by the media, distrusted by his subordinates, dismissed by his countrymen, *Newsweek* labels U.S. CEOs "corporate killers" for downsizing the workforce. Scott Paper's CEO, Al Dunlap, is dubbed "Chainsaw Al" for his quick trigger to terminate staff. And AT&T's CEO, Robert Allen, is ambushed by *60 Minutes* and made to justify his salary before 20 million Americans.[2]

Mr. Eaton writes that in just one year—1993—the CEOs of American Express, IBM, Westinghouse, Apple Computer, Eli Lilly, Eastman Kodak, Scott Paper, and Borden were bounced, in no small measure due to pressure from institutional investors.[3] Unfortunately, in the past ten years we have seen perhaps more profiteers than leaders in industry, and the cost–benefit trade-off between economic considerations and the public good has gone awry. We read that some of last year's successful organizations are in trouble or are no longer with us. In most cases, we don't have to speculate why because, on close examination, the primary cause is obvious—poor management. There has been a failure by management to manage. Why? What are the obstacles to effective management? Can they be eliminated? How well are managers performing? Are our organizations being managed by the best and the brightest? Is the word to describe the norm regarding organizational performance "excellence" or is it "mediocrity"? Are today's managers more interested in managing their careers or in managing their organizations? Are managers properly prepared for their jobs? Why are there poor managers? What managerial sins do managers commit? Which ones are fatal? Is the organizational norm to "look good at any expense"?

Answers to these and other related questions regarding managerial performance are very important to managers, potential managers, students of management, business educators, investors, and the general public. Yet, very little has been written based on research findings, even though much has been written about organizations in general.

In 1979, *Time* magazine asked a group of prominent Americans to identify "what living American leaders have been most effective in changing things for the better." Leaders who have given voice to criticisms of traditional leadership, such as Ralph Nader and Gloria Steinem, were mentioned,

"When you catch up to this, Harris, we'll issue a 'Think Big' sign."

(Appeared in *Harvard Business Review,* September–October 1992.
Used with permission.)

but no one named Gerald Ford, Richard Nixon, Jimmy Carter, or any other political leader. Nor did they agree on leaders of large organizations in business or academia. One person said: "I can't think of any leaders."[4] Isn't that sad? If the same question were posed today, would the results be the same?

Throughout history, it has been recognized that the difference between success and failure, whether in war, business, a protest movement, or sports, can be attributed largely to leadership.[5] The intensity of today's concern about leadership is highlighted by recent observations such as the following:

> Business in America has lost its way, adrift in a sea of managerial mediocrity, desperately needing leadership to face worldwide economic competition. Once the dominant innovators in technology, marketing, and manufacturing, American business has lost ground to foreign competition.[6]

In recent years, many theorists and practitioners have debated and emphasized the difference between managers and leaders. For example, Warren G. Bennis recently noted that, "To survive in the twenty-first century, we are going to need a new generation of leaders—leaders not managers. The distinction is an important one. Leaders conquer the context—the volatile, turbulent, ambiguous surroundings that sometimes seem to conspire against us and will surely suffocate us if we let them—while managers surrender to it."[7]

In an article appearing in *Fortune* entitled "Rambos in Pinstripes: Why So Many CEOs Are Lousy Leaders," Richard Hagberg, an executive development consultant who has been advising chief executives on the fine points of leadership and who compiled a database on the characteristics of 511

CEOs, was asked why so many fail to inspire loyalty in their troops. Based on CEO personality tests and evaluations from thousands of their coworkers, his research showed that:

> Many who stumble are impatient, impulsive, manipulative, dominating, self-important, and critical of others. Moreover, Hagberg has concluded that the number of Rambos in pinstripes is increasing. Five years ago only half of his CEO clients were classified as loners; today, the figure is closer to 70%.[8]

Hagberg responded to the following two questions: (1) "Your studies have found that many CEOs don't have what it takes. What exactly is it about their leadership skills that's lacking?"

> We find there are three pillars of leadership: One is to be the inspirational evangelist for a vision. A lot of CEOs, we found, are mechanical and machine-like, and it is hard to be inspired by a problem-solving machine. Another pillar is to manage implementation—which many are good at—and a third is to build relationships with subordinates. We discovered that many CEOs are very egocentric. They don't think the third step is important, because the world doesn't exist beyond them. Therefore, they have a hard time developing talent. They are Rambo-like individuals who create a survival-of-the-fittest atmosphere.[9]

(2) "How do these CEOs get their companies into trouble?"

> Under the stress and pressure that go with the job, many CEOs become reactive, listen less, and act impulsively without thinking. Their impatience drives them to focus on financial goals, which means they fail to build relationships with their boards or their employees. One result is that people stop buying into their solutions. As a group, CEOs tend to be domineering and strong-willed: they state their opinions forcefully. As they distance themselves from others, it becomes harder for people to disagree with them. When that happens, they stop getting bad news or the benefit of a give-and-take conversation.[10]

This book is written as an attempt to better understand the reasons for the CEO's triumphs and failures. It sets the stage not only to examine delicate, sensitive, and important issues, but also to suggest corrective action. Through interviews and through the use of a comprehensive survey involving many individuals who are knowledgeable about the business community, coupled with in-depth research on the subject, the book provides valuable and insightful information regarding this important yet somewhat neglected area.

It is intended to evaluate the manager's ability to manage and to explore and understand the real reasons why many managers fail in their task "to manage." By understanding why they fail, perhaps failures can be avoided. The title is used to draw attention to a serious concern regarding erosion of managerial competency. The recent forced resignations and firings of executives sends a message to the business community that all is not well in our corporations. This book is intended to serve as a "wake-up call." The collapse of many businesses, the removal of well-known managers, the mounting fines against many organizations, and the numerous indictments brought against managers have caused many to question the competency and performance of U.S. managers and to scrutinize their corporate responsibility and accountability. People are asking: Who is "watching the store"? Do managers really know what they are doing? What recourse is available to those who are harmed—be they stockholders, employees, or customers?

The Evaluators, The Survey, The Interviews

After many years of studying, researching, and teaching about the management environment, it is only natural that I have formed some opinions regarding managers and managerial performance. However, in writing this book, those opinions had to be set aside until the research was completed, to assure that it would not be biased. To that end, the objective has been achieved.

The task became one of gathering information to report on the managers who lead our nation's organizations—the privately held and the publicly owned, the small and the large, the for-profit and the not-for-profit, those that manufacture goods and those that provide services. To find out how managers perform and to determine whether the evidence really supports some of the widely held beliefs about managers, a survey was developed to measure the performance of top U.S. manager (i.e., chief executive officers). The next step was to decide who should receive the survey.

The survey to rate managerial performance was carefully constructed, and the 65 questions (50 close-ended and 15 open-ended) were tested to assure their objectivity and reliability. Then the evaluators, or "panel of experts" (those who were to answer the questions), were selected. The panel consisted of presidents and/or CEOs of Fortune 500 companies, presidents and/or CEOs and senior managers picked randomly from companies other than the Fortune 500, directors of various corporate boards, union officials, business news editors representing the media, college and university business school deans, and university business professors teaching business policy courses at the graduate and undergraduate levels.

In addition, authors of business books, management scholars, and a number of CEOs and/or presidents of large as well as small organizations were interviewed in depth. The findings of the research are reported and analyzed throughout the book. However, to stop there would not do justice to the research or the book. The acts and deeds which have been identified as causing the problems, termed "sins," are also explored and analyzed. In addition, some suggestions for how to correct and avoid these problems are offered. The "sinners" have to be shown the road to redemption! Finally, the book provides a glance at—an opportunity to meet—an "ideal" CEO.

Notes

1. Martin R. Smith, "Common Sense Antidotes to Business Fads and Fallacies," *Management Review*, April 1992, p. 47.
2. Robert J. Eaton, "In Defense of the CEO," *The Public Relations Strategist,* Volume 2, Issue 2, Summer 1996, p. 6.
3. Ibid., p. 7.
4. Michael Maccoby, *The Leader: A New Face for American Management* (New York: Simon and Schuster, 1981), pp. 13–14.
5. Fred Luthans, *Organizational Behavior,* 6th edition (New York: McGraw-Hill, 1993), pp. 268–69.
6. Ibid.; citing Alexander Zaleznik, "The Leadership Gap," *Academy of Management Executives*, February 1990, p. 9.
7. Luthans (note 5), p. 269.
8. Linda Grant, "Rambos in Pinstripes: Why So Many CEOs Are Lousy Leaders," *Fortune,* June 24, 1996, p. 147.
9. Ibid.
10. Ibid.

CHAPTER 4

The Verdict—The Analysis

He uses statistics as a drunken man uses lamp posts—for support rather than illumination.
   —Andrew Lang

I don't believe in statistics. You can't measure a ball player's heart...
   —Red Auerback

Not everything that counts can be counted, and not everything that can be counted counts.
   —(Attributed to Albert Einstein)

In the art of governing, one always remains a student.
   —Queen Christina of Sweden (1626–1689)

It has been said: "It is not so bad to make a mistake; it's bad not to learn anything from it."

Standards for Managerial Competency—Can They Be Defined?

No real and meaningful assessment of managerial competency can be made without first determining the criteria/attributes of a "competent" manager. The question that needs to be addressed at the outset is: What characteristics must a manager possess before he or she can be "labeled" a competent manager? Once those characteristics are identified, the task becomes manageable. Let's try to identify them.

Since management is not an exact science, there will be no agreement, even among "professional" managers, as to what these characteristics are. Even if there were agreement, the definitions would still vary. Take, for example, the characteristic "risk taker." The prevailing questions are: What exactly do we mean by "risk taker"? At what point does risk taking become good and when does it become bad (when does risk taking amount to gambling)? Is or should the risk be judged when it is taken or after the fact (a little Monday morning quarterbacking)?

If we decide that one of the characteristics is success, then the following questions need to be answered: What is success—how do we define success? Can an organization be termed successful during a particular year even though it lost money during that year? After all, an organization can be successful in the short term, yet it may not stand the test of time. What about the statement "Companies don't succeed...people do"? It is important to note that if an organization does not provide innovative products and does not continue its product development, the market may march on without the company. Even though an organization may get customer input, it cannot wait for customers to tell it what to do. It needs to provide leadership and offer customers a better way of doing things. It has been said that "the organization gives birth to the product, but the customer gives life to it." It is important to separate short-term from long-term success.

Even if agreement cannot be reached as to the characteristics or traits of a good manager, just as there is no agreement regarding the traits of a leader, there are some characteristics that appear in many lists. For example, a good manager is a visionary, a creative decision maker and a problem solver, a good delegator, an innovator, and a good communicator. He or she focuses on people, inspires trust, is goal oriented, has strong people skills, is ethical, is able to set priorities, is able to equitably balance the interests of the various stakeholders, asks what and why, is a straight shooter, and leads by reason rather than by force.

One CEO who was said to be among the best and the brightest was cited for his growth and profit, vision and dedication, willingness to reevaluate and change the company, ethics, goal setting, viewing people as an asset, excellent performance, risk taking, changing himself and his company to be much more open, his leadership and commitment to principles and vision, being a doer, his vision for the future, his simplistic approach to organization and problem solving, and for taking a company in dire straits to profitability.[1]

The general manager has to be a strategist, an organizational builder, and a doer. Generally, managers have no problem acknowledging these as necessary functions and abilities to perform their tasks. The area where managers have great difficulty is in realizing what precisely these roles require them to do. No manager, for example, would claim that he or she is not a doer or a strategist or, for that matter, an organizational builder. The problem arises in how a manager attempts to perform these tasks and how he or she accomplishes them. Being good in these roles means more than recognizing them and accepting responsibility for them. It means having the ability, the knowledge, and the training to do them. This is critical. There may be some legitimate difference of opinion, backed by logical and sound arguments, about how these skills are acquired (i.e., inherited or learned), but there is concurrence as to their importance and necessity in order to be an effective and excellent manager. Because managers are able to recognize these skills, it becomes too painful to admit that they are deficient in these areas; consequently, they psychologically block out their weaknesses and see themselves as possessing these skills.

When their confidence is low and they recognize that others in their organizations may notice their deficiencies, they often tend to pull away from the limelight. They don't want to give others the opportunity to scrutinize them. Delegation is reduced, almost non-existent, because they fear they will be exposed. They hire employees whom they perceive as less talented than they are. They begin to withdraw and seem to spend their time in their offices, not wanting others to invade their turf. As a matter of fact, it is fairly safe to say that in 80% of the cases, a general manager who closets himself or herself is an incompetent manager. The sad part is that because of the power held by the manager, very little can be done to remedy the situation. There is usually no gradual correction. If and when correction takes place, it is drastic—usually resulting in the forced ousting of the manager. Of course, in many cases this does not happen until it is too late, until the organization suffers a severe or even fatal blow.

On the other hand, those who have confidence in themselves, even though they may have some deficiencies, may be saved by using good judgment and analytical skills. Many are good at recognizing and calling on those who can help them. Their confidence gives them a sense of stability in their work and keeps them from being threatened by those whom they employ. Some managers seem to underestimate intuition and "street smarts." Yet, both can be powerful tools when used with other positive managerial qualities. Managers who possess them, and who properly utilize them, can benefit immensely.

In addition, the manager must be able to project the image that he or she truly possesses these characteristics. Perception is key. Often, it is more important than reality. The manager must be perceived as a "winner" by those whom he or she manages. This is crucial to the success of the manager, as well as the organization. In many cases, ability without the right perception is not enough.

We need clear answers to questions regarding CEOs, but often the answers are hazy and complex at best. Consider, for example, the following questions posed by an author and former CEO: "Are CEOs special people, unusual men and women destined from birth to be leaders? Or, do they reach the top through some combination of talent and lucky circumstances? Do they owe their selection to some arbitrary god possessed of more humor than justice? And if some CEOs have 'lucked out' over people more worthy than they, does their experience, once they reach the top, somehow transform them? For that matter, are CEOs really any different from ordinary mortals?"[2] How would you answer these questions?

Many people, including some "self-styled managers," unfortunately have only a vague understanding of the true meaning of management. Some go so far as to say that anyone can manage. For example, if one were to walk into a first-year MBA organizational behavior class, made up of a cross-section of business students, engineers, doctors, lawyers, communication majors, and the corporate sector, and begin to lecture about management, the students would appear to be very comfortable, as though many were very familiar with the subject. This scenario, however, would not repeat itself in a physics or an engineering class. Why? Many perceive managing to be an easy task, something that they can do given the opportunity.

As a case in point, consider a U.S. senator with a background in law or some other non-management field, who has come up through the political ranks. Suppose he has done an outstanding job representing his constituents, has championed the right causes, and is a great orator and a good politician. He now decides to run for president of the United States. Is it fair to ask what qualifies him to manage the United States? Is he able to "effectively" manage and "efficiently" govern? It troubles many management professionals that the question of whether a candidate is able to effectively manage is seldom, if ever, addressed. The media focuses on the candidate's political philosophy, ethics and morals, charisma, or physical appearance, but the subject of managing is seldom mentioned, much less used as a serious criterion for selection. What message does this convey about management? What should the message be? Should we really be surprised that some elected officials fall short of accomplishing their mission? Is it fair to conclude that government crises are inevitable?

The Perception of Others—The Survey

To better understand managers, many professionals who are familiar with managers and their tasks were surveyed. The purpose was to determine the overall opinion of these professionals representing the various publics as to how U.S. organizations are being managed and with what levels of managerial competency. Their specific comments and analysis will be discussed in subsequent chapters, as will the strengths and weaknesses of managers. In addition, subsequent chapters will deal with acts and attitudes that affect managerial performance. Before doing so, however, several comments need to be made to set the overall stage.

Let's begin by considering the responses given by university business deans to the statement: "Most companies fail because of poor management." Eighty-one percent of those responding either agreed or strongly agreed with the statement, while only 10% either disagreed or strongly disagreed. The responses of university business professors were similar to those of the deans; 76% either agreed or strongly agreed with the statement, while 20% disagreed or strongly disagreed, and 4% neither agreed nor disagreed. Furthermore, when the same question was asked of CEOs, 81% agreed or strongly agreed, while only 5% disagreed. Union presidents felt the same way; 77% agreed or strongly disagreed, while 11% disagreed. The responses of business news editors were in line with the others; 77% agreed or strongly agreed, while 23% disagreed.

When the business deans were asked to respond to the statement "American organizations are being managed by the 'best' and the 'brightest,'" 44% either disagreed or strongly disagreed, while 26% agreed and 2% strongly agreed. Twenty-eight percent neither agreed nor disagreed. When it came to business professors who were teaching business strategy courses, 53% either disagreed or strongly disagreed, 20% agreed, less than 2% strongly agreed, and 25% neither agreed nor disagreed. As for the CEOs, 25% disagreed with the statement, 31% agreed, 6% strongly agreed, and 38% neither agreed nor disagreed. Responses from union presidents indicated that 56% strongly disagreed, while 44% disagreed. No one agreed or strongly agreed with the statement. Of the business news editors, 54% disagreed or strongly disagreed, 31% agreed, and 15% neither agreed nor disagreed.

The following tables depict the responses of these groups to three statements concerning managerial performance and the abilities of managers:

The word to describe managerial performance is "excellent."

Survey Panel	Disagree Strongly	Disagree	Neither Agree Nor Disagree	Agree	Agree Strongly
University business deans	6%	51%	31%	12%	0%
University business professors	7%	69%	18%	2%	4%
CEOs	0%	38%	44%	18%	0%
Union presidents	45%	33%	22%	0%	0%
Business news editors	31%	46%	8%	15%	0%

The word to describe managerial performance is "mediocre."

Survey Panel	Disagree Strongly	Disagree	Neither Agree Nor Disagree	Agree	Agree Strongly
University business deans	2%	34%	24%	37%	3%
University business professors	4%	18%	29%	45%	4%
CEOs	0%	69%	19%	12%	0%
Union presidents	0%	11%	11%	56%	22%
Business news editors	0%	15%	23%	54%	8%

American organizations are being managed by the "best" and the "brightest."

Survey Panel	Disagree Strongly	Disagree	Neither Agree Nor Disagree	Agree	Agree Strongly
University business deans	8%	35%	28%	26%	3%
University business professors	11%	42%	25%	20%	2%
CEOs	0%	25%	38%	31%	6%
Union presidents	56%	44%	0%	0%	0%
Business news editors	23%	31%	15%	31%	0%

An examination of the responses to these questions clearly reveals that managerial performance certainly cannot be described as excellent. A better word to describe managerial performance is mediocre. What can be concluded is that, on the average, all the groups surveyed labeled U.S. managers, in general, as mediocre. If that assessment is correct, we have to ask why.

Farcus

by David Waisglass
Gordon Coulthart

6-24
© 1993 Farcus Cartoons/Distributed by Universal Press Syndicate

WAISGLASS/COULTHART

**"It seems to me, Flemming, you have the
skills to join our management team."**

(Farcus ©Farcus Cartoons. Distributed by Universal Press Syndicated.
Reprinted with permission. All rights reserved.)

In the United States, perhaps the greatest industrialized country, where business reigns as king, where people from all over the world come to the best business universities to learn how to manage their businesses, American managers, in general, are labeled mediocre. Surely we can do better. We must. We owe it to our constituents and to our stakeholders. As Herbert Hoover said, "The future of America rests not in mediocrity, but in the constant renewal of leadership in every phase of our national life."

In order to take a more in-depth look at this area, an open-ended question was posed to the same panel: "Overall, how would you rate the performance of U.S. managers?" Some responses were general (poor, fair, mediocre, good, very good), but others were more specific, as reflected in the following sampling of responses from each group.

University business deans:

- If other professionals handled their professional work the same way, we would probably have a revolution.
- Mediocre—We are, as Warren Bennis asserted (perhaps by quoting someone else), overmanaged and underled.
- Poor—They don't really know what they are doing. They're fumbling in the dark.
- Good—but must do a much better job to be world class.
- Good but getting better.
- No better than fair.
- Generally, tolerable but certainly below par. Far from where they should be.
- Imperfect but best in the world and trying hard to improve.
- Overall, I would have to say they are far below from where they should be. Many are just micro managing. Their vision is blurred at best.

University business professors:

- I think performance is improving as public pressure to be accountable beyond just dollars increases.
- You would think with all the business schools they would do much better.
- Unfortunately many organizations are driven to profitability by their products rather than by their managers. Many managers can manage much better if they don't let their egos get in their way.
- Mediocre—much too driven by a "bottom line."
- Improving fast. The younger generation will be a lot better.
- In most instances "OK." A lot of room for improvement but could be worse.
- 1920–1940s, good; 1950–1980s, improving in some areas.
- Although some are very good, many are far from being designated professional managers.

CEOs and chairmen of boards:

- Wide range—but overall better than government–academia or non-U.S. management.
- Satisfactory, better than 10 years ago.
- On a scale of 1–10, about 6–7.

- Most are weak, or there would not be continuing write-offs in public companies.

Union presidents:

- Very bad.
- Very poor.
- Poor/terrible.
- Very bad.
- Lousy.

Business news editors:

- Poor, short sighted.
- Disappointing.
- The smaller the company, the better the management.

Here are some of the panel's representative responses to the following open-ended question: "The main weakness of most managers today is..."

University business deans:

- The quest for personal gain overshadows their true organizational missions.
- Lack of depth in knowledge.
- Short term focus.
- Lack of integrity and professionalism.
- Lack of leadership commitment.
- Fad driven.
- Lack of vision. (this comment appeared over and over)
- Apathy.
- They are "forced" into short-term solutions rather than being allowed to do long-term planning.
- Short-term thinking.
- Lack of ability to think creatively.
- They do not strongly identify with the long-run success of the firm.
- Their egos and self-interest stand in their way of being what they ought to be.
- Short-term frame for evaluation.
- Coaching and developing others. Changing from power-command model to coaching model.

- Fear of challenging the status quo.
- Their inability to really listen to what their employees are saying.
- Spread too thin.
- Effective communication.
- Out of touch with operations.
- Short-term planning.
- A climate that forces them to avoid responsibility while making them assume authority.
- Narrow vision.
- Understanding global changes—empowering their workers.
- Commitment to the organization.
- Lack of leadership and an organizational structure to support it.
- Seeing the big picture.
- Working to comply with excessive legislation rather than risk-taking to gain market share or enter new markets.
- Short-term perspective.
- Inability to use people to their potential.
- Failure to fully develop human capital.
- Interpersonal skill, development of subordinates is inadequate.
- Managing change.
- Inability to communicate.
- Lack of long-term vision for the unit.
- Difficulty in delegating responsibility.
- Incompetence in human resource management.
- Long-term focus.
- Form of external (to organization) constraints.
- Lack of loyalty, too qualitative in their approach.
- Lack of shared mission.
- Lack of character.
- They are overwhelmed by complexity and lack information necessary for success—leads to uncertainty.
- Judging performance on a quarterly profit or loss.
- A mis-match between authority and responsibility—not enough of the former.
- Team building.
- Lack of appreciation of employees.
- Become so involved with the tasks of management that they lose touch with people and organization purpose.
- Lack of long-range ethical vision/too tied up in operations.
- Lack of skills at managing in a rapidly changing environment.

- Short-sightedness.
- Failure to articulate and follow an overall and progressive vision.
- Lack of strategic vision.
- Lack of vision; lack of organizational mission; lack of concern for employees.
- Not enough practical experience in the functions they manage.
- Too bureaucratic and lack of risk taking.

University business professors:

- Loyalty.
- I am the "king" attitude. Either bow to me or you're out—no debate about that.
- Too much focus on own career.
- Lack of overview.
- Allowing themselves to be pulled in too many directions so they become focus-less and too "urgency-centered."
- A too narrow focus on their specialty area and an acceptance of the old paradigm.
- Focus on short-term results.
- Pressure for profit and government regulations.
- Excessive emphasis on short-run profit.
- Short-term focus.
- Narcissism.
- Concern for their own PYA files rather than other affected parties.
- Dealing with uncertainty.
- Paying attention to politics instead of the marketplace.
- Focus on day-to-day problems and short-term objectives.
- Concern for bottom line.
- Interpersonal skills.
- Commitment, risk-taking ability, vision, clarity regarding company objectives/goals.
- Lack of understanding that 1) people are different, 2) different strokes for different folks can be accomplished with a little effort.
- Narrow, functionalistic views.
- Vision and understanding.
- Lack of personal vision and vision for organization.
- Willingness to take responsibility. And this problem is created by a situation over which he/she has no control.
- Decision making under uncertainty.

- Too much emphasis on the short term.
- Narrow knowledge base.
- Communication skills and ability to develop employees.
- Ability to communicate.
- Lack of vision.
- Short sightedness.
- A tendency to autocratic style.
- An uninformed public or misinformed public who, if they only knew the facts, would love them!
- Pressure to perform well in the short run; lack of value of the work force.
- Future thinking or lack of it.
- Narrow focus, time, discipline, cognitive level.
- Putting their self-interest ahead of the corporation.
- Lack of training in bringing out the best in other people.
- Tunnel vision—poor decision habits.
- Lack of operations experience.
- Not thinking systemically.
- Ability to manage and see change.
- Lack of commitment and leadership.
- Overwork, time constraints.
- Lack of vision and the ability to communicate this vision throughout the organization.
- Inability to recognize the strengths of their employees and the need to tap these strengths.
- Self-interest.

CEOs and chairmen of boards:

- Leadership competencies.
- Fear and complacency.
- Setting and holding people to high standards of performance.
- Experience.
- The inability and/or desire to keep up or stay current.
- Hesitance to take best advantage of the opportunities they see.
- Taking accountability.
- Short-term view, hierarchical organization.
- Lack of focus and purpose.
- Lack of communication skills.
- Lack of leadership skills.

- Ability to manage change.
- Indecision.
- To handle all aspects well of the very demanding and wide-ranging scale.
- Lack of commitment to the long term.

Union presidents:

- Lack of leadership.
- Inability to view the work force as an asset deserving of care and investment (training).
- Poor training and lack of ability.
- Survival syndrome.
- Too much pay.
- Utter lack of historical, social/economic context of their action.
- Commitment to the company and to fellow officers and employees is lacking. To much "me!!."

Business news editors:

- Politics are more important than performance.
- Lack of basic intelligence; lack of ability to communicate and empathize with lower-level workers.
- Inability to combine fairness with toughness.
- Overworked with huge list of responsibilities and not enough staff.
- Fear of failure.
- Failure to step back and develop cohesion.
- Inability to plan effectively for an uncertain future.
- Lack of genuine commitment.
- Fear of doing something bad that will hurt/end their career.
- Isolation from "real world"; arrogance.
- People skills.

What about managerial strengths? What are the strengths of our managers? To gain better insight, the panel was asked to complete the following statement: "The greatest strength of most managers is..."

University business deans:

- Communication ability.
- Ability to work well with others.

- Desire to succeed.
- New concern of customer and service.
- Background.
- Availability of technology.
- Good technology training.
- They are well educated.
- Qualitative skills.
- Their interpersonal skills in building team work throughout.
- Technical knowledge/skills. (many times)
- Risk taking.
- Ability to plan, organize and delegate.
- Experienced in the political environment.
- Better education. Too bad that they fail to use it in many business decisions.
- Analytical skills.
- Ability to network and establish linkages with others who can influence company success.
- Total access to information.
- Self-confidence.
- Getting the job done.
- Experience in problem/decisional situations.
- Financial knowledge.
- Focused goal-oriented management.
- Technical competence.
- Commitment to the organization.
- Work ethic; they work hard.
- Quantitative analysis.
- Hardworking/dedicated.
- Financial planning.
- P&L management.
- Spirit, ambition.
- Trying, but never knowing when they will be terminated.
- Adaptability.
- Organizational skills.
- Leadership.
- Aggressiveness and self-confidence.
- Ability to change when they see a need.
- Technical skills in their area.
- Ability to learn.

- Experience in the field; however, this does not necessarily lead to ability to manage/work with people.
- Motivation and loyalty to company and job.
- Their physical health.
- Well-educated and intelligent.

University business professors:

- Technical skills.
- A new recognition of the value of difference—it's okay to change rules and do things differently than in the past.
- Self preservation.
- The ability to at least make something happen.
- Technical qualifications.
- Hardworking.
- Intelligent, high achievers.
- Leadership.
- Ability to follow policies and procedures and execute "technical" requirements of the job.
- They are well educated.
- Willingness to take responsibility.
- Drive and energy.
- Understanding.
- Good educational and technical background.
- Desire to succeed.
- Education managers today know so much or should that they strive to be very good at their job.
- Hard work.
- Action-oriented approach.
- Interpersonal skills.
- Formal education. However, not always used in a constructive manner.
- External appearance.
- Technical knowledge and analytical skills.
- Information.
- They are task oriented.
- Incredible brainpower and ethics.
- Understanding that profit is necessary.
- Business sense, decision-making quickness.
- Motivation.

- Hard worker.
- Individual desire to succeed.
- Analytical skills.
- Flexibility and trained.
- They work hard—they want to do the best.

CEOs and chairmen of boards:

- Bottom-line focus.
- Care for customers and subordinates.
- Intelligence.
- Ability.
- Should be communication ability and people skills.
- Hard work, commitment and loyalty.
- Communication.
- Global perspective, greater willingness to take risks.
- Experience and ambition.
- Technical.
- They are ready to deal with changes.
- Ability to keep a cooperation moving in the agreed upon direction.
- Concentrate on the most critical aspects.
- Increased intelligence.

Union presidents:

- Being sensitive to "the bottom line."
- Familiarity with operations and commitment to organization.

Business news editors:

- Great training opportunities.
- Savvy.
- Dedication.
- Knowledge.
- Commitment, enthusiasm, desire to do well and do good.
- Team work and leadership.
- Fear of failure.
- CYA.
- Brains, guts, stamina.
- Bean counting.

It would be misleading to end this chapter with the impression that all U.S. managers are mediocre. That is certainly not the case. There are great, even outstanding, managers and leaders. We are proud of their performance. Many perform their jobs as CEOs and general managers very well indeed. We are pleased to have them lead our organizations. That statement is practically undisputed. Many people would like to be a part of these great organizations, to work with these great leaders. Indeed, many investors are very happy with their performance, as are customers and suppliers. Some organizations are in existence and are performing excellently due to the great leadership—to the stewardship—of these leaders. The success of many of these organizations is primarily due to good managerial performance rather than to the unique products they sell. These organizations are management driven rather than product driven. However, these two "drives" are not mutually exclusive; indeed, they often complement each other very well.

The purpose of the survey and this study is to gain insight into overall managerial performance. The discussion should not necessarily be viewed as a criticism but rather as a wake-up call—a call to take a closer look at the present situation. A call to do better. Organizations need to determine where they are, where they want to be, and precisely how to get there.

Notes

1. Brian S. Moskal, "CEOs Speaking Out...On Their Careers, 23rd Annual CEO Survey," *Industry Week*, November 21, 1994, p. 14. Reprinted with permission.
2. Thomas R. Horton, *The CEO Paradox: The Privilege and Accountability of Leadership* (New York: AMACOM, American Management Association, 1992), pp. xiii–xiv.

PART III

Managerial Performance: Obstacles to Effective Leadership— Corporate Confessions

CHAPTER 5

The Fatal Managerial Sins:
Deadly Misdeeds

People ask the difference between a leader and a boss. The leader leads and the boss drives.
—Theodore Roosevelt

We are what we repeatedly do. Excellence, then, is not an act, but habit.
—Aristotle

The superior man seeks what is right; the inferior one, what is profitable.
—Confucius

Lead, follow, or get out of the way.
—Anonymous

Corporate Chaos—Where Many Thrive and Many Die

Are you happy with your job? How about your friends—are they happy with their jobs? Surveys estimate that between 60 to 80% (depending upon which survey one reads) of U.S. employees respond negatively to that question. These estimates are probably accurate, but even if they were cut in half, the picture would still be gloomy and frustrating. Think of how many millions of people get into their cars every morning to go to a place where they don't want to be, where they will spend at least eight hours doing a job they don't enjoy doing. They spend forty of their best hours every week someplace they'd rather not be. We live in a country where there is lots of wealth and opportunity, yet something is missing. Shouldn't an alarm be sounding? What is wrong? What are we doing about it? What can be done about it? How? By whom? When?

According to Dun and Bradstreet, approximately 50,000 U.S. companies reached the point of failure in 1989. By 1992, that figure rose to 97,000. Why the 94% increase? Perhaps competition, unfavorable legislation, and economic conditions could be part of the explanation, but the overall cause, in practically all cases, had to be bad management, lack of proper leadership. That is inexcusable. After all, good leaders, visionary, proactive leaders, should have anticipated the problems and found remedies to prevent the failures. Why didn't they?

Let's look at the responses to a statement that was posed to the panel:

Most companies fail because of poor management.

Survey Panel	Disagree Strongly	Disagree	Neither Agree Nor Disagree	Agree	Agree Strongly
University business deans	0%	10%	9%	61%	20%
University business professors	4%	16%	4%	48%	28%
CEOs	0%	6%	13%	69%	12%
Union presidents	0%	11%	11%	45%	33%
Business new editors	0%	23%	0%	39%	38%

Obviously, the data leave no doubt, at least from the panel's point of view, about why most companies fail. In view of that, we need to address why we have poor management. To gain insight into this, let's again turn to our panel. The responses to the next two statements shed some light on why there is poor management.

There are employees that are promoted to managerial positions not because they possess the proper qualifications, but rather for political or personal reasons.

Survey Panel	Disagree Strongly	Disagree	Neither Agree Nor Disagree	Agree	Agree Strongly
University business deans	1%	6%	6%	64%	23%
University business professors	2%	7%	5%	51%	35%
CEOs	6%	31%	13%	50%	0%
Union presidents	0%	0%	0%	56%	44%
Business news editors	0%	23%	8%	54%	15%

Do you find the results surprising? Probably not! Nevertheless, they are disturbing, to say the least, in light of the fact that those who do the hiring do not, in most cases, own the company. Where is their loyalty—their responsibility? When organizations hire or promote managers who do not possess the proper qualifications, what do they expect the result to be? Can we say that is management at its best?

Let's take a look at the responses of the panel to the following statement:

Managers do an excellent job in placing (matching) employees in the right job (doing the right tasks) in the right organizations.

Survey Panel	Disagree Strongly	Disagree	Neither Agree Nor Disagree	Agree	Agree Strongly
University business deans	7%	49%	24%	19%	1%
University business professors	7%	55%	20%	16%	2%
CEOs	6%	31%	25%	38%	0%
Union presidents	33%	45%	22%	0%	0%
Business news editors	16%	46%	23%	15%	0%

Managing is not an impossible job; indeed, managing can be easy. It begins with the right people, the right managers, adhering to certain principles. High on the list should be the careful selection and placement of the right person (employee) in the right job (task) in the right organization. Easy? It can be, but as is evident from the data above, this principle is violated much too often. Complicating things is the fact that even if an employee has been initially placed in the right job, the manager has not necessarily completed the task. The manager must review each employee periodically to determine whether each is still properly placed. Maybe, just maybe, one of them has outgrown his or her job!

In order to determine the overall management climate in the United States, the panel was asked to respond to the following statements:

The word to describe the overall management climate in corporate America is "mediocre."

Survey Panel	Disagree Strongly	Disagree	Neither Agree Nor Disagree	Agree	Agree Strongly
University business deans	3%	31%	23%	35%	8%
University business professors	2%	25%	22%	42%	9%
CEOs	19%	44%	37%	0%	0%
Union presidents	0%	0%	0%	44%	56%
Business news editors	0%	15%	15%	62%	8%

**The word to describe the overall management climate
in corporate America is "excellent."**

Survey Panel	Disagree Strongly	Disagree	Neither Agree Nor Disagree	Agree	Agree Strongly
University business deans	7%	51%	26%	14%	2%
University business professors	17%	61%	15%	5%	2%
CEOs	0%	25%	50%	25%	0%
Union presidents	67%	33%	0%	0%	0%
Business news editors	23%	46%	16%	15%	0%

Oren Harari writes, "When managers tolerate a culture of mediocrity, they reinforce the most pernicious barrier to change. Mediocrity insidiously works its way through every nook and cranny of the corporation. It anesthetizes people into passivity and, even worse, creates a quicksand of generalized inertia that continually frustrates those who attempt to shake things up toward real change."[1]

In order to get a better and more focused view of the managerial climate, the panel was asked the following open-ended question: "How would you describe the overall management climate in corporate America?" The responses point to a disorganized and generally unhappy environment. It is consistent with what has been said so far. Some of the responses follow.

University business deans:

- Selfish and inconsistent.
- First my pocket book, second, my job and then the rest of the stakeholders.
- Unfocused, reactive.
- Scared and reactive.
- Lots of lip service but no follow-through.
- Companies thriving and failing in chaos.
- Tense and anxious.
- Discouraging...downsizing without logic.
- Behind, backwards and not ready for the 21st century.
- Sadly reactive rather than pro-active.
- Self-centered and out for themselves in the shortest time period.
- Very good—but not without some/many serious problems. We are in a culture change period.
- Strong and improving.

- I have mine, you try to get yours.
- Myopic, self-centered.
- Opportunity abounds in our society, but government regulations are oppressive.
- Cautious, poor risk takers.
- Average at best—too much focus on the short term.
- Suspicious of one another, those above and below.
- Exciting and frustrating.
- Cost and productivity conscious; more aggressive and proactive than ever.
- Nervous, scary, not representing an attractive career path it once did.
- Very little leadership capabilities.
- Good but management in a state of anxiety.
- Poor—misoriented by "catch up" philosophies and stockholder driven.
- Doubt, fear; lack of clear vision.
- Ego-oriented, but frustrated due to lack of power.

University business professors:

- Competitive and manager-centered.
- Most managers fail to instill a sense of urgency and purpose in their employees.
- No time to plan for the future—eyes too focused on the bottom line.
- Competitive and overwhelmed by change.
- Chaotic because of downsizing.
- Companies driven by and for the bottom-line.
- Middle managers are discouraged, angry, unhappy due to downsizing and poor leadership.
- More power seeking than success thinking.
- Threatened and threatening.
- Easily confused and distracted by media and trends.
- Shaky for middle managers.
- Intense, competitive, complex, dynamic.
- Challenging.
- Terrible when Lincoln Electric, Drucker/Deming are not listened to.
- Cautious.
- Unsettled, shifting to new paradigms.
- Managing for the short term, applying reactive rather than proactive techniques.

- Mediocre, more reactive than proactive.
- Politically oriented internally.
- Stressful.
- Old fashioned, narrow.
- Personal gain that is characteristic of short-term thinking.
- Rather than suffocating, they are caught in the short-run financial treadmill.

CEOs and chairmen of boards:

- Demanding—insecure—competitive.
- Positive and improving.
- Intense, highly stressed, short-term oriented.
- Reasonably healthy with managers more socially aware than their counterparts of 20 years ago.
- Good.

Union presidents:

- Focus on simplistic fix.
- Dog eat dog.
- Self—first and foremost.
- Poor/terrible.
- Winning is all—angry, surly, mean, nasty.
- Oppressive—too much focus on downsizing.

Business news editors:

- Back-stabbing.
- Becoming more proactive.
- Stressed and paranoid.
- Difficult.
- Very questionable, overpaid/overcompensated and not accountable.
- Poor.
- Nervous.

It is obvious that the foregoing words do not place managers in the best light. Not many are "raving" about their performance. The focus by senior managers on short-term results, on realizing immediate profits, on shareholders' dividends, and on promoting their own careers has significantly contributed to both the demise of many organizations and the negative image of the manager's ability to manage. While it is true that some or even considerable blame should be shared by the various members of the organization, ultimately the blame lies with the senior managers and, in the end, with the CEO. After all, the implication is that the CEO's strategy was wrong; it wasn't the proper strategy to meet and respond to the organization's challenges. The CEO failed to properly assess the various variables and was not a visionary; in sum, the CEO was not a competent manager/leader. In the words of Malcolm Kent, creative director of advertising and author of several business titles, "One of the greatest failings of today's executive is his inability to do what he's supposed to do."

Facts: several years ago America's CEO, the president of the United States, was not re-elected but rather forced to leave office. The governors of Texas and New York are forced to take early retirement. The Speaker of the House was not re-elected. Cabinet members lost their jobs. Questions: Why? What does that say about their managerial ability? Is there any reason to question their managerial ability? Is there a message here for managers? What about leaders from the private sector who were forced to leave or left their organizations at an age and at a time when retirement is not usual? Consider, for example, William Agee from Bendix Corporation and later from Morrison Knudsen, John Akers from IBM, Joseph Antonini from K-Mart, Samuel Armacost of Bank of America, Donald Burr from People Express Airlines, Steven Jobs from Apple Computer Company, Paul Lego from Westinghouse Electric Corporation, John Shields of Computervision, and Roger Smith from General Motors. Jeffrey H. Erickson, fifty-one, president and chief executive of Trans World Airlines, Inc., announced his resignation shortly after the airline posted a $14.3 million quarterly loss that was linked to the July 1996 explosion of one of its jetliners. The list can be extended for pages and pages. Why were these chieftains separated from their organizations? What effect did these, and so many others, have on their organizations? What about their influence on other employees in their organizations?

Why Do Managers Fail? Obstacles to Effective Management

It should be made clear that just because a CEO or senior manager is let go does not necessarily mean that he or she lacks managerial competency or is a weak manager. Many would argue that a case in point here is Lee Iacocca. He was let go from Ford Motor Company and then, at least for a number of years, successfully led the Chrysler Corporation. CEOs are entrusted with great responsibility; some would argue that their responsibility is awesome!

The way the system is supposed to work, at least in theory, in the private sector is that stockholders elect the right board of directors, who then hire the right CEO for that organization—the individual who will properly lead the organization. In theory, CEOs are supposed to have reached the top because of their qualifications, their past accomplishments, and their predicted potential. In many instances, things go as planned; the assessment is accurate, and they perform well. Unfortunately, there are those instances when things don't go as planned. What then?

In order to answer that question and remedy the situation, it is extremely important to understand why things didn't go as planned. Was the board wrong in its assessment? Did the board overevaluate the CEO's qualifications and/or potential? Could it it be that even though the CEO had the right qualifications and the potential for the job, he or she didn't properly exercise them, didn't put them to proper use, and thus failed? The reasons why organizations get into trouble are not always easy to determine. Often, they are interwoven and difficult to separate. However, in many cases, the reasons are fairly obvious if we look for them objectively. The analysis has to start at the top. Organizations are made up of people, and they depend on their leaders. When we ask why organizations fail, the answer to that question can be found in the answer to another question: Why do people at the top of the organization fail? Consequently, the problem must be dealt with at the top.

Having generally assessed the current status regarding managerial competence in U.S. organizations, we need to shift our focus to the reasons for the present condition. How and why did they get where they are? To answer that question, we first need to determine and define the obstacles to effective management. What are these obstacles? Can they be eliminated? What are the acts, attitudes, and behaviors of practicing managers which are or could be fatal mistakes or misdeeds—managerial sins? What do managers do that in the long-run adversely impacts both them and their organizations?

These precise questions were posed to our panel of experts throughout the United States, as well as to a number of CEOs through in-depth interviews. The panel was asked to respond to the following question: "What are the obstacles to effective management?" Here's a sample of the responses.

University business deans:

- Poor supervision—no mentoring—political decision making.
- Government regulation. Short-term focus of shareholders and analysts.

- Greed, short sightedness and lack of accountability.
- The environmental (social, political, legal) constraints.
- Governmental controls, too much litigation. Change the legal climate; have government work with companies toward common society goals.
- Complacent workers. Leadership.
- Greed, lack of peripheral vision and lack of accountability.
- Self-centeredness, personal bias, loyalty, work ethic.
- Incapable boards of directors.
- Short-term thinking, rewarding short-term performance—rewarding only profits. Delay compensation for future years.
- Tradition, fear, shareholders.
- Management control of the firm. Effective control by the unpaid board of directors would go a long way toward providing an incentive structure for effective management.
- Union work rules.
- Stupidity and arrogance.
- As in all professions, keeping up. Continuous learning is essential.
- Fear of failure. Managers must be held accountable, but at the same time can be encouraged to take reasonable risks in pursuit of the organization's goals. It would help if reasonable risk-taking was rewarded and "playing it safe" punished.
- Politics inside the organization. Power hungry people who feel the need to do this to amass more power. Inability to listen with an open mind. People have to care more about the organization than their own advancement.
- I think the barrier is pride. It is more a character issue than a competence issue. It can be overcome through both spiritual awakening and teaching.
- Government.
- Lack of clear goals.
- Emphasis on short-term profits.
- "Rights." Everyone claims to have rights but few claim to have responsibilities! Everyone wants satisfaction up front instead of a reward for achievement. Management wants everyone to do more with less. To overcome, it needs to build a work culture within a company. It takes years. Difficult to change.
- Lack of vision on the part of the manager. It is not always easy to overcome—egos and other things get in the way.

- Personalities. Weak boards of directors that do not hold managers accountable.
- Long-term vision and commitment. It is hard to overcome without a "re-focus" for long-term survival and growth.
- A lack of understanding of how to manage and implement change. Too "chicken" to blow up the organization and start over.
- To overcome the obstacle there is need for education—benchmark with successful change programs.
- Rapid change. Not enough investment in people! There is a need for change in approach/attitude; maybe have a new type of manager with strong ethics and broad training.
- Unions, liberal federal government policies, taxes, all of which divert attention from progress to fighting fires.
- Pressure of quarterly results which leads to short-term focus.
- Security, loyalty, lack of vision, improve adaptation to change, not investing in employees.
- Lack of communication, lack of trust.
- Conditions changing too rapidly for coping behavior to be developed; short-term thinking, overcoming the adversarial relationship between owners/managers and employees, and the lack of employees' and managers' commitment to organizational goals in the post-social contract era.
- Bonuses that focus on short-term goals which may be unrelated to long-term viability.
- Organizational politics.
- Lack of integrity.

University business professors:

- Politics, morale.
- Arrogance and insensitivity.
- Bottom line.
- Effective managers are in short supply.
- Incompetent superiors, lack of risk-taking environment. Too much concern on bottom-line strategies.
- Lack of control. Give a manager accountability/responsibility— and the wherewithal to do it. If he/she does—reward them. If they don't, replace them.
- Weak board of directors.
- The "we–they" syndrome between managers and workers— brought on mainly by managers not having participative management as a means of operating.

- Mixed signals from the top.
- Us vs. them mentality.
- Obsession with short-term results driven by Wall Street. Interest in personal gain to the detriment of what is best for the organization.
- Marriage to the old command-and-control paradigm, unwillingness/inability to listen and give credit to others, paying too much attention to financial analysts.
- Failure of boards of directors to do their jobs. Extreme individualism and personal competitiveness, excessive ego.
- No reward for excellence.
- Lack of clear vision.
- Inability to recognize the strengths of their employees and the need to tap into these strengths.
- Terrible managerial education. Not only is it woefully inadequate, graduates think it is complete.
- Egotism, short sightedness, lack of accountability.

CEOs and chairmen of boards:

- Inability of managers to move from doers to leaders.
- Fear of taking risks. Need teamwork, empowerment so everyone takes risk together.
- Lack of self-confidence.
- Unrealistic expectation at any level in the organization; misunderstood goals; poor communication.
- Bureaucracy.
- Government regulation.
- Too much short-term orientation rather than balance. Lack of training and support. Lots of people in management lack the strategic skills and interpersonal capabilities to really be good at it.
- Fuzzy objectives, poor communication.
- Union.

Union presidents:

- Office politics.
- Dishonesty, pride, manipulating the bounds of the law (including labor law) for the wrong reason. Insensitivity to people, inability to be an all-inspiring leader.
- Stagnation—poor training.

- Managers.
- Ideological bias, greed, stupidity.
- Too much to do. Nothing gets done well. Too much attention to industrial politics, which detracts from focus on real problems.
- Lack of proper ethics.
- To eliminate the obstacles, need better screening of prospective managers, better education in business schools and in internal programs, realign pay to performance, and let the people who know how do what they do best. Eliminate politics.
- Government regulation and oppression, lack of foresight ahead of time.
- Management is possible if the directors truly represent shareholders and are continually vigil. Also, many new managers had no personal responsibility during their youth.

Business news editors:

- Entrenched power structure that encourages managers to put self-interest above all else.
- Poor top leadership.
- Capital limitations and staff limitations.
- Time, resources and knowledge.
- Organizations that lack vision.
- Getting genuine commitment.
- Respect for individual contribution to overall product and well-being of company.
- The dominion of corporate decisions by "The Street."
- Politics, corporate dividends and executive bonuses.

Exploring the Roots Underlying Managerial Failures

Each panel member was asked to respond to the following statement: "Please list acts, attitudes, and behavior of practicing managers which you feel are fatal managerial sins." A sample of the answers follows.

University business deans:

- Dishonesty.
- Lack of loyalty to corporation.
- Focus on personal advancement.

- Lack of long-term vision.
- Arrogance and myopia.
- Ego.
- Economic motivation only.
- Short-term orientation.
- Not utilizing partnerships more effectively.
- Lack of clear vision—foresight.
- Making decisions on short run vs. long run.
- Poor reward system.
- Not getting all the facts.
- Inconsistent decision making.
- Talking teamwork and rewarding individuals.
- Failure to develop their people, processes and structure—to meet competitive conditions.
- Failure to make use of interval level power.
- Resisting change/embracing status quo.
- Promotion without merit but due to political pressure and/or seniority.
- Fighting present fires.
- Difficulty in delegating.
- Out of touch with the customer.
- Out of touch with the employees.
- Empire building.
- Not following through on something promised—paying lip service.
- Failure to take reasonable risks.
- Downsizing to salvage your own future.
- Surrounding yourself with "yes" people.
- Lack of trust in fellow workers/subordinates.
- Rigidity.
- Closed door policy—never seen but gives orders.
- Does not know how to empower others and give up "control."
- Inability to deal with complex issues.
- Short sightedness, egotism, lack of ownership.
- Too much power in one position.
- Perks.
- Inflated egos.
- Failure to develop people to fullest.
- Failure to execute.
- Not open to new ideas.

- Lack of controls.
- Sexual misconduct.
- Poor analytical skills.
- Inability to accept a "sunk cost" and move on.
- Failure to create employee commitment and loyalty.
- Not hearing what is said.
- Poor leadership skills.
- Rigid organizational structure.
- My way is the only way.
- Colleague envy.
- Avoidance of conflict.
- Tunnel vision, focus on self.
- Limited/underuse of technology.
- Lack of character/integrity.
- Failure to recognize contributors to success—not saying thanks often enough.
- Burning people out—using and abusing contributors.
- Failure to purge the non-contributors.
- Wasting time and resources on popular panaceas or "management fads."
- Waiting too long to seek help.
- Lip service to quality without the commitment.
- Treating employees as commodities.
- Lack of people skills.
- Failure to empower others.
- Failure to be "in the trenches."
- Trying to hide mistakes.
- Ignoring the needs of his subordinates to do their jobs.
- Failure to go "out on a limb" for his people.

University business professors:

- Unethical, lack of long-term vision, focus on personal advancement.
- Obsession with personal ego, failure to admit mistakes, short-term mentality, failure to utilize resources of all employees, lack of leadership, failure to provide a vision for the organization.
- Lack of professional ethics and integrity, poor communication skills, prejudices (gender, race, age), self-preservation decision making, lack of creativity, narrow vision of future, fear of risk taking, blaming others.

- Focus on short-term profits.
- Seeking personal wealth rather than opportunity to make positive difference, too willing to take the path of least resistance, too quick to blame almost everyone but themselves, isolation from everyone but their peers in public sector.
- Concerned for short-term performance, not organization building, allowing political agendas to overrule good judgment.
- Arrogance, narrow mindedness, lack of ethics, lack of awareness of responsibilities to people in organization, lack of trust.
- Failure to give good example in private life, failure to develop staff, failure to see the big picture, not considering all the stakeholders, not keeping current.
- Myopic vision, selfishness, ethnocentrism, no guts, poor HR skills, lack of intelligence, inability (or fear) to delegate.
- Poor decision making, lack of creativity.
- Lying, inability to face problems as they arise.
- Short term/quick fix thinking, adversarial approach to employees, inflexible—resistant to change, complacency.
- Power hungry. Lack of integrity. Greed. Lack of accountability.
- Closed mindedness, management by numbers, no concern for employee welfare, inability to motivate.
- Failure to represent the interest of the owners, doesn't understand strengths and weaknesses of firm.
- Not investing in the future, not investing in employee training, lack of understanding of manufacturing and technology.
- Indecisiveness, failure to plan, inability to recognize the strengths of their employees and the need to tap these strengths, a lack of willingness to share the rewards with all the employees, lack of accountability.

CEOs and chairmen of boards:

- Lack of result delivery, lack of focus, lack of leadership skills, lack of vision.
- Lack of sensitivity and shareholders' value, responsibility to community, customer focus.
- Fear/lack of confidence to take position, ignorance/lack of intellect to understand and compete, lack of care for customer and/or employees.
- Lack of integrity, poor judgment, lack of knowledge of the business, poor people manager, poor communicator, inflexible.

- Put own interest above company, intolerant.
- Lack of purpose, false expectations, inconsistent behavior.
- Arrogance, lack of listening skills.
- Satisfaction with status quo, short-term view, unwillingness to take risks, rigid organizational structure, have not kept up with technology.
- Doesn't tell the truth, rules through fear, no sense of consistent direction, blames others for his/her mistakes or failures, withholds vital information, doesn't communicate.
- Inability to get ego out of the business decision, unethical (or even marginally unethical) behavior, honesty to self and others, inability to stay current in terms of knowledge, inability to balance extremes: short term vs. long term, etc., inability to know when to make a decision, inability to laugh at oneself.
- Lack of honesty, not treating people as you want to be treated, lack of vision, bad communicator, risk averse, lack of effective delegation, adverse to change.
- Lack of integrity, lack of vision, inability to communicate adequately and inspire.

Union presidents:

- Family influence to obtain position, lying, lack of knowledge, not trained.
- Dishonesty, abuse of employee's rights, lack of openness in dealing with subordinates, ignorance of the labor law, abuse of managerial privileges.
- Tunnel vision, going "by the book," selfishness.
- Self at all costs, self at every point, self at every decision.
- Self-aggrandizement, lack of respect for others, dishonesty, failure to listen to advice, rigidity in attitudes.

Business news editors:

- Dishonesty, favoritism, self-interest, incompetence (failure to stay current), subversive subordinate (afraid of being shown up by younger talent).
- Blames everyone else but himself/herself for poor performance, shortsighted, "bosses people around" without teaching, thinks he/she is better than everyone else.
- Managing for personal gain, managing for the short run only.

- Not being truthful, asking employees to do something you consider to be "beneath" your job description, following double standards, demanding that employees give 110%—should create an environment that fosters productivity.
- Underutilizing talent and abilities of staff, sloppy or arrogant assessment, failure to listen or hear.
- Self-absorption, lack of respect for fellow workers, lack of personal integrity, inability to inspire others for quality workers.
- Hypocritic "don't do as I do, do as I say" with staff, favoritism/familiarity with certain staffing, too protected with compensation, perks, and pension.
- Not knowing the names of individual employees and what they do in the company, not having a clear vision for company and plan of how to get there, not being able to communicate the goals, not being able to motivate employees, favoritism, not promoting based on merit, inflexibility.
- Arrogance—both personal and institutional, complacency, isolation from rank and file, the product, the company, greed (personal), myopia, narrowness of perspective—usually financial, lack of candor.
- Keep company success or failure from the employees, authoritarian attitude.

In examining the responses, it is evident that a number of managerial sins appear in all the lists. How frequently they are committed, their potential damage, and whether they can be prevented will be explored in depth in the chapters that follow.

The Seven Fatal Managerial Sins

A thorough review of the literature, the results of in-depth interviews with CEOs, as well as the results of our national survey of experts present a less than complimentary picture of U.S. managers' managerial ability to manage. The evidence shows that many of those who are leading our organizations are not the best and the brightest. That, of course, is a disturbing fact, especially when we take into account the fact that they are capable of doing better. It is not that the United States doesn't have plenty of "bright" people to manage; there are plenty of them out there. What is lacking, in many of our managers, is the qualities that are needed to make professionals—true professional managers.

We need managers to manage our organizations professionally. We need people who know what to do and who do what is needed properly and in a timely manner. When a leader fails and is fired, forced to resign, or voted out of office, the impact is far-reaching. It affects not only the leader, but many others. Often, others are brought down with the leader. As we have seen in the previous discussion, there are a number of identifiable acts and attitudes of practicing managers that are fatal managerial sins, which in the long run severely and adversely impact both the manager and the organization. In addition to the many small (cardinal) sins that managers commit, which jeopardize their effectiveness and tenure in the organization, our study reveals and identifies seven major sins. These sins are fatal. Committing one or more can and often does result in serious damage to the organization and/or the manager's career. In many cases, that damage can be fatal. The seven fatal sins are: (1) the character flaw: erosion of trust and integrity; (2) blind ambition: focus more on managing own career than managing the organization; (3) "short-term scare" mentality: managing for survival—the simplistic fix; (4) indecisiveness: unclear on when and who decides; (5) blurred focus: the fuzzy vision; (6) employees perceived as an expense, not an investment; and (7) managing unchecked: lack of real accountability.

The next seven chapters are devoted to a thorough examination of these sins. If we can fully understand them, perhaps we may be able to avoid them. The discussion should be viewed not as a criticism of present managers, but rather as a way to do better in the future. Past failures can be lessons for the future. Even though bygones may be bygones, we can learn from them. As the saying goes, "None of us can change our yesterdays, but all of us can change our tomorrows." It is not so bad to make a mistake as it is not to learn anything from it. As a prelude to the discussion of the seven fatal sins, a statement by Professor Fred Friendly, made before he began a discussion on ethics, is appropriate: The purpose of the discussion which follows "is not to make up your mind but to open your mind and to make the agony of decision-making so intense you can escape only by thinking."[2]

Notes

1. Oren Harari, "Why Don't Things Change?" *American Management Association*, February 1995, p. 31.
2. Lisa Newton, *Ethics in America* (Preview Packet). Produced by Columbia University Seminars on Media and Society (Upper Saddle River, NJ: Prentice-Hall, 1988), p. 9.

CHAPTER 6

Sin #1:   The Character Flaw: Erosion of Trust and Integrity

Matters of principle stand like a rock.
—Thomas Jefferson

Stand with anybody that stands right, stand with him while he is right, and part with him when he goes wrong.
—Abraham Lincoln

The unexamined life is not worth living.
—Socrates

At a time when the reputation of business is generally low...one would expect corporate executives to be especially sensitive even to appearance of conflict of interest...yet this seems not, on the whole, to be the case...
—Irving Kristal

Protect your own credibility...One of the highest—and most beneficial—accolades for a manager is the comment "If he says so, you can bank on it."
—James L. Hayes

You get the behavior you tolerate.
—Plato

On the first day of every MBA business ethics class, I pose the following question: Do you believe that you can succeed in business today without some deception? I also pose the same question to the participants of various business ethics seminars that I conduct. Approximately 90% of the members of both groups are working professionals. How do you think they answer that question? Perhaps a more important question is: How should they answer it?

Approximately 80% of both groups answer "no." What they are really saying is that a businessperson cannot succeed today in business without some deception. Why do you think that these sophisticated bright students respond as they do? Do you feel that their perceptions of what is going on are accurate? Are their responses accurate in light of what is taking place in the business world? Do they represent the views of American businesspeople?

I follow up that question by asking: How many of you want to succeed? Obviously, the answer to that question is predictable—all of them. When we combine the two answers, it seems that what we have is young professionals flocking into business schools to receive a business education so they can work at a job and in an environment where deception will be inevitable in order to succeed. Are we comfortable with that conclusion? Are we far from having someone demand a course to teach students the latest deceptive business techniques? Business in our organizations should be conducted and pursued in such a way that it is not only socially responsible but also commands respect for its integrity and for its positive contribution to society. Integrity should never be compromised.

Why are so many of yesterday's CEOs no longer on their thrones? Has "booting the boss" become the trend of the moment in corporate America? What causes their untimely demise? It may be safe to conclude that of all the reasons for replacing a CEO, poor earnings is the most obvious. However, it can also be concluded that poor earnings is a symptom of other, less treatable corporate ailments that will be explored hereinafter. Our thesis is that generally the CEO's demise is attributed to one or more of the fatal managerial sins.

Corporate Ethics: Fact or Fiction?

In order to put the first managerial sin—*the character flaw: erosion of trust and integrity*—in perspective, we need to delve into corporate ethics. Let's begin by asking where we are today in business ethics. Are we happy with the ethical standards of our businesses? How does business ethics compare with the ethics of other professions? As an example, consider the following scenario. Suppose you have just moved to a new city, several hundred miles from your previous home. While at work one day, you develop a severe abdominal pain that persists for several hours. Since you do not know any doctors in the area, you ask other employees for the name of a good doctor. Your inquiries take you to the office of Dr. Smart. After a few routine tests, he tells you that his suspicion has been confirmed; it is your gall bladder, and it must be taken out the next morning. Would you take his word and lay on the operating table the next morning? Why? Would you trust him? Would you be worried that he may need money and your operation could help him toward that end? Would your reaction be the same if a mechanic told you that your car needed $500 worth of repairs? Why? Are the ethics of the two professions different? Should they be?

Has there been a decline in managerial ethics during the last two decades? Here is how the panel responded to a related statement:

There has been a decline in the last twenty (20) years in managerial ethics.

Survey Panel	Disagree Strongly	Disagree	Neither Agree or Disagree	Agree	Agree Strongly
University business deans	6%	26%	27%	29%	12%
University business professors	4%	36%	11%	40%	9%
CEOs	19%	62%	13%	6%	0%
Union presidents	0%	0%	0%	33%	67%
Business news editors	8%	22%	31%	31%	8%

It is interesting to note that 100% of the union presidents either agreed or strongly agreed with the statement. Is that the way it ought to be? Forty-nine percent of the university business professors agreed or strongly agreed. We are talking about ethics, and ethics do matter in business transactions. What is the message here? Are CEOs trying to correct this situation, or are they only interested in keeping themselves and their organizations out of legal trouble and economically sound?

How does one keep his or her job in the organization? How does one move up the corporate ladder? You may think that it takes hard work and making good and sound decisions, yet close analysis of what is happening in corporate America today reveals that while, in some cases, hard work and sound business decisions may help some to rise to the top, they are by far no guarantee.

Is loyalty alive and healthy in corporate America? Is job security a myth or a reality? Are loyalty and job security closely allied and closely connected? Many argue that loyalty and job security, in the workplace, are almost extinct. Do you agree? Can employers who deliver satisfying work in an honest atmosphere expect a new form of commitment from workers? The panel was asked to comment on the following statement:

Managers possess less loyalty and integrity to their organizations than they should.

Survey Panel	Disagree Strongly	Disagree	Neither Agree or Disagree	Agree	Agree Strongly
University business deans	2%	29%	21%	40%	8%
University business professors	6%	28%	20%	37%	9%
CEOs	12%	38%	25%	25%	0%
Union presidents	11%	11%	11%	56%	11%
Business news editors	8%	46%	8%	38%	0%

Forty-eight percent of the university business deans and 46% of the university business professors agreed or strongly agreed with that statement. Should organizations be proud with such results? Why? Should we tolerate people who are less than 100% loyal to their organizations? Is it sound and proper to argue that any employee who is less than 100% loyal to the organization should be viewed with suspicion or be dismissed?

The results of this survey are consistent with other recent surveys of American workers that depict a work force which has little loyalty to its employers. If you want ethical companies, you must have ethical bosses. Ethics start at the top. Lawrence Blockman, former president and CEO of Microdot, Inc., in his review of the book *The Unknown Iacocca* by Peter Wyden writes, "When Bunkie Knudsen was installed as Ford's president, over the head of Iacocca, Lee noted, 'Nobody at Ford expressed much loyalty towards Knudsen, therefore, he was without a power base. He failed to bring over any of his top people from G.M. A decade later—when I went to Chrysler—I made sure not to repeat that mistake.'"[1]

In his autobiography, Lee Iacocca states that "Robert McNamara, while at Ford, had such high standards of personal integrity that he could sometimes drive you crazy...Once, for a skiing vacation he planned, he needed a car with a ski rack. 'No problem,' I told him. 'I'll put a rack on one of our company cars out in Denver, and you just pick it up.' But he wouldn't hear of it. He insisted that we rent him a car from Hertz, pay extra for the ski rack, and send him the bill. He resolutely refused to use a company car on his vacation, even though we loaned out hundreds of courtesy cars every weekend to other VIPs.[2] McNamara used to say "that the boss had to be more Catholic than the Pope—and as clean as a hound's tooth. He preached a certain aloofness, and he practiced what he preached. He was never one of the boys."[3]

In *Profiles in Courage*, John Kennedy writes that each man's self-respect "was more important to him than his popularity with others. His desire to win or maintain a reputation for integrity and courage was stronger than his desire to maintain his office...His conscience, his personal standards of ethics, his integrity or morality...was stronger than the pressures of public disapproval."[4]

We need to judge CEOs and top executives on personal and corporate integrity and long-term results—at least five to ten years of solid accomplishment. Jack Welch states, "We have the ultimate chance at G.E. during the 1990s to create a corporate atmosphere where it's culturally acceptable to speak out—where telling the truth is rewarded and where bosses who yell at people for speaking up are not."[5] Should anything less than that philosophy be acceptable?

Max DePree defines integrity as, "A fine sense of one's obligations. That integrity exhibits itself in the company's dedication to superior design, to quality, to making a contribution to society—and in its manifest respect for its customers, investors, suppliers, and employees. Integrity comes out in lots of little ways. For example, while executives in other companies were busy 'taking care of number one' by arranging Golden Parachutes for themselves, in 1986 Herman Miller introduced Silver Parachutes for all its employees with over two years of service. In case of an unfriendly takeover of Herman Miller that led to termination of employment, the Silver Parachute plan would offer a soft landing for the kind of people in the ranks of the organization whose welfare is ignored in most organizations."[6]

"The first characteristic of the professional," says Dr. Langhorne, an industry consultant, "is integrity." He continues, "Integrity also needs a behavioral definition. Integrity is doing what you say you are going to do. Many of the people we work with often will say one thing and then do something entirely different. Think about the people you work with that you respect and trust. They are almost certainly people who carefully monitor what I call their 'say/do' ratio. What they promise they deliver and if they cannot, you are soon informed. For such people 'the check is in the mail' is not a joke." This say/do characteristic, he states, "is probably the foundation for self-esteem. Remember what the Bard said: 'To thine own self be true. And it must follow, as the night the day, thou can't not then be false to any man.' Probably the best piece of advice in English literature. Mark Twain also said it rather well: 'Do what is right; it will gratify some people and astonish the rest.'"[7] Excellent managers live their commitment to people—and above all, to their employees. Integrity has to be kept in tact. It has been said that "once integrity is gone, everything comes easy." The only questionable competitive advantage any business has is its reputation. The same statement can be made with respect to individual businesspersons.

Ethics sometimes is lost in the shuffle, as it was in the competitive shuffle of the 1980s. Why do we have problems in business ethics? Perhaps its deterioration can be attributed to several factors. It can be argued that unethical conduct sometimes can be and, unfortunately is rewarded in the short term. That fact becomes significant when we consider the important role short-term mentality plays in today's business environment. Compounding the situation is the fact that the vast majority of companies are not privately owned and are operated by CEOs who are not the owners. They are under pressure to produce—to show a profit every quarter. They constantly think about what the stockholders will say and do if the quarterly report is negative. Such thought is unbearable for many CEOs. Consequently, the temptation is to show a profit at almost any expense. So much for integrity! Compromise sets in. Rationalization takes over. They "reason" that they need to go "out of bounds" just this one time, but will make up for it later. The problem is that such does not stop after the first time; it generally continues and grows. Indeed, often there is a need to cover up. It has a tendency to balloon, to get bigger and bigger—a snowball effect.

Unquestionably, the loss of ownership has had a significant impact on CEOs' ability and desire to manage their organizations. This is evident in the panel's responses to the following statement:

Lack of ownership has affected the degree of commitment to the operation of the organization.

Survey Panel	Disagree Strongly	Disagree	Neither Agree or Disagree	Agree	Agree Strongly
University business deans	1%	16%	10%	63%	10%
University business professors	4%	22%	4%	59%	11%
CEOs	0%	19%	19%	56%	6%
Union presidents	0%	0%	33%	56%	11%
Business news editors	0%	15%	16%	69%	0%

Seventy-three percent of the university business deans and 70% of the university business professors agreed that lack of ownership has affected the degree of commitment to the operation of the organization. So what is the answer? Stock ownership? Profit sharing? What about returning to the basics—instilling more integrity and loyalty in the employees? To do that, of course, it is necessary to begin at the top. Can we do that?

Two simple stories illustrate the power of ownership. An MBA student stopped by my office and told me that he had recently bought a small mini-mart and was preparing to open the next day. He said he spent all afternoon cleaning, scrubbing, and doing repairs in the bathrooms. He wanted the bathrooms to look nice for the customers. He continued by saying, "Boy was that tough work! I certainly wouldn't have done that for somebody else's business. But, I really didn't mind doing it because it is mine." Many of us have probably heard similar stories. A simple story perhaps, but a great big management principle at work.

Compare that with another "manager" of a mini-mart. A regular customer stopped by and asked for change for a dollar. The "manager" opened the cash register and saw that he had sufficient change, but said no. After some conversation, the "manager" reluctantly offered some help. "There is a bank up the street," he said. "It will be open shortly. Why don't you go there?" That alone would have been bad enough, but there is more to the story. As the customer was leaving the store, but was still within hearing distance, the "manager" said to another customer, "This is not a bank. If he gets mad, if he doesn't want to come back, that's his problem. I don't get paid enough to worry about that." Would the manager have handled the situation differently if he owned the store or received a commission for his sales? The power of ownership over motivation is alive and well!

A related statement regarding ownership was presented to the panel:

Lack of ownership has affected managerial performance.

Survey Panel	Disagree Strongly	Disagree	Neither Agree or Disagree	Agree	Agree Strongly
University business deans	1%	20%	11%	57%	11%
University business professors	4%	22%	5%	56%	13%
CEOs	0%	25%	13%	56%	12%
Union presidents	0%	11%	22%	56%	11%
Business news editors	0%	15%	23%	62%	0%

Again, the results paint a disturbing picture. However, the point here is not to say that publicly held and run organizations are bad, but rather to identify what may need to be done to make sure that managerial performance is not diminished.

It is not that CEOs don't know or can't do the right thing. Indeed, in most cases, they do and can, as long as doing the right thing doesn't interfere substantially with the bottom line or with their careers. The pressure to do good has forced many organizations to come up with a code of ethics or a code of conduct. Today, adopting a meaningful "codes of ethics" is being recognized as necessary for long-term corporate survival. Some 75% of the top 1,200 U.S. companies now have written ethical codes. In addition, many multinational corporations require every employee to receive training in business ethics. The studies also indicate, however, that many organizations pay little attention to them; there has been very little effort to implement and enforce them. They are there for "show," like ornaments on a Christmas tree—just there to look good.

Students in a business ethics class were asked to draw up a code of ethics. In doing so, they mailed letters to a number of large organizations, explaining who they were, what they were doing, and requesting a copy of each organization's code of ethics. Quite a few organizations sent in their code of ethics. The fact that many of the codes were very general and superficial was bad enough, but what was really disturbing was that a number of organizations wrote back and said, "Sorry, we can't send you a copy of our code of ethics because it is confidential." Isn't it fair to ask why the code of ethics is confidential? A number of other organizations responded as follows through their director of public relations or human resources: "We have reviewed your letter and resume, and even though it is very impressive, at the present time, we don't have a job which matches your qualifications." What resume? Who was asking for a job? What happens to the "real" job applications? It would probably be safe to state that a large number of mid-level jobs which are advertised have been spoken for and, in effect, someone has been picked before all the applications are received. The organization had someone already "wired" to the job. In those cases, the whole process, including the interviews, is meaningless, a waste of time. Moreover, such conduct is demeaning to all concerned. Even more disturbing was that several of the responses from corporate officials stated that they were keeping the students' resumes on file for a year in the event a job in the future would match their qualifications. What resumes were they talking about? None were sent!

The integrity, reputation, and profitability of a company ultimately depend upon the individual actions of its employees. Establishing a code of ethics or improving an existing one won't convert the corrupt into the virtuous, but it will give individuals access to a body of knowledge and create a climate in which the organization and its employees are better able to make informed judgments. The ethical performance of the organization is the sum of the ethics of all its employees. If employees maintain high personal ethical standards, the organization will achieve its desired level of ethical standards. The code also stresses that the organization should maintain ethical standards well above the minimum level required by law. Ethical behavior contributes to the organization's reputation for integrity.

There has been a lot of talk about trust and integrity in the corporate sector. When it comes to the sin of erosion of trust and integrity, often the perception of "wrongdoing" can be as harmful as if it were real. The manager has to be careful about the image he or she projects, even though it may be difficult to control the way others perceive you, especially when you are doing the right thing. Take, for example, William Agee at Bendix Corporation, who promoted one of his employees, Mary Cunningham, from executive assistant to vice president of strategic planning fifteen months after she graduated from the Harvard Business School. Even though he denied rumors of an affair, the perception was different. Perception, rightfully or otherwise, prevailed. The corporate staff saw it as conduct that was not proper. That action, along with the failed hostile takeover bid of Martin Marietta, may have cost him his job. His retirement may have been voluntary, but many perceived it as one of "necessity."

Instead of taking an approach which says, "I am your manager. I am not better or worse than you, but I do have different responsibility, authority, and accountability than you have," many managers give the impression that they are way above the rest in the organization. They become arrogant and display hypocrisy, greed, and lust; in sum, they become "titans" who rule their "kingdoms" autocratically. When it comes time to leave the job, the boss just hangs on, often undermining and firing potential successors. As a Fortune 500 CEO put it, somewhat jokingly, when asked how he managed to stay at the top for so long: "I just identify the person who is to replace me," he said, "then I fire the S.O.B!"

What about trust? Our survey demonstrates how weak trust is in our organizations. It certainly can be argued that the most important thing that keeps an organization together is trust. Trust ties leaders and followers together. Lack of trust leads to deterioration of the organization. Compare the situation to a marriage without trust. Can it last and flourish? Point to a CEO who doesn't have the trust of his or her employees and in 90% of the cases you are pointing to a "has-been" CEO—if not now, in the very near future. Is it a fatal sin? You bet! Is it a terminal? Unquestionably, yes.

Without trust, you cannot properly lead. In an article entitled "Ten Lessons for Leaders and Leadership Developers," the authors, Professor Barry Posner and Jim Kouzes, chairman and CEO of the Tom Peters Group/Learning

Systems, discuss their research regarding what it takes to get extraordinary things done in organizations. In discussing Lesson 5: "Without trust, you cannot lead," they state:

> ...Without trust, people become self-protective. They are directive and tightly hold the reins on others. Similarly, when there is low trust, people are likely to distort, ignore and disguise facts, ideas, conclusions, and feelings. People become suspicious and unreceptive. A trusting relationship between leader and constituents is essential to getting extraordinary things done.[8]

Another primary task of leadership is to create a climate in which others feel powerful, efficacious, and strong. In such a climate, people know they are free to take risks, trusting that when they make mistakes, the leader will not ask, "Who's to blame?" but rather, "What did we learn?"[9]

Without trust, can there be integrity? And without integrity, how can one "effectively" manage? Unless there is trust, how can one lead and command respect. What happens without respect? It has been said that "leading should be by reason, not by force." Instilling and maintaining organizational trust has to be one of the most important tasks confronting a CEO. Can there be organizational cohesiveness without trust? How can effective change—real, acceptable change—take place in an organization without trust? Those managers who advocate and run their organizations based on a "results at any cost" mentality cannot endure for long. It is important, indeed necessary, that managers patch up and, where necessary, reinstill trust between themselves and their employees. In *Servant Leadership*, Robert K. Greenleaf puts forward the notion that the leader is really the servant of his followers and that he removes obstacles that prevent them from doing their jobs.[10] Lack of trust, either real or imagined, causes statements made by managers or projects advocated by them to be questioned—to become suspect.

One may ask: If this sin is so obvious, why do so many CEOs commit it? The answer is simple. Many CEOs' thirst for power and greed for personal gain seem to blind them. For many, the greed leads to lack of integrity and trust, which becomes ingrained in their systems and their personalities; it ends up infecting them—it becomes a disease. Furthermore, many CEOs transmit the disease involuntarily and sometimes voluntarily to others in the organization. Speaking about this, Jack Welch said, "We cannot afford management styles that suppress and intimidate. Trust and respect between workers and managers is essential." In Mr. Welch's view, the sort of manager who meets numerical goals but has old-fashioned attitudes is the major obstacle to carrying out these concepts. This is the individual who typically forces performance out of people rather than inspiring them—the autocrat, the big shot, the tyrant.[11] Trust was also a very important factor on the management list of Col. Harland Sanders, founder of Kentucky Fried Chicken. He put a lot of trust in the goodness of the people around him, and he trusted his franchisees to be fair and honest with him. The result was that everyone was handsomely rewarded.

The panel was asked about trust between employees and managers in the following statement:

There is a lack of trust between employees and managers.

Survey Panel	Disagree Strongly	Disagree	Neither Agree or Disagree	Agree	Agree Strongly
University business deans	0%	14%	16%	58%	12%
University business professors	2%	5%	7%	62%	24%
CEOs	0%	25%	6%	63%	6%
Union presidents	0%	0%	11%	22%	67%
Business news editors	8%	15%	8%	38%	31%

Eighty-six percent of the university business professors and 70% of the university business deans believe that there is a lack of trust between employees and managers. Furthermore, 89% of the union presidents agree with the statement. Not one of the union presidents disagreed. What does that tell us? Should we expect top quality from these people? Should we be surprised if we don't get it?

There is little if any disagreement that the key ingredient that keeps a relationship together and makes it work and flourish is trust. Whether this lack of trust is characterized as real or imagined is not as important as the fact that there appears to be a lack of trust. And as long as there is a lack of trust, an organization cannot prosper and be the best it can be. Trust, honesty, and fairness are essential to successful leadership. Employees wouldn't really willingly follow any other kind of leader. A successful leader has to be trusted completely. Consequently, he or she has to be trustworthy.[12] Why is there so much distrust? What are the people at the top, the "chieftains," doing to remedy the situation? Honesty, integrity, and caring form the foundation of the company and should flow everywhere and through everything the organization does. Are organizations built from the bottom up or from the top down? James Case Penney said, "Golden Rule principles are just as necessary for operating a business profitably as are trucks, typewriters and twine."

Notre Dame football coach Lou Holtz says that character and integrity have to be the cornerstone of every decision. Consequently, lack of integrity leaves a hollow person, and we know what hollow people generally accomplish. Character, said Theodore Roosevelt, in the long run, is the decisive factor in the life of an individual and of nations alike. We need executives who make decisions from both the head and the heart, who truly trust their inner voice over outside advisers who want to go along with what may be politically expedient. Goals don't start in the brain—they start in the heart. Obviously, sincerity is an ingredient of integrity. Truth is part of sincerity. However, even truth can be dangerous if it is improperly used. It has been said that "a truth that's told with bad intent beats all the lies you can invent."

It has been argued that because some employees may not be loyal to the organization and/or the CEO, the CEO may be justified in reciprocating. Obviously, such arguments falter in light of what we know about management. Just as ethics starts from the top of the organization, so do trust and integrity. Consider a newly hired employee who is asked to sign a contract that gives the employer the right to terminate the employee with or without cause. Does such a relationship or such conduct foster trust? What about an employee who is required to punch a clock? What goes through the employee's mind? We need to be realistic about these matters. Let's not try to rationalize and justify something that isn't so. It may be possible to argue that employees are required to punch a clock in order to keep better records, but the following examples point to the real purpose.

A new president is addressing key employees in the organization and says to them: "I can't trust you, because I don't know you, but you've got to trust me because I am your president." What is the result? A subordinate wants his supervisor to verify whether certain things are going to happen in the organization next week. The supervisor's response is, "I don't know anything about that." A few days later, things happen just as the subordinate thought. What is the result? The subordinate thinks either the supervisor lied to him or the supervisor was not given the information because she is not trusted with such information, even though everybody else seemed to know. What does this do to the supervisor's image? Shouldn't we be open and up front with our employees? Of course, we are not talking about top secrets, but not many top secrets exist in an organization. Aristotle said, "All men by nature desire to know." Members of the organization should know first, before the rest of the world gets the information. They are like the members of a family. Shouldn't family members be informed before the rest of the world?

Trust, loyalty, and integrity must be earned, not bought. You must do what you say you will do, when you say you will do it. Is it easy? Maybe not, but it's not hard to do. Is it important? You bet. Is lack of trust and integrity detrimental to the organization? The answer is obvious. Is it detrimental to the CEO? If not the number one fatal managerial sin, it certainly is tied for the top spot.

We have witnessed a decline of the work ethic. Many managers work in an organization as a means to an end. Many obey state and federal laws but ignore the inner voice that speaks to them—they ignore their conscience. Their loyalty is focused on short-term goals which are primarily geared toward the advancement of their careers. Managers need to maintain the highest standards of honesty, integrity, and ethics in all aspects of the organization's affairs. This, of course, must include interactions with customers, suppliers, employees, stockholders, creditors, corporate directors, governments, and society at large; at the same time, they must comply with the laws of each country and community in which they operate. In sum, they must properly and ethically balance the interests of all stakeholders. Anything short of that should not be tolerated.

Downsizing, for example, when viewed as a short-term solution, can and often does result in the loss of trust between the CEO and the employees. It is not easy to let employees go and ask those who survive to be upbeat, innovative, and loyal. Coupled with the fact that the average worker will change jobs seven times during his or her career, it is easy to see why loyalty has declined. Furthermore, the decline of integrity is highlighted if we add to that whistle-blowing, back-stabbing, and political games.

Caring and commitment are missing in many managers. Many employees are not treated with dignity as individuals. Managers fail to maintain an open atmosphere where direct communication with employees affords the opportunity to contribute to the maximum of their potential and fosters unity of purpose with the company.

The Personal Conscience and the Corporate Conscience—Can They Be Separated?

When discussing business ethics, it is not uncommon for individuals to assume rather cynical postures: "There is no such thing as business ethics." "Business ethics is a contradiction in terms, an oxymoron." "The business of business is business; ethics just isn't relevant." Although these remarks represent the cynical extreme, the attitude that business must play by a different set of rules is a common one. As a matter of necessity, business practice must rest on a moral base. If it did not, business practice would be impossible. The enterprise of business presupposes that the participants in business transactions must sub-scribe to a set of universal moral norms.

Can the two consciences—the private and the corporate—be separated? Many tend to conclude they can, but the reasons given for their conclusion don't seem to support their case. The two consciences are intermingled, and a line cannot be drawn between them. Consequently, our personal ethics do influence our corporate ethics; in turn, we have to acknowledge that there is no way to divorce ethics from our decisions. In decision making, we take objective data and enter that data into our minds. Our minds are made up of our intelligence, our prejudices, our backgrounds, our morals, our ethics, etc. When data enters our minds, it is culled and influenced by what is in our mind. As a result, we generally end up with subjective decisions. That's why two people may have the same data and reach different decisions. Minds are not objective computers. Henry Clay said, "Statistics are no substitute for judgment."

The author of *Managing with a Conscience* states:

> In the turbulent, frenetic, dog-eat-dog times of the past decade, many believed that the only way to achieve success was to be unscrupulous. Acting like slum lords, corporations let their assets deteriorate by mistreating employees, squeezing suppliers, and taking advantage of customers. What was forgotten in the pursuit of short-term profits, however, was that by such behavior, individuals and organizations alike significantly damaged their ability to perform long term. The book spells out a better option for improving long-term success: restore traditional values and inject trust and integrity into all business practices and relationships. *Managing with a Conscience* is about replacing the old 'we' against 'them' mentality with a new perception of 'us' that encourages the growth of profitable relationships with employees, customers, clients, suppliers, and alliance partners. It's about stimulating creativity, adapting to change, decreasing time to market, promoting service excellence, communicating in a world of information overload, building trust, and energizing the decentralized work force. In such a culture, people work at a higher level, exceed customer expectations, and ensure that products are flawless and produced on time and within budget. To make this a reality, remember that although the golden rule may be considered a cliché, it still has value. When you act in a way that instills trust, that trust is returned. Acting honorably also does something else: It makes you feel good about yourself—and that is reflected in the way you look and the way other people look at you.[13]

When a CEO's integrity is diminished, when the trust between the CEO and the employees declines, the CEO positions himself or herself in the "firing line."

The foregoing discussion lends credibility to the fact that when a CEO has a character flaw, when and where there is erosion of trust and integrity, the CEO is suffering from a serious managerial disease—a terminal disease. That disease results from improper managerial acts. It amounts to a serious corporate sin and is a fatal managerial sin. The penalty for those who commit such a sin can be, and often is, managerial death. This sin can be prevented. It must be prevented; otherwise, damage and suffering will result. The sad thing is that this suffering often befalls innocent people. In the end, the CEO must be guided by the "Disclosure Rule" in relationships with others and in his or her decisions. The rule states: "Ask yourself, if the full glare of examination by associates, friends, even family were to focus on your decision, would you remain comfortable with it? If you think you would, it probably is the right decision." Or to put it in more familiar words, "Do unto others as you would have them do unto you." St. Francis DeSales said, "Make yourself a seller when you are buying, and a buyer when you are selling, and then you will sell and buy justly."

Notes

1. Peter Wyden, *The Unknown Iacocca* (New York: Morrow & Company, 1987). Copyright ©by Peter H. Wyden, Inc. Used by permission of William Morrow and Co., Inc.
2. Lee Iacocca, *Iacocca: An Autobiography by Lee Iacocca with William Novak.* Copyright © 1984 by Lee Iacocca. Used by permission of Bantam Books, a division of Bantam Doubleday Dell Publishing Group, Inc., p. 42.
3. Ibid.
4. John F. Kennedy, *Profiles in Courage* (New York: Harper and Row, 1955).
5. Stephen W. Quickel, "Welch on Welch," *Financial World*, April 3, 1990, p. 62.
6. Max DePree, *Leadership Is an Art* (New York: Doubleday), p. xvii.
7. John E. Langhorne, "3 Attributes Define a Real Professional," Langhorne Associates, Iowa City, IA, November 17, 1986, p. 1.
8. Barry Z. Posner and James M. Kouzes, "Ten Lessons for Leaders and Leadership Developers," *The Journal of Leadership Studies,* Summer 1996, pp. 6–7.
9. Ibid.
10. Robert Greenleaf, *Servant Leadership: A Journey into the Nature of Legitimate Power and Greatness* (New York: Paulist Press, 1977), p. 7. Reprinted from *Servant Leadership* by Robert K. Greenleaf; ©1977 by Robert Greenleaf; ©1991 by the Robert K. Greenleaf Center. Used by permission of Paulist Press.

11. John Holusha, "A Softer 'Neutron Jack' at G.E.," *The New York Times,* March 4, 1992, p. D1.

12. James F. Lincoln, *A New Approach to Industrial Economics* (New York: The Devin-Adair Company, 1961), p. 153.

13. Frank K. Sonnenberg, *Managing with a Conscience*: *How to Improve Performance Through Integrity, Trust, and Commitment* (New York: McGraw-Hill, 1994), pp. xi–xii.

CHAPTER 7

Sin #2: Blind Ambition: Focus More on Managing Own Career Than Managing the Organization

We have committed the Golden Rule to memory; let us now commit it to life.
—Edwin Markham

The fundamental premise of the new model executive...is, simply, that the goals of the individual and the goals of the organization will work out to be one and the same. The young men have no cynicism about the "system" and very little skepticism...They have an implicit faith that The Organization will be as interested in making use of their best qualities as they are themselves, and thus, with equanimity, they can entrust the resolution of their destiny to The Organization...[T]he average young man cherishes the idea that his relationship with The Organization is to be for keeps.
—William H. Whyte, Jr.
The Organization Man (1956)[1]

I have never been able to conceive how any rational being could propose happiness to himself from the exercise of power over others.
—Thomas Jefferson

The world has enough for everyone's needs, but not enough for everyone's greed.
—Mahatma Gandhi

I made mistakes and I learned the importance of humility.
—President Bill Clinton

Watch out for CEOs who have too much power.
—Donald C. Burr, People Express Airlines, Inc.

CEOs should rise to the occasion and ensure the interests of their organizations by asking, "Is it good for the company and not just for me?" Sadly, but nonetheless true, there are many CEOs today whose primary goal is to promote and advance their own careers. They don't seem to have a problem with using the organization as a means to achieving their own personal goals; they thirst for power and personal gain. Oftentimes, these managers center on their own image and become defensive, outspoken, and extreme in their goals, opinions, and focus. They want to be in the spotlight, and as long as the result is good, they love to hog the credit!

The Conflict: Subordination of Interests— Whose Interests?

In order to gain insight into managers' priorities, the panel was asked to respond to the following statement:

Generally, managers are more interested in managing their careers than in managing their organizations.

Survey Panel	Disagree Strongly	Disagree	Neither Agree Nor Disagree	Agree	Agree Strongly
University business deans	8%	38%	17%	30%	7%
University business professors	4%	31%	20%	38%	7%
CEOs	38%	50%	6%	6%	0%
Union presidents	0%	11%	11%	45%	33%
Business news editors	8%	46%	0%	38%	8%

It is interesting to note that 37% of the university business deans and 45% of the university business professors agreed or strongly agreed with the statement. That number is almost double (78%) when we look at the responses of the union presidents. The question, then, is whether these results are good or bad. It would appear that the results represent bad news for corporate America. If it happens that the interests of both are compatible, then things are fine, but if not, as is often the case, then corporate interest has to prevail over personal interest. Otherwise, we would have people pulling in various directions and the organization would suffer. What is needed is to place employees in organizations whose interests are congruent with the interests of the organization.

To gain better insight in this matter, the panel was asked the following open-ended question: "Do you feel managers today, in general, are *more* concerned with managing their careers than managing their organizations?" Here are some representative responses from the various groups.

University business deans:

- Yes, and why not: "Loyalty" is out the window, so it's "me" first, more than ever = survival.
- Yes, corporate America has proven it has no loyalty to its people, so it has become every man for himself.
- Yes, unfortunately! Most feel uncomfortable with empowered employees, managing change and global concerns.
- Not necessarily. However, as more get bumped out of jobs, they need to be concerned.
- No. Most managers are so engrossed in doing their jobs well that they tend to put career issues on the back burner.
- No. I do not believe that managing their career is necessarily in contrast to managing their organization.
- Yes. Downsizing/rightsizing has created an every man/woman for himself/herself environment.
- Unquestionably yes!
- Somewhat, but particularly true in some industries.
- Generally yes. Their careers come first; however, in many cases the two are compatible.

University business professors:

- Definitely they're mercenaries.
- In large organizations yes, caused by trends in downsizing not true of smaller businesses of 75 employees or less.
- Yes, but they try to rationalize it by believing it is in line with the corporate union.
- Yes, but not as bad in companies as it is in academia. I think business organizations do better aligning these interests.
- In my experience usually this is so.
- Yes, nature of the beast.
- Me first and organization second.
- Only to the extent that the organization is not loyal to the manager.
- Yes, but justifiably so. Do organizations care much about their employees?

- Cause/effect managers realize they must "cause" organizational success in order to advance.

CEOs and chairmen of boards:

- Some are and some are not.
- It varies a lot, but I guess this is true in general; however, there are plenty of exceptions.
- I am sure some are, but I don't think it's a majority by any means.
- Yes, by looking at their insistence on pay packages in public companies.

Union presidents:

- Yes—everyone must go down with the ship except the manager!
- Yes—they've been abandoned by their companies.
- Definitely, yes.

Business news editors:

- Yes, they are interested in their career first.
- Appears to be the case.
- Yes. Many high level managers "jump ship" for more challenges.
- Survival mode causes them to behave this way when forced to choose.
- Yes, not willing to risk something if it may not help their careers.

In answering the question, a CEO, after stating he believed there are some managers who are mainly interested in managing their organizations and then there are those who are mostly interested in their careers, went on to say, "Those who are more interested in their careers at the sacrifice of peers and subordinates—over time will become self-destructive and will have limited growth potential as a manager."

One of Henri Fayol's 14 Principles of Management is that there should be subordination of individual interest to the general interest—to the interest of the organization. It has been pointed out by Dr. Archer, professor of management, that, "The abuse of power, the subjection of the general welfare and exploitation of labor tend to increase in degree as the general interests of the organization are subordinated to the interests of an individual or

Farcus

by David Waisglass
Gordon Coulthart

WAISGLASS/COULTHART   © 1992 Farcus Cartoons/Distributed by Universal Press Syndicate   11-20

**"Someone is stealing paper clips
on the second floor. Take 'em out."**

special interest group within the organization and tend to decrease in degree as the interests of the individual or special interest group are subordinated to the general interests of the organization. (When the activities of the organization serve only the interests of one person or a chosen few, the majority of employees will suffer abuse and exploitation.)"[2] Self-conceit could and often does lead to self destruction.

Ideally, managing a successful organization and a successful career should be compatible. A manager's managerial success is, or should be, directly related to his or her personal success. If the manager runs the organization poorly, he or she will look bad; if the manager looks bad, his or her career will be damaged. On the other hand, if the actions and decisions of the manager benefit the organization, peers and others will recognize those actions. They will also remember those actions when making career decisions that affect the manager. Thus, there is incentive for the manager to do whatever he or she can to make the organization a successful one. But that is easier said than done. Unfortunately, it doesn't happen as often as it should. Why?

It should be reemphasized that many business problems would be easily solved if organizations could or would place the right person (employee) in the right task (job) and in the right organization (structure). Is this an easy task to accomplish? It could be. Is it often done? Not really. Why not? Who should take the blame? Who should be responsible? Even if initially the requirements of the job are congruent with the employee's interests and the employee is properly placed when hired, it is important that the situation is monitored throughout the employee's career to assure that a "perfect fit," or a near "perfect fit," is maintained. If that is accomplished, there is a win–win situation. Then, by accomplishing one's personal goals, the organization's goals are also accomplished. The reverse is also generally true; accomplishing organizational goals leads to the accomplishment of personal goals, for they are compatible.

Unfortunately, many organizations do an average and, in some instances, a poor job of selecting and placing employees. What generally happens when there is a job opening is that the focus is on filling that job with someone who can do the work, without too much concern as to what happens to the employee in five or ten years when he or she outgrows the present job. Even if the employee is asked during the hiring interview where he or she sees himself or herself in five years, the dialogue is short. Consider what would happen if the interviewee asked the interviewer/manager, "Where do you see me in five years?" What the interviewee would probably see is a "blank" look on the interviewer's face. Many organizations are guilty of such conduct, and generally the blame can and must be placed on the human resources department. Even if the match happens to be good at the outset, things change as time passes. Just because an employee was happy with what he or she was doing in a job the previous year doesn't mean that the employee is happy with what he or she is doing now or will be happy in the future. The situation has to be monitored frequently. There really is no other satisfactory or acceptable alternative.

When a manager faces a difficult situation which he or she perceives as forcing a choice between personal career and the organization's goal, which may happen to be inconsistent, the manager has to be strong enough and find a solution that is consistent with the organization's goal. If not, chaos is likely to occur, and sooner than later the CEO will find himself or herself in a dangerous predicament. If the situation happens to be significant, the CEO begins a downward journey in the organization, and his or her departure appears to be almost imminent. The problem is that many CEOs either don't realize this or don't care to. After all, being the little kings that some are, they feel indestructible. Recall the passage in *King Lear* upon the monarch's departure: "I am the King himself...Aye, every inch a king! When I do stare, see how the subject quakes."

Some leaders sacrifice their careers for the organization. Lee Iacocca writes how John Rucardo sacrificed his career at Chrysler to save the company when he brought in Iacocca. He states: "John was sacrificing himself to save the company. Although it meant the end of his own career, he bent over backward to make sure that the transition would go as smoothly as possible. He blew himself out of the water to bring Chrysler back to life. And that is the test of a real hero."[3]

In order to better understand why many managers today are more interested in managing their careers than their organizations, we need to look into where business has been, where business is, and where it is headed. In the past, there was substantial ownership by those who managed the company; many were family owned. The reins were often passed from father to son, as a king passes the throne to a prince. Each knew his boundary and stayed within it. Eventually, if people paid their dues, they would get their turn. It was almost predictable. Someone looked out for them. There was some sense of order, respect, and loyalty.

Today's business environment is, or at least appears to be, different. Managers seem to have more pressures, more concerns. The employee's so-called "birthright" is almost non-existent, even when the employee has played by the rules. Downsizing, not for the sake of rightsizing but rather to meet a short-term objective, has caused many employees to lose confidence and has shattered their loyalty. Oftentimes, managers use their current positions as means to more attractive, more lucrative positions within the same or with another organization. In itself, this may not be bad; in some cases, however, what makes it bad is that many managers don't want to play by the rules; they don't want to pay their dues before the next step. They are ready today to go through, around, or over anyone who stands in the way of their advancement, using whatever means may be necessary, as long as they see themselves as staying within the law.

Unfortunately, many managers don't want to be bothered by their employees; they aren't there for them anymore. They will do and say what is expedient and politically correct. They turn with the wind. What we have witnessed is that downsizing and corporate reengineering have been interpreted by many, rightly or wrongly, as a means of accomplishing an obligation placed on them—to manage their own careers. It used to be the responsibility of the employer to develop and enhance the employee's skills. Furthermore, it was the employer's responsibility to guide the employee along a defined career path, with detailed organizational charts showing progression. It was done with care, loyalty, and sensitivity and was done ethically. It was methodical, precise, sincere, and simple. This led to promotions which were expected and received. Consequently, it was more the rule than the exception for a person to spend thirty to forty years with the same company.

Many managers don't think they are being fair to themselves and to their families if they don't prepare themselves for the unavoidable and inevitable, that is, the next career move. Their reasoning is, "The 'company' is not going to look out for me, so I must look out for myself." Consequently, networking sets in. Managers feel it is their responsibility to become not only good managers but to manage their careers so they will be ready for the next career move, if and when it occurs.

Many managers today, whether because of the size of the organization, or a lack of care, or a combination, don't know or worry about the dreams and ambitions of their employees. Employees are often seen as expenses which can be manipulated, rather than assets to be nurtured and encouraged. The training that most employees receive today is not the meaningful, rewarding, growing, learning experience it used to be, but rather is used as a way to help managers meet their organizational goals. The underlying theme in many U.S. companies is "every man for himself!" Managers blatantly see their jobs as stepping-stones to reach positions to which they aspire. Consequently, employee training, in many cases, is done for the wrong reasons. However, some CEOs take a somewhat different approach, as evidenced by the comments of one CEO: "I tell my employees that I can't guarantee them a career with our organization, but I will help them prepare their careers. One way to accomplish that is by encouraging them to get as much education as possible."

A manager who is concerned about job security will not put the organization high on his or her priority list. That manager will be more concerned with his or her own survival in a volatile environment. If we expect managers to shift their concern from themselves to their companies, there must be less political influence, more job security, and a stronger, more trusting relationship between the company and its employees. Unfortunately, these conditions are presently lacking in many organizations. There is not a lot of loyalty between managers and their organizations. The organization doesn't instill a sense of trust. Frequent layoffs, rampant politicking, and bureau-cracy are some of the factors which dampen the morale of the employees.

Unfortunately, some negative effects are not noticeable until later. Many managers move along the fast track so quickly that no one has time to notice the destruction they leave in their path. They are moving too fast to be seen. This is consistent with the attitude of many managers that the important thing is to look good in the short term. Often, this can be accomplished by produc-ing short-term results. They see greater rewards in the short term than in the long term. In many situations, managers know the right thing to do, yet they aren't strong enough to do it. They hide behind labor laws, internal and external politics, corporate policy, or they just plain blame somebody else. Such situations become more apparent during downsizing and reorganizing. When a manager decides to look out for his or her career above all else, the result is loss of employee respect, a tarnished reputation, and a shaky future with the company, at best.

Managerial Arrogance—Greed and Glory

One of the symptoms associated with this sin is greed for power and glory. Bertrand Russell was led to the thought that power, along with glory, re-mains the highest aspiration and the greatest reward of mankind.[4] Power is the possibility of imposing one's will upon the behavior of other persons.[5] Many of the CEOs in this category are like the jungle fighter described in Michael Maccoby's *The Gamesman.*[6] Maccoby writes: "The jungle fighter's goal is power. He experiences life and work as a jungle (not as a game), where it is eat or be eaten, and the winners destroy the losers…Jungle fight-ers tend to see their peers in terms of accomplices or enemies and their subordinates as objects to be utilized. There are two subtypes of jungle fighters: lions and foxes. The lions are the conquerors who, when successful, may build an empire; the foxes make their nests in the corporate hierarchy and move ahead by stealth and politicking."[7]

Some of these CEOs will do anything to be noticed and view such con-duct as fair. Some even have their own "publicists" to make them look good at the company's expense. They find it necessary to have control and achieve it at any cost. They view stepping on others, if necessary to succeed, as their corporate duty. Egotism is at work and, in some cases, is very visible. Harold Geneen, a former CEO of ITT Corporation, said, "The worst disease which can afflict business executives in their work is not, as popularly supposed, alcoholism; it's egotism."

Other words to describe their conduct are arrogance, hypocrisy, and lust. The following description of a manager puts it in perspective: "Sometimes he so arrogantly assumes victory that he does not fight. He has stationed himself behind the back line. It is not so with his opponent (competition). He is in the front line, side by side with his troops, and he has placed the rear of his regiment next to the river. His commitment to die in order to win will beget the troops' commitment in turn. Just as the babbling brook, which rushes in one direction, carries the paper easily while the large lake cannot, so is it that a regiment small in size but unified in commitment will win. Remember, weaponry and manpower are important, but it is the general's commitment that determines victory."[8] We have to be careful what message we want to give. As one football player said of coach Vince Lombardi, "When he says 'sit down,' I don't even look for a chair."

As might be expected, such conduct can place them in pretty powerful positions at the outset. It is not that their conduct goes undetected; indeed, it is the opposite. Because they lead by force rather than by reason, those who notice their behavior don't want to get involved because they fear for their jobs. However, in time, real resistance forms, and these chieftains are ultimately brought to their knees. When that happens, it is not a pretty picture.

Looking down at others in the organization—the class system—is not the exception. Lee Iacocca, in his autobiography, writes about his early days at Ford Motor Company:

> Those were the days of wine and roses. All of us who constituted top management in the Glass House lived the good life in the royal court. We were part of something beyond first class—royal class, perhaps, where we had the best of everything. White-coated waiters were on call throughout the day, and we ate lunch together in the executive dining room.
>
> This is no ordinary cafeteria. It was closer to being one of the country's finest restaurants. Dover sole was flown over from England on a daily basis. We enjoyed the finest fruit, no matter what the season. Fancy chocolates, exotic flowers—you name it, we had it. And everything was served up by those professional waiters in their white coats.
>
> At first we paid all of $2.00 each for those lunches. The price had started at $1.50 but inflation hiked it to $2.00. We got into a discussion of how much those lunches really did cost the company.

In typical Ford style, we ran a study to determine the real expense of serving lunch in the executive dining room. It came out to $104 a head—and this was twenty years ago [1964].[9]

If you were a Ford employee, how would you feel about this "cafeteria"? How would you feel about an executive who wanted to refurbish his office with antiques costing $1.25 million at the same time the battle was on to keep the minimum wage down? We aren't talking about executives who don't know what is happening; we are talking about intelligent people who have lost perspective of the situation. They aren't just employees; they see themselves as little "monarchs," and they believe that they can do no wrong.

You don't see many of them walking around their organizations talking with their employees (certainly no Sam Waltons); they "closet" themselves in their offices. They don't want to be confronted or challenged by others. There is a lot of truth to the previously mentioned statement: "Show me an executive that closets himself and I will show you, in most of the cases, a chieftain that is incompetent for the job." When these chieftains are finally exposed—when someone dares to stand up to them— they make one last "pitch" for a "money deal" and then "just fade away." Up to that time, however, they "promote" a chaotic environment and display flagrant arrogance.

It is important not to confuse the excitement, or the action and power, which enables the CEO to accomplish the mission of the organization with the power that corrupts. John F. Kennedy said, "I run for President because that is where the action is." We should not confuse the action to which President Kennedy refers with the absolute power which corrupts absolutely. CEOs have to be careful not to lose sight of who they are.

Oftentimes, it is easy for leaders to develop an elevated opinion of themselves. The following story puts this in its true perspective. During his reign as heavyweight champion, Muhammad Ali was in the first-class section of an airliner waiting for takeoff, when a stewardess asked him to buckle his seat belt. Ali looked at her and said, "Superman doesn't need a seat belt." The stewardess looked right back at him and said, "Superman doesn't need an airplane, either." That's what people at the top need—someone who can bring them gently back to earth when they get too carried away with themselves and their accomplishments.

Jumping Ship—Overly Ambitious

In the "good old days," because of part ownership in and loyalty to the company, employees worked for the same company for a long time. Some would spend their entire career with one organization. Was that good? The answer is complex and not easily ascertainable. However, what is certain is that was how organizations were being operated, in contrast to what is happening in most organizations today. As one CEO said, "Employees in today's organizations are primarily interested in preparing and shaping their careers rather than preparing themselves for their present jobs."

How long do managers stay at the top of their organizations? What happens when they leave their organizations? Have you ever met a CEO shortly after he or she left a position? Most do not cope too well. Many know what awaits them, so they spend a lot of time preparing for life after the company instead of devoting their time to achieving the company's goals. To some, reaching the top means they have reached the pinnacle of their life, the ultimate success. They feel that from there, they can only go one way—down. Of course, we know that such reasoning is faulty. It has been said that "success is never final." Even though success may be defined differently by different people and in some instances not defined at all, make no mistake, we can recognize success when we see it.

On the average, a CEO stays at the top of an organization for approximately six years. That being the case, what happens to those who are overly ambitious? Are they preparing for their next tour of duty with another organization? Are they preparing and positioning themselves to jump ship? Should they be? Why? In this vein, consider the fate of José Ignacio López de Arriortúa, who went from General Motors to Volkswagen. And when these managers arrive at their new homes, which generally are competitors of the organizations they formerly headed, what then? What impact does that have on the former organizations? When CEOs are "dethroned," what happens to them? What happens to all the power they possessed as CEOs? It must be remembered that the likelihood for success of each employee can be better assured when the long-term prosperity of the organizations can be assured.

It doesn't take three strikes before the person at the top is out. In many cases, one or two strikes will suffice. While there are unethical, unscrupulous managers who violate the trust placed in them by discussing confidential information with outsiders, most managers aren't so blatantly disloyal. They are better characterized as indifferent, undermotivated, sources of untapped potential, or as opportunists always ready to pounce upon the moments which will further their personal agendas.

The Contagious Terminal Disease—"Manageritis" or "Presidentitis"

Another symptom of this sin is "manageritis" or "presidentitis." These "chieftains" believe that now that they have reached the top, they are indestructible. Apparently, many think that their power is derived from themselves and not from the office. Wrong—the office giveth and the office taketh. What happened to President Richard Nixon's power following his resignation? Remember, what goes up must come down. They are ready to play politics, organizational politics. They try to avoid controversy at any expense; their plan is to "just look good." This scenario may at first appear as though it provides the CEO with a safe haven. For a short time, that may be true, but if indeed it does, it certainly doesn't last long. Within time, the CEO is history; he or she has committed one of the "unforgivable" sins of management. What many managers don't realize is that long-term success can best be attained by putting the employees above short-term profits. President Richard Nixon was quoted as saying, in essence, that there are two kinds of people who want to be president: The first kind want to be big; the second kind want to do big things.

The people at the top have to realize that the organization may be led from the top, but it runs from the bottom. Sam Walton, and then David Glass, current CEO of Wall-Mart, and a small cadre of senior executives used that strategy at Wal-Mart. Wal-Mart says that through their company doors pass ordinary people on their way to accomplishing extraordinary things. The top people in the organization cannot be allowed to become bottlenecks. As Peter Drucker puts it, "the bottleneck is always at the head of the bottle and this can often apply to an organization." We need confidence in our leaders, for confidence is what keeps the company and its suppliers glued together. We need people at the top who inspire, protect, and nurture, not hinder and destroy. At celebrations marking her one-hundredth birthday, Edward Kennedy said about his mother, Rose Kennedy: "In the chaos of our household, she was the quiet at the center of the storm, the anchor of our family, the safe harbor to which we always come." Wouldn't it be great if that could be said of all our leaders.

Speaking at a college, the chairman of Remington Electronics, Inc. said: "What you are, our country will be. You have an absolutely idealistic opportunity to change the world for the better." CEOs have the same opportunity to change their organizations for the better and affect their employees and the rest of the stakeholders. Wouldn't it be great if all of our leaders rose to that challenge. What a business world that would be!

Some of these chieftains enjoy telling subordinates what to do, but as Don Shula says, "They don't provide the example. If they got the stuff of greatness, then they should use that to change things for the better—now rather than later." They should adopt, and really put into practice, a philosophy similar to Ford Motor Company's stated mission: "Our people are the source of our strength. They provide our corporate intelligence and determine our reputation and vitality. Involvement and teamwork are our core human values."

Most managers today aren't going to put their careers on hold while promoting their organizations. Many find that inconsistent with their personal goals. On the other hand, they need to know that if they put their careers way ahead of their organizations, they set in motion the beginning of the end of their tenure with their organizations. That sounds fatalistic, but it really is not. Managers must find ways that allow them to meet both goals at the same time. It is not easy but it can be done. After all, what is the alternative? In the words of Immanuel Kant, "Act only according to that maxim by which you can at the same time will that it should become universal law."

Notes

1. William H. Whyte, *The Organization Man*, (New York: Simon and Schuster, 1956).
2. Earnest R. Archer, "What Happened to the Principles of Management?" *Business Review*, Volume 17, Number 1, Spring 1991, pp. 7–8.
3. Lee Iacocca, *Iacocca: An Autobiography by Lee Iacocca with William Novak* (New York: Bantam Books, a division of Bantam Doubleday Dell Publishing Group, Inc. 1984), p. 145.
4. John Kenneth Galbraith, *The Anatomy of Power* (Boston: Houghton Mifflin, 1985), p. 1.
5. *Max Weber, Law in Economy and Society* (Cambridge: Harvard University Press, 1954), p. 323.
6. Michael Maccoby, *The Gamesman: The New Corporate Leaders* (New York: Simon and Schuster, 1976), p. 197.
7. Ibid., p. 80.
8. W. Chan Kim and Renee A. Manborgne, "Parables of Leadership," *Harvard Business Review*, July–August 1992, pp. 123–28.
9. Lee Iacocca (note 3), pp. 95–96.

CHAPTER 8

Sin #3   "Short-Term Scare" Mentality: Managing for Survival— The Simplistic Fix

A poorly observed fact is more treacherous than a faulty train of reasoning.
—Paul Valery, French philosopher

We are now strategically positioned to capture the wealth of opportunities that exist for us.
—Dexter Corp. '90

When a man does not know what harbor he is making for, no wind is the right wind.
—Seneca

Just Look Good at Any Expense—Are the Numbers Right?

The pressure is on. It is already August 21, and September 30 isn't far away for Mr. I.M. Scared, the president of the Produce or Die Corporation. He took over the corporation as president and CEO on January 11 and has already had to endure two big stories in the financial news. The papers played up how Mr. I.M. Scared has failed to show profits for the corporation. The corporation had to report losses for two consecutive quarters—six long months! Now the due date, September 30, for the third-quarter report is fast approaching.

Unfortunately, things don't look good for the third quarter either. It is almost midnight, and he is driving home from a meeting. The night is peaceful, but he seems restless and preoccupied with the constant thought of what will happen on September 30 if he is unable to show a profit. Is the company in danger? How will the financial media treat the news? What will they say about him? What about his career? Oh, how hard he politicked to get where he is—now his world seems to be crumbling. Will those troubling numbers take him down? Can he survive three bad reports? He knows, or at least he feels, that he is doing a good job for the company; he is positioning the company for the future, but the figures don't show that. Worse yet, two news reports during the year didn't mention that; in fact, the focus was on him, the head of the company. In bold print, they said that Mr. Scared has been a disappointment.

He ponders what he should do. Can he take a chance and continue along his course to strengthen and position the company for the future, even if the figures show a third-quarter loss? Should he focus on the figures so the bottom line will show a profit? What about downsizing? The numbers associated with that option sometimes work almost like magic.

We are reminded of one of the commercials in the last presidential race. One of the presidential candidates appears on the television screen and shows a chart of stick men representing the employees in the federal bureaucracy. With the click of his fingers, we are told he can slice this bureaucracy by one-third. As a matter of fact, in the next second, we are shown a picture of our government "neatly" cut by a third. Then the chief executive assures us that now our budgetary problems are over. We are assured of all that in thirty seconds. And you say managing is hard—it's magic! Are you a little skeptical?

Are there other options which could make the numbers look better? How about the old numbers game? As Andrew Lang said, "He uses statistics as a drunken man uses lamp posts—for support rather than illumination." Mr. Scared thinks about the final option when all else fails—manipulate the data!

Obviously, the Produce or Die Corporation is a fictitious company. The names may have been changed to protect the "guilty"—but the facts have not. Tragically, the facts fit far too many organizations and their CEOs.

Seeing Through the Haze

CEOs complain that investors are fixated on quarterly dividends, and they feel the heat. As dividends shrink, the heat becomes more intense, and their focus turns to the bottom line. They complain that academia and the general public don't appreciate their plight. They complain that academicians overlook, underplay, or simply ignore management's key word—survival. That word, they say, is unfairly missing from the discussion.

It cannot be denied that their complaints are valid. No one can deny that investors are interested in profits. To think otherwise would be ludicrous. No one can deny that survival is a must for any organization. Having said that, the question is how. What are the steps that need to be taken by management to make sure these goals are accomplished? These are tough and sensitive issues that need to be not only discussed but managed. The question is how.

What has happened in the 1990s is that many managers have shifted the emphasis from long-range strategic planning to just managing for "survival." Here are the panel's responses to the following statement:

"Managing for survival" is the norm today in corporate America.

Survey Panel	Disagree Strongly	Disagree	Neither Agree Nor Disagree	Agree	Agree Strongly
University business deans	2%	24%	13%	49%	12%
University business professors	4%	15%	9%	57%	15%
CEOs	6%	25%	44%	19%	6%
Union presidents	0%	0%	0%	33%	67%
Business news editors	8%	0%	23%	61%	8%

How are managers managing for survival? The panel was asked to comment on the following statement:

Generally, managers are interested in and focus on the "simplistic fix."

Survey Panel	Disagree Strongly	Disagree	Neither Agree Nor Disagree	Agree	Agree Strongly
University business deans	5%	34%	13%	41%	7%
University business professors	4%	19%	9%	55%	13%
CEOs	19%	44%	0%	37%	0%
Union presidents	0%	0%	11%	56%	33%
Business news editors	8%	17%	25%	33%	17%

There is 100% agreement among the union presidents; in fact, 67% of them strongly agreed with the statement. The responses of the university business deans, university business professors, and business news editors indicate that they, too, strongly agree with the statement. Is this good and sound management strategy? Are our corporations properly positioning themselves for the future?

Unless someone can equate "managing for survival" and the "simplistic fix" with managerial excellence, today's managers are generally reactive rather than proactive. They are profit oriented rather than wealth oriented. Should they be? Where does such a strategy lead the organization in the short term? How about in the long run? Pose these questions to CEOs who followed such a strategy—if you can still find any around! What response do you expect from them?

One can make a fairly strong case that managing purely for survival may work in the short run. However, even if it does work, the organization's future will be shaky. Why? The answer is quite simple. What happens when a temporary building is put up? The future of that building doesn't look too bright. Will it fall? Probably. When? Maybe not immediately, but given sufficient time, it will. And that is, and should be, unacceptable conduct for the professional manager. After all, the life of an organization should not be one or two years. An organization is not formed, at least in theory if not in practice, for one or two years. In fact, it has a perpetual life! Or does it?

Do the Figures Represent Reality—Have the Books Been Cooked?

Obviously, the best way to manage for survival, using the simplistic fix, is to show positive figures to all those who are concerned with figures. Often, coming up with figures is easy, sometimes too easy. But how meaningful are they for both the short term and the long term? It is easy for corporations today, if they choose, to manipulate the figures by doing some creative accounting. Such creativity is not necessarily always illegal or unethical, but the figures could be almost meaningless in terms of determining the status of the organization. Even worse, the figures may only give a static picture of the corporation at a specific moment, even though there could be a dramatic change in the near future.

This can be likened to an individual who is suffering from a serious illness. There may be a lot of pain associated with that illness; indeed, the pain may be one of the real symptoms of the illness. If the individual is given sufficient medication, the pain may temporarily subside or even go away. Does that mean the patient is in good health? Indeed, no; as a matter of fact, the patient's overall condition may have deteriorated. For the moment, however, the pain has subsided and the individual is perceived as being better. Therefore, what is perceived as real may not be. The same can and does happen in many organizations. At best, there may be temporary relief, but that relief may be far from a cure—far from making the patient well.

Because of the "short-term scare" mentality, the simplistic fix appears to some to be a necessity—just what the doctor ordered! It is not necessarily that managers want to fool those who rely on the figures, but they feel that it is their duty to place the organization in the best light possible. They know of no better or safer way to do that. Thus, while the organization appears to be doing well, in reality, it is sinking; it is having real problems.

It is the CEO's responsibility to properly position the organization for the present as well as the future. Otherwise, neither the organization nor the manager will endure for long. In the long run, these figures can't keep the manager afloat, but the organization may look good for a while to those who are not privy to the total picture, those who do not have or do not understand the true figures, those who do not have the vital statistics.

Consequently, the bottom line does not always represent the true picture. Often, the bottom line has been manufactured to represent a temporary solution to a problem. It is a quick, hollow solution. In many cases, it can be likened to quicksand. Managers who realize what is taking place begin their journey of exiting the organization before the bottom drops out or at least before the real condition becomes apparent to others. This is precisely what frequently happens in government. Some politicians, be they the president or the governor of a state, time their departure from office just before the real problems begin to surface. They are good planners, or should we say good manipulators; that is, they are able to stay afloat, and look good while in office, by applying one quick fix after another to get them through their tenure. Shortly after they leave, the bottom falls out, and woe to the person who takes over that position! Often, their replacement gets the blame. Is it fair? Not really. Unfortunately, it is reality, which makes the situation very troubling. Some chieftains set their goals so that the problems surface after their tenure is up. If their goals are successfully achieved, they take the credit; if not—you guessed it.

Sometimes the timing is bad, and the manager runs out of quick and/or simplistic fixes before his or her tenure is over. When that happens, the CEO's tenure is involuntarily ended. The sin is detected and the CEO pays a heavy price, often his or her job. If that were the end, it wouldn't be so bad, but often managers take others down with them—many who have not committed any sins or even knew that the CEO was sinning. They are the innocent victims who trusted and believed in their leader. But now their leader has failed them, knowingly or otherwise, and brought them down with his or her demise.

Can conduct that ends up being a fatal sin be detected and prevented before it happens? The answer is "it depends." Timing and accountability are crucial in this area. The board can, if it takes its job seriously, help detect and often prevent the harm. Generally, however, good responsible board action is the exception rather than the rule. Again, the problem is that the focus is on the bottom line as a measure of success. That being the case, the CEO's strategy revolves around that mission. Is there safety in numbers? Get the wrong information, make the wrong decisions, and one can quickly find the organization in a financial crisis. It is a given that the world of the manager is filled with facts and quick fixes.

W. Edwards Deming compared the U.S. economy to a big ship, traveling at full speed, requiring distance and time to turn. He warned that those who expect quick results are doomed to disappointment. He said that one of the deadly diseases which can cause failure in any business is emphasis on short-term profits. Business and organizations, he said, are driven by "now" money and the fear of collapse. Norio Ohga, president and CEO of Sony Corporation, commented on the bottom line as a measure of trade between countries: "I feel that focusing solely on the 'bottom line'—the net value of goods traded between America and Japan—misses the larger picture entirely." In the same vein, the former CEO of Ben & Jerry's said, "It's our objective to run Ben & Jerry's for long-term financial and social gain. We are becoming more comfortable and adept at functioning with a two-part bottom line, where our company's success is measured by both our financial and our social performance. We are convinced that the two are intertwined. And, we are convinced that attention to excellence, quality, and the social needs of our communities will lead to solid, stable growth of both our bottom lines."[1]

What is the relationship between success and the bottom line? Here are the responses of the panel:

Most managers generally see the bottom line as proof of success.

Survey Panel	Disagree Strongly	Disagree	Neither Agree Nor Disagree	Agree	Agree Strongly
University business deans	0%	2%	4%	77%	17%
University business professors	2%	0%	5%	69%	24%
CEOs	0%	6%	0%	81%	13%
Union presidents	0%	0%	0%	56%	44%
Business news editors	0%	0%	8%	92%	0%

How would you respond to the statement? How does your response compare with the panel's? Here, we see almost unanimity in the responses. However, there may not be unanimity in how these results should be interpreted. Are the results good or bad?

"Don't Rock the Boat" Syndrome

Closely allied with the simplistic fix is the "don't rock the boat" syndrome. Many insecure managers feel that "rocking the boat" will get them noticed, and if their actions are viewed by others as less than "perfect," they run the risk of damaging their reputations. Consequently, they believe that the "status quo" is the way to go. This has been the philosophy, if not the motto, of many older managers. As long as everything is going fairly well, why upset things? Their reasoning is there is less risk associated with that philosophy. Is there less risk? Again, in the short term the answer may be "yes," but what about in the long run? What happened to the principle: "the higher the risk, the greater the profit; the lower the risk, the lower the profit"? Is that principle applicable to the overall management philosophy? After all, risk isn't always found where you expect it to be. It has been pointed out that one cannot discover new oceans unless he or she has the courage to lose sight of the shore.

There has been considerable discussion in the literature regarding this matter. Many young managers don't like the way older managers manage. Privately, they take the position that the present way of managing in the United States is bad and should be changed. They say that as soon as they get to the top, they would change things and manage by "the book." That sounded good to some academicians and students of management. They saw it as a sign that things were going to change for the better. After all, the majority of CEOs are nearing retirement age and soon will be turning over their helms to the new breed of managers—the college-trained MBAs who have been climbing the ladder. Many who are presently at the top entered the business world when business education as we know it today was somewhat in its infancy. In the early and mid-fifties, business schools generally didn't attract the best and the brightest students. In those days, it was "fashionable" for educators to advise students that if they couldn't make it in engineering, medicine, or law, they could always enter the school of commerce. Things have changed since then, and many of the best and brightest students have been enrolling in the business schools, which, in turn, has elevated business education to a profession worthy of notice and respect.

But what has been happening is not what was expected to happen. Many of the business graduates, when they took over the helm, looked around and had a sudden change of heart. Instead of changing their organizations, as they had contemplated all along, and taking the necessary risks associated with such actions, these new managers decided that it may be better and safer to continue to manage the same way as the "chieftains" whom they replaced.

Perhaps they reasoned that now that they had reached the top, why rock the boat and risk becoming controversial? After all, the old style of management served their predecessors well. Why take a risk by changing?

Many present CEOs reason that it may be better to let something marginal go on than to try to change it for the better and risk rocking the boat. Lee Iacocca relates how he lost an election for captain of the student patrol when he was in the sixth grade because some kids voted twice. When he complained to the teacher, she said, "Let's leave well enough alone." She covered it up. She didn't want any scandal.[2] She didn't want to take the risk that someone would accuse her of wrongdoing. Unfortunately, too many CEOs follow that same reasoning. What about the statement "if you are standing still, you are falling behind"? Isn't risk taking one of the manager's responsibilities? To shed some light on this, let's look at the responses of the panel:

Managers today tend to take fewer risks than they have in the past.

Survey Panel	Disagree Strongly	Disagree	Neither Agree Nor Disagree	Agree	Agree Strongly
University business deans	2%	30%	26%	36%	6%
University business professors	2%	29%	24%	43%	2%
CEOs	0%	62%	19%	19%	0%
Union presidents	0%	11%	11%	33%	45%
Business news editors	0%	38%	15%	39%	8%

Short-term mentality leads to a more conservative management philosophy. Managers are afraid to take risks. Yet we know that often some calculated risks are necessary. Thus, the panel's responses are consistent with the short-term mentality but inconsistent with management philosophy as we read it and understand it.

Resistance to Change—Change Is for the Future!

The managers who commit this sin are those who are more apt to resist change. They associate change with problems. They view change as problem driven rather than vision led. They reason that things are going pretty well, so why change. They prefer to wait until there is a need for change. Often, such an approach is damaging to the organization.

There are no valid written rules in corporate manuals which state or mandate that change should occur only when things are bad, when the organization is in trouble, or when it is showing a loss. Consider, for example, the restructuring of Pepsi-Cola and the recent restructuring of Ford Motor Company. Both companies were healthy at the time the changes were initiated and took place. Why shouldn't we operate from a position of strength instead of weakness? Why should we wait until there is a crisis? Wouldn't it be better to be in control of what needs to be changed?

We begin with the proposition that change is difficult but inevitable. Back in the fourteenth century, Machiavelli stated that the hardest thing to do is to change the order of things. Those who oppose the change will fight you, and those who believe in the change will be lukewarm because they don't know how it will turn out. Machiavelli wrote in *The Prince*, "There is nothing more difficult to take in hand, more perilous to conduct or more uncertain in its success than to take the lead in the introduction of a new order of thinking."

We need to plan for change and try to implement it when the timing is best for it. Sure, there will be disagreements and resistance, but what is the alternative? As long as people are affected by change, there will be conflict. Conflict is inevitable, indeed necessary for progress. A Yiddish proverb states, "If we all pulled in one direction, the world would keel over." William Wrigley, Jr. said, "When two men in business always agree, one of them is unnecessary."

Change is for the future. No one has a "perfectly" clear vision of the future. Often, we don't know what will happen in the next five minutes. Just because the risks in predicting the future cannot be eliminated doesn't mean that we shouldn't take the future into consideration. We make decisions and changes taking the future into account. If our decisions are accurate, that is good; if not, we try to minimize the losses and move on. It has been said that "to try and fail is at least to learn; to fail to try is to lose the inestimable loss of what might have been." Obviously, change for the sake of change is neither the answer nor what is being proposed. Unfortunately, reorganization has sometimes been used for the wrong purpose, for the quick fix. Organizations must change in order to grow. However, change for the sake of change often results in additional problems. To be effective, change must be carefully planned. We need to be mindful that a bend in the road is not the end of the road—unless you fail to make the turn.

Petronius spoke of this in 210 B.C. "We trained hard," he said, "but it seemed that every time we were beginning to form up into teams, we would be reorganized…we tend to meet any new situation by reorganizing, and a wonderful method it can be for creating the illusion of progress while producing confusion, inefficiency, and demoralization." Gilbert Keith Chesterton said, "Don't ever take a fence down until you know the reason why it was set up." Let's examine the panel's responses:

When it comes to managing change, managers generally do an "excellent" job.

Survey Panel	Disagree Strongly	Disagree	Neither Agree Nor Disagree	Agree	Agree Strongly
University business deans	12%	65%	17%	6%	0%
University business professors	22%	67%	5%	4%	2%
CEOs	0%	63%	31%	6%	0%
Presidents of unions	22%	56%	22%	0%	0%
Business news editors	23%	54%	15%	8%	0%

Since an important duty of managers is to handle meaningful change, the responses to the statement add more credence to the fact that, in general, managerial competency is not what it ought to be. These responses are very troubling. Organizations in the future will be faced with the demand for faster and more drastic changes in order to survive, and it would serve CEOs well to hone their tools in this area. If they don't, they many find themselves outside looking in. Maurice Maeterlinch, the Belgian poet and essayist who won the Nobel prize for literature in 1911, said it best: "At every crossing on the road that leads to the future, each progressive spirit is opposed by a thousand appointed to guard the post."

Management theorists, as well as practitioners, have recently focused on the importance of restructuring. Tom Peters says he is now a "radical structuralist." If a new product or an existing product is eliminated or a new CEO is brought in, the company's structure needs to be reexamined. It's like changing your will after getting married or having a child. How well do managers respond to restructuring? Here are the responses of the panel:

Corporate restructuring today is *generally* problem-driven rather than vision-led.

Survey Panel	Disagree Strongly	Disagree	Neither Agree Nor Disagree	Agree	Agree Strongly
University business deans	2%	12%	7%	58%	21%
University business professors	3%	2%	4%	63%	28%
CEOs	6%	31%	13%	44%	6%
Union presidents	11%	0%	0%	33%	56%
Business news editors	0%	8%	15%	62%	15%

The responses depict a picture of CEOs primarily responding to problems geared for the short term. Obviously, this defies our management theory. Isn't one of the functions of top management to have a clear sense of vision for the organization's future? It is important that managers manage proactively instead of reactively. For organizations to stay healthy and succeed in the future, they must be vision led, not problem driven. Organizations that get to the point where they must be managed by managing existing problems end up managing crises.

What do managers consider to be the barometer for measuring the success of the organization? The following statement posed to the panel addresses that issue:

The main factor in determining whether the organization is "winning" is whether it is making a profit for the shareholders.

Survey Panel	Disagree Strongly	Disagree	Neither Agree Nor Disagree	Agree	Agree Strongly
University business deans	3%	31%	8%	50%	8%
University business professors	5%	35%	9%	46%	5%
CEOs	0%	12%	13%	50%	25%
Union presidents	11%	34%	22%	11%	22%
Business news editors	0%	31%	8%	61%	0%

Milton Friedman said that there is one and only one social responsibility of business: to increase its profits—its economic performance. How does that statement fit in with the panel's responses? There is little dispute that economic performance is very important; it is a key responsibility of a business. The economist would argue that a business that doesn't show a profit at least equal to its cost of capital is irresponsible; it wastes resources. Perhaps we need to begin there if an organization wants to continue, wants to be a contributor to society, and wants to be able to discharge other responsibilities. But we must remember that there are other important responsibilities which an organization has to perform.

Which Is It: Downsizing or Rightsizing?

Do managers really understand the difference between downsizing and rightsizing? Is there a difference between the two? Do managers focus on downsizing or rightsizing? We asked our panel to respond to the statement:

The focus of managers is on "downsizing" rather than "rightsizing."

Survey Panel	Disagree Strongly	Disagree	Neither Agree Nor Disagree	Agree	Agree Strongly
University business deans	2%	22%	22%	42%	12%
University business professors	2%	24%	7%	52%	15%
CEOs	6%	63%	19%	12%	0%
Union presidents	0%	11%	0%	45%	44%
Business news editors	0%	8%	61%	23%	8%

It is obvious from the responses that the emphasis is more on downsizing than rightsizing. Union presidents certainly seem to agree with that. If downsizing is not rightsizing, a company can expect problems. While the problems may not be around the corner, they certainly aren't far away.

Every working day, thousands of American workers learn that they will be losing their jobs. The paternalistic model of long-term employment is a thing of the past. Corporate America is driven by a mission to rid itself of "excess" workers. People used to be rewarded for loyalty, but that isn't the case anymore. Employees have to be prepared for the possibility that their jobs may disappear. Only about half of workers believe that their company offers security to those who perform well.

Today, there are approximately one-third fewer people working for Fortune 500 companies than in 1979. Big corporations have been slicing away big time. Companies such as Sears, IBM, General Electric, Ford, Boeing, United Technologies, McDonnell Douglas, and AT&T are in the midst of this reduction. The idea was that this would be the fastest and easiest way to cut business costs, be more competitive, and raise profits. However, there is mounting evidence that this slashing is backfiring. Studies indicate that a number of companies that trimmed their work forces not only failed to see a rebound in earnings but found their ability to compete eroded even further.[3] George M.C. Fisher, chairman and CEO of the Eastman Kodak Company in Rochester, New York, states: "In the late '80s and early '90s, for example, Kodak reduced its Rochester work force by half, to 34,000 employees, cutting the payroll by $1 billion. Some of these terminations were voluntary. Afterward Kodak still experienced some of the same business problems it grappled with before the downsizing, but those problems were compounded by the fact that employee anxiety was at an all-time high."

While the millions of employee layoffs did help corporate America cut expenses, there is growing evidence that the strategy known as downsizing produces destructive side effects that range from demoralized workers to job burnout.[4] Furthermore, researchers and strategists believe that the attempt to strengthen profits and productivity through cutting layers of workers may have cost many companies billions of dollars.[5] "Much of the downsizing of the last 10 years has been an enormous waste of time and energy, and in many cases has been spectacularly unsuccessful."[6] A consultant specializing in reengineering efforts estimates that 70% of the corporate cost-cutting he has observed has not achieved the anticipated results.[7] A survey of top executives shows that about two-thirds are not satisfied. In hindsight, many said they should have planned more carefully.[8]

The downsizing that many CEOs use to make their companies look better is like "corporate surgery." Initially, it seems to be only minor surgery. The reason for this misconception is that the patient (the organization) seldom dies on the operating table when the procedure (downsizing) takes place. Following the operation, however, an infection, known as "corporate anorexia," sets in. Generally, the infection alone is not fatal, but coupled with other corporate "viruses," it can and docs often bring companies down, resulting in their demise. About a month before Montgomery Ward and Co. filed for bankruptcy protection from its creditors (Chapter 11), it had announced that it was cutting 22 percent, or 400 employees, from its corporate staff in an attempt to avoid bankruptcy.

It is difficult to properly treat many of these "infected" companies. Often, the system rejects the attempted treatment. An associated problem is that "corporate anorexia" may often go undetected in the short run, and the organization looks healthy. In time, however, the quick fix is no longer effective, and the organization is left in worse shape than before the fix.

There are both obvious and hidden repercussions to downsizing. Consider, for example, what happens when downsizing gets to a point where the organization can't produce enough widgets to meet the demand of its customers. The customers turn to competitors. A case in point is what happened recently to ALCOA. When AT&T recently announced it was downsizing, its stock went up. Sometimes, that is precisely the reason why some companies downsize. Unfortunately, Wall Street investors, at least in the short term, usually react favorably to cost-cutting. Stock prices often rise when companies terminate workers.[9] But how would the organization look if we were to fast forward? What often happens is that when jobs are cut, rather than using the savings for necessary repairs, the savings are redistributed in the form of higher raises for the top people in the organization. When the organization needs to add people later, more money has to be spent just to put the organization back where it was before the job cuts.

Sometimes budgets can be balanced by cutting expenses, and when organizations get into financial trouble, that is the first thing many CEOs do in the hope it will solve the problem. In the short run, such action seems to work. However, the unknown is the potential damage it may have on the organization's long-term survival. Some organizations may even show a short-term profit, but such a profit does not translate into wealth maximization. When will those managers learn that there is another way to balance the budget—it is called increasing revenue! Many avoid it because, in some instances, to do so the organization must first increase expenses, and that is viewed as more risk taking, which makes many of them nervous.

Perhaps one of the worst things managers do in this area is to "decree" that there be a certain percentage cut across the various departments. Talk about a simplistic fix that can seriously damage an organization's long-term survival! While some departments may be able to sustain the cuts, others not only can't afford them but need additional resources. Often, the reason for an organization's downfall is the inequity of resources among the various departments. Is that poor management? That's putting it mildly.

There are two things about across-the-board cuts that excite poor managers. First, such managers feel that they are meeting a present need: to run an organization that appears profitable. Second, and even more important to them, they are doing it in an equitable manner; every department is getting the same percentage cut. To those who think this helps their careers, such conduct appears to be what the doctor ordered—good medicine. Their hero is the person who came up with the term "downsizing." He provided them with a rationale and a mechanism to save their jobs. However, those who see management as a profession view those who advocate and champion downsizing as having considerable impact on organizations failing and at the same time managers losing their jobs as "chieftains." Think of the organizational rewards if managers had never heard of or focused on downsizing, but rather focused on rightsizing. Some organizations and CEOs have become symbols of corporate greed, promoting self-interests and shortsightedness. These unprincipled organizations and managers failed to serve their various constituents and in the end didn't even serve the stockholders.

If cutting costs becomes necessary, it must be done logically and sensitively instead of "mechanically." This is not only important but necessary, whether it means eliminating employees or parts of the business or consolidating operations. It must be accomplished with both a short-term and a long-term objective in mind. It takes more than short-term recoveries. The situation becomes much more troublesome when managers try to get their employees to focus only on the bottom line. Managers must see the big picture, not only internally but externally as well. Managers cannot and should not work in a vacuum. Herein lies the short-term mentality approach—the simplistic fix.

A better approach is to develop effective teams that are able to focus on the entire organization and assess it accordingly. Anything short of that places the organization on the edge of a cliff. Its survival will depend on what lies ahead—on the oncoming storms. Some organizations are "terminally ill," and it may only take a small storm to bring them to their knees and ultimately to a premature death. For some organizations that are sick, whether they make it or whether they fail depends on whether their managers are able to diagnose the problem early enough and prescribe the proper medicine. The manager whose conduct amounts to "managerial malpractice" is understandably on the verge of bringing down the organization. Once that conduct is discovered, the manager's career in that organization is, for all practical purposes, finished.

That is why weak managers don't want others in the organization to know exactly what is taking place. Many managers see employees who work together and departments that interact with other departments as threatening. They see such interaction as a plan to undermine them, and they become paranoid. Organizational functions need cohesion. This, of course, helps prevent a corporate evil known as complacency. Complacency destroys the right organizational focus and the vision for the organization. Without that planning, the heart of the CEO's responsibility is compromised, even tainted.

The consequence is organizational discord, resulting in an organization whose sails are affected and guided by very slight wind movements. The organization is so loose and so fragile, without a proper foundation, indeed, in many cases without any foundation, that its survival is guaranteed by chance rather than by design. Managers must not manage by chance, even though chance sometimes enters the managerial process. The key is to take the necessary precautions to ensure the organization is rightsized, which, in turn, will enable the organization to be properly steered so it can better weather anything that is not consistent with its survival.

These weak managers often, following the quick fix—the simplistic approach—give across-the-board raises. They don't want to risk offending anyone. They think they are being fair by giving everyone the same percentage raise. Is it fair? What about motivation? What is the alternative in light of the fact that some of them don't know their employees or how they performed? CEOs need to focus on rightsizing and develop a strategy to implement it which is consistent with the corporate mission.

A note of caution: The preceding comments should be viewed in their true perspective. They must be sensitively treated and understood. In certain instances, downsizing is indeed necessary. Our concern here is primarily when downsizing is done out of fear, without proper analysis, as a quick fix, solely for the organization to look good, now and in the near future. We cannot afford to mismanage this important matter. It goes without saying that downsizing in the form of lost jobs has resulted in the loss of trust between employees and managers. Employees often feel betrayed by their former employer.

Jack Benny told a story about going to the doctor for an exam. After the doctor saw his x-rays, he told Benny that he needed an operation which would cost $400. Benny said to the doctor, "I don't have $400, but for $25 would you touch up the x-rays?" A quick fix indeed! We must be cautious that any cut, any reduction, is well thought out. It is easy to balance our personal budget by cutting expenses. We can, for example, cut our car payment by getting a smaller car, cut our house payments by getting a smaller house, cut our grocery bill by eating less, and on and on. But what would the result be after we do all that?

Early Retirement: Benefit or Detriment—Who Wins?

In the last decade or so, we have seen a heightened increase in early retirement. Why is this happening? Is it because of managers' concern for their employees? Is it a sound business strategy? Does it help or harm the organization? Who really benefits from early retirement? Who generally takes early retirement? Because the concept of early retirement is fairly new in corporate America and the jury is still out, there are no clear answers to these questions. What is clear, however, is that it has raised serious concerns. Many are demanding accurate answers to these questions because early retirement has a significant impact on both the organization and its employees.

Is early retirement generally a result of the short-term scare mentality? Is it another example of the simplistic fix? Early reports seem to validate rather than invalidate such an assumption. For many insecure managers, early retirement looks like a win–win situation. When they are faced with present or potential corporate loss, the issue of what to do becomes a serious concern. An obvious solution is to cut costs. Which costs? Salaries? To some, the option of early retirement seems like a better solution than layoffs. This, of course, is somewhat in line with the previous topic of downsizing.

Managers are faced with a dilemma. They perceive cutting costs, even in the short run to make up losses, as positive for their careers, but doing so may be viewed negatively. It is controversial, which, of course, is something weak, insecure managers want to avoid like the plague. They think they have to come up with a win–win situation. After some deliberation, they come to the conclusion that early retirement is the answer. They reason that there can't be much objection and think their employees would welcome such an option. They think that only the less desirable employees will be affected. Those who are really not interested in the organization in the first place, the "disloyal" employees, will be the ones who will exercise the option of early retirement. The good, loyal, and efficient employees will stay with the organization. Generally, that reasoning is wrong.

From the limited studies available, the evidence is disturbing. It appears that the good, efficient employees are much more likely to take early retirement. They perceive their so-called option to take early retirement as being not an option but rather a demand. If the manager really wanted them to stay, he or she would have informed them. The manager would have tapped them on the shoulder and asked them to stay. If they fail to voluntarily take early retirement, the alternative is that they will be given early retirement anyway, by being forced out of the organization. They probably will be laid off without severance pay. Marginal employees aren't really interested in early retirement. They know that it won't be easy to find a job in another organization, and the early retirement pay is not enough to support them and their families. The unfortunate result is that because so many good employees decide to take the early retirement, the company is left with a lot of poor performers. If the company let them go and hired new ones to do the work, litigation might ensue.

Another concern is what happens to those good employees in their late forties or early fifties who take early retirement? Some may be hired back as consultants, but the majority will be hired by other organizations. Which organizations? You guessed it—competitors. Competitors could certainly use all that experience, knowledge, and expertise. All the training that these employees received will now be used to compete against the organizations that trained them. Is that fair? Maybe not, but that is what is happening. To many analysts, the answers to whether early retirement is good or bad for the organization and who wins and who loses seem obvious. For further insight, let's turn to our panel:

Early "optional" retirement, as presently administered in corporate America, is sound.

Survey Panel	Disagree Strongly	Disagree	Neither Agree Nor Disagree	Agree	Agree Strongly
University business deans	3%	27%	29%	39%	2%
University business professors	7%	26%	24%	39%	4%
CEOs	6%	19%	13%	62%	0%
Union presidents	22%	22%	45%	11%	0%
Business news editors	0%	23%	39%	38%	0%

Overall, early retirement benefits the organization rather than the employees.

Survey Panel	Disagree Strongly	Disagree	Neither Agree Nor Disagree	Agree	Agree Strongly
University business deans	0%	21%	30%	45%	4%
University business professors	2%	29%	20%	44%	5%
CEOs	0%	44%	12%	44%	0%
Union presidents	0%	11%	11%	45%	33%
Business news editors	8%	23%	23%	38%	8%

Are the responses in line with good management policy? What is the impact of these responses for both the short term and the long term? Would another solution have been better for the organization under the circumstances? Simplistic fixes often have a tendency to discourage managers from exploring solid, effective solutions. Analysis should come before solutions. Analysis does not have to become paralysis, but it certainly should be adequate.

What we have are organizations in search of easy ways to downsize and cut costs without laying off employees, and early retirement looks like a good option. In practice, what actually happens is that a company offers employees an early retirement package that management feels is equitable. Knowing the company is downsizing, employees feel pressured to take early retirement rather than be forced out later with less. Thus, vital employees that the company would like to keep sign up. The company then needs to hire and train others to fill those vital positions. In the end, the company winds up spending as much on hiring and training as it would have if it had kept the existing employees.

These measures are generally implemented to curb corporate expenses, add to the bottom line, or put the organization back in the black. There is little, if any, advance planning. Early retirement, in many instances, is a reactive rather than proactive response to a perceived need. In sum, it is generally used as a quick fix.

If It Isn't Broken, Why Bother It?

We hear it over and over again: Why do you want to change that? There's nothing wrong with it. "If it isn't broken, don't fix it" is the attitude of many managers who want to maintain the status quo. Consider the panel's reaction to the following statement:

Managers today, in general, adopt the philosophy, "If it ain't broke, don't fix it!"

Survey Panel	Disagree Strongly	Disagree	Neither Agree Nor Disagree	Agree	Agree Strongly
University business deans	2%	28%	18%	47%	5%
University business professors	0%	24%	9%	62%	5%
CEOs	12%	44%	13%	31%	0%
Union presidents	0%	0%	56%	11%	33%
Business news editors	0%	38%	8%	54%	0%

Do the responses represent what is happening in corporate America? More importantly, are you comfortable with the responses? What needs to be done? In general, our panel's responses appear to agree with what is taking place in our organizations.

Was the abacus broken before the slide rule was invented? Was the slide rule broken before the calculator was developed? Was the calculator broken before the computer was invented? Should we have waited until they were broken before coming up with their replacements? Where would we be today if that philosophy had been followed? What does that say for long-range planning?

This philosophy is another example of the simplistic fix. Maintaining the status quo is much safer than trying to come up with something better. To a weak manager, it appears to be less risky; consequently, there is much less chance for potential controversy. Is that what management is all about? Is that what we expect of professional managers?

What a CEO "inherits" is often a major factor. If you had the chance to become the CEO of either a failing company or a successful company, which one would you take? When MBA students were asked this question, most picked a failing company over a successful one, their reasoning being there is less risk associated with a failing company. They felt that they would not be hurt as badly if the company failed. Many would disagree with their choice. After all, what is wrong with some calculated risk? It has been argued that one can't reach his or her goals without occasionally taking "some long shots." The higher the risk, the greater the profit; the less risk, the less profit. In other words, "no guts, no glory." As Will Rogers said, "You've got to go out on a limb sometimes, because that's where the fruit is."

Let's briefly examine the 1996 federal budget crisis. Why did it become a crisis? Shouldn't a crisis be something that is completely unanticipated? Didn't the parties involved know what would happen in the near future? Shouldn't they have known that it had to be managed? Isn't managing a big part of a politician's responsibility? Could it be that these people really meant well, but just couldn't manage effectively and responsibly? Or does it mean that they were more interested in managing their careers than the government? Managing responsibly should be a major part of their job, yet many politicians see managing as a side issue, a minor part of the job. The cynics may argue that the budget crisis was an orchestrated event to put forth an agenda. If that is true, then what does it say about the responsibility of politicians to their stakeholders, to their constituents, to the nation? Are they putting their personal interests ahead of the nation's interest? Perhaps something was learned from all that when we look at what happened this year!

Some basic questions need to be asked here: What are the prerequisites to managing responsibly and effectively? Are they the same prerequisites required to lead effectively? Can these prerequisites be easily identified? Are they discussed in the press or political forums? Should they be? Perhaps this sheds some light on why governments operate as they do.

Very little respect is given, consciously or unconsciously, to the prerequisites needed to properly manage. To fix things only when things are broken is to adopt, in effect, a problem-driven rather than vision-led management philosophy. Are we ready to follow a leader who adopts such a philosophy?

Does It Make Me Look Good? Go for It!

Unfortunately, many managers today make managerial decisions based on whether it will make them "look good." They rationalize that their decisions will also help the organization. In many cases, they also rationalize that such conduct is acceptable. Such decisions may look good in the short term, but often by the time the real impact is felt in the organization, the manager has moved on to another organization.

A new-product manager described this approach as follows: "When you are about to introduce a new product which you have been working on, you should move from that position to another position prior to the introduction of the product in the marketplace. If the product is successful, you can claim the credit. If the product is a failure, you can blame the new manager who introduced the product. That way, you cover yourself if the product is a failure and at the same time, position yourself to look good if it is a success." For some managers such conduct is viewed as a win–win situation. If things go wrong, you can argue that if you were still the product manager, this wouldn't have happened!

A manager may be able to get by with that kind of logic in the short run, but eventually it will catch up with him or her. As the saying goes, you can fool some of the people some of the time, but you can't fool all of the people all of the time. The bottom line is: Beware of the quick fix! Professional managers need to roll up their sleeves and prepare for the future of their organizations. Careful planning and analysis are critical. They may take time, but so be it. Complex problems cannot be solved in an hour; that only happens on television. Socrates said, "All good things are achieved through hard labor." Success usually does not happen by accident; it has to be achieved. When success is the result of hard work, it is more appreciated and more fulfilling. After all, "success without fulfillment is failure."

Summary

Many managers today primarily "manage for survival." They use the quick fix to solve organizational problems. Short-term answers with short-term results are the norm in corporate America. Our present business culture seems to support quick and easy solutions as a way to obtain quick and tangible results. Unfortunately, many managers are convinced that if they don't produce steady, stair-step increases in profits, investors will sell out, raising the specter of takeover. A "want it yesterday" attitude has invaded corporate America.

"Business myopia" is a phenomenon used to describe every aspect of business today. Market myopia is lack of vision in defining customers and markets. Organizational myopia is lack of planning, strategy, and vision. Operational myopia is the "if it's not broken, don't fix it" mentality applied to processes.[10] More and more business analysts, researchers, and CEOs are identifying shortsightedness as a problem throughout organizations. As problems are identified and defined, solutions are proposed and implemented.

In *Short-Term America: The Causes and Cures of Our Business Myopia*, Michael Jacobs describes the overall problem as the "adversarial relationship between capital providers (shareholders and lenders) and capital users (managers)." The problem has been brought about by the American financial system.[11] Responsibility for short-term scare management rests not only with management but with the corporate financial structure in America and has resulted in an erosion of America's competitiveness worldwide. It is a "catch-22" situation. When managers must show profits to remain managers, fear takes over. The lack of long-term wealth building may mean a company is open bait for a takeover. The problem is as complex as the solution. Managers can begin by attempting to get the board of directors and investors involved in the vision of the company. Managers can begin by campaigning for their companies to look to the future in terms of training, research and development, and capital investments. By being up front with investors concerning the lack of initial profits and emphasizing the need to look to the future and build wealth to remain in business, managers may be able to win over investors. Pepsi's CEO called it "choosing probable death over certain death."[12] It is important that CEOs lead their organizations with positive vision rather than negative vision, which surfaces when things go wrong. Negative vision is reactive management and a short-term approach. "Managers," says Harold Geneen, CEO of ITT, "in all too many companies do not achieve the desired results because nobody makes them do it. Management must manage; and that means management must manage effectively and efficiently."

Notes

1. Fred Lager, *Ben & Jerry's, The Inside Scoop* (New York: Crown Publishers, 1994).
2. Lee Iacocca, *Iacocca: An Autobiography by Lee Iacocca with William Novak.* (New York: Bantam Books, a division of Bantam Doubleday Dell Publishing Group, Inc. 1984), p. 15.
3. Bernard Banmohl, "When Downsizing Becomes 'Dumbsizing'," *Time*, March 15, 1993, p. 55.
4. Lisa Genasci, "Corporate Downsizing Has Adverse Side Effects," *The Fort Wayne Journal Gazette*, July 10, 1994, p. 3F.
5. Ibid.
6. Ibid.; quoting Michael Hammer, a consultant.
7. Ibid.
8. Ibid.; quoting the consulting firm Arthur D. Little.
9. Ibid.
10. Michael Jacobs, *Short-Term America: The Causes and Cures of Our Business Myopia* (Boston: Harvard Business School Press, 1991).
11. Brian Damaine, "Times Are Good? Create a Crisis," *Fortune,* Volume 127, June 28, 1993, p. 124.
12. Peter M. Senge, "The Leader's New Work: Building Learning Organizations," *Sloan Management Review*, Volume 32, Fall 1990, p. 14.

CHAPTER 9

Sin #4   Indecisiveness: Unclear on When and Who Decides

If no one ever took risks, Michelangelo would have painted the Sistine floor.
   —Neil Simon

Be willing to make decisions. That's the most important quality in a good leader. Don't fall victim to what I call the "ready-aim-aim-aim-aim syndrome." You must be willing to fire.
   —T. Boone Pickens

Not to decide is to decide.
   —Harvey Cox

I have an absolute rule. I refuse to make a decision that somebody else can make. The first rule of leadership is to save yourself for the big decision. Don't allow your mind to become cluttered with the trivia. Don't let yourself become the issue.
   —Richard Nixon

Accept rigorous debate and then make a decision. You're the one who has to do it, you can't just hope it will evolve by some mystical group process.
   —Abraham Zaleznik

When it comes to fatal managerial sins, managerial indecisiveness has to be one of the deadliest, if not the deadliest. For openers, a manager who cannot confront a problem and make a decision causes stress among his or her employees and places the organization at risk. How do managers rate in this area? Are they good decision makers? We posed the following statement to our panel of experts:

**"Indecisiveness" (unclear on when and who decides)
is a trait of many managers.**

Survey Panel	Disagree Strongly	Disagree	Neither Agree Nor Disagree	Agree	Agree Strongly
University business deans	6%	37%	14%	38%	5%
University business professors	2%	51%	15%	25%	7%
CEOs	6%	38%	19%	37%	0%
Union presidents	0%	22%	0%	45%	33%
Business news editors	8%	38%	8%	31%	15%

Forty-three percent of the university business deans either agreed or strongly agreed with the statement. As for union presidents, 78% either agreed or strongly agreed. Is there reason to be concerned? Are our managers making timely and proper decisions? Is there room for improvement? General George C. Marshall said, "Don't fight the problem. Decide it!"

Who Says No Guts, No Glory?

"Congratulations on your new position. We always knew you were made of the 'right stuff' and that one day you would be sitting in that chair. It couldn't have happened to a better person. All that hard work and perseverance paid off. Now you are on easy street!"

"Excuse me, Mr. President, you are wanted on the phone. As Commander-in-Chief, it is your call whether we should drop the A-bomb. We are ready to carry out your decision. Should we proceed with the mission?"

"Ms. President, we have just been informed of another death caused by our product. Should we recall all of the product? The retail value? It's approximately $100 million."

"Mr. President, according to the weather forecast, there is a 95% chance of rain at the time of graduation this afternoon. Should we hold graduation inside? Yes, some guests will have to stand, and it will be very hot and stuffy."

"Ms. President, we just completed a thorough search of the plane, and we didn't find any explosives. Yes, we had another call, and the caller insists that he has planted a bomb on the plane. Should we proceed with the flight? We are already one hour and twenty-two minutes behind schedule, and some of the passengers are very upset."

"Governor, this is the warden. Have you reached a decision on the execution? As you know, it is scheduled for seventy-two minutes from now."

These kinds of tough decisions are not rare, which is precisely why we need good and honorable people at the helm. Mediocrity should not reign at the top. It is true that complex and sensitive issues that need to be carefully analyzed often confront managers. But the complexity of the issues should not deter the proper decision makers from calmly and professionally analyzing the problem and arriving at the best possible decision under the circumstances. Some managers cannot, for a number of reasons, deal with rough issues. That's why we need the very best and the brightest at the top—only good decision makers belong at the top. That's what led one writer to comment:

> ...good men belong in the heat of the battle, where issues are confused, where you're never sure you're right, where good and bad are inextricably fused with the partly good and the partly bad, where often you can't do one worthy thing without endangering some other worthy thing.[1]

President Harry Truman said:

> All my life whenever it comes time to make a decision, I make it and forget about it, and go to work on something else, and when these things came before me, as President of the United States, I made the decision on them, and went into the next thing. You never have time to stop. You've got to keep going because there's always a decision just ahead of you that you've got to make, and you don't want to look back. If you make a mistake in one of these decisions, correct it by another decision, and go ahead.

Lee Iacocca writes in his autobiography:

> If I had to sum up in one word the qualities that make a good manager, I'd say that it comes down to decisiveness. You can use the fanciest computers in the world and you can gather all the charts and numbers, but in the end you have to bring your information together, set up a timetable, and act.
> And I don't mean act rashly...
> Actually, my management style has always been pretty conservative. Whenever I've taken risks, it's been after satisfying myself that the research and the market studies supported my instincts. I may act on my intuition—but only if my hunches are supported by the facts.[2]

Few would disagree that decisiveness is a key quality of a good manager. The question that needs to be addressed is why so many managers have problems in this area. However, before exploring why so many CEOs are indecisive, we need to put decision making in its true perspective. A better understanding of how decisions are made will help us to understand the way they should be made. The following statement gives an insight into the ingredients of "real" decision making:

> Decision making is...complex, redolent with feedback and cycles, full of search detours, information gathering, and information ignoring, fueled by fluctuating uncertainty, fuzziness, and conflict.[3]
>
> In real decision situations, one seldom observes...clear, step-by-step process...steps in the process proceed simultaneously, some steps are skipped, some are repeated....There are obvious interactions, feedbacks, and cycles. Also, decision situations intermingle, decisions are imbedded in decisions. All these complications are quite real and usually quite rational.[4]

In a study of strategic organizational decisions, it was concluded that:

> ...a strategic decision process is characterized by novelty, complexity, and open-endness, by the fact that the organization usually begins with little understanding of the decision situation it faces or the route to its solution, and only a vague idea of what that solution might be and how it will be evaluated when it is developed. Only by groping through a recursive, discontinuous process involving many difficult steps and a host of dynamic factors over a considerable period of time is a final choice made. This is not the decision making under uncertainty of the textbook, where alternatives are given even if their consequences are not, but decision making under ambiguity, where almost nothing is given or easily determined.[5]

In *Crises in Organizations*,[6] the author, Lawrence Barton, relates how the then nation's CEO handled the Cuban missile crisis: "Every president, like every manager in industry, tends to see his decision-making skills mature during his tenure during office." He quotes a comment by historian Theodore H. White reflecting on President Kennedy's handling of the crisis. It offers an analogy for every manager who aspires to cope well under stress:

> Like all presidents, he was groping. They all do as they try to reach for controls of the levers and pedals in their first few months—as a buyer gingerly tests the brakes and gas pedals of the new car he has

driven off from the dealer's. Kennedy, however, was groping not only for control of unfamiliar instruments; he was pushing out into an unknown stream, guiding the power around the bend into a new country, new times, and the unexplored landscape of the 1960s...After the instant disaster of the Bay of Pigs and the taut confrontation with the Russians on access to Berlin, by his first autumn in office he had brought his instruments well in hand and, then, gradually moved to the mastery of the missile crisis and the test-ban treaty.[7]

The Organizational Maze

The authors of an article on decision making pose the following questions: Who would suggest that Albert Einstein should have been President of the United States? Or that Franklin Roosevelt should have understood the intricate details of atomic structure? Each of these men had particular abilities—one to deal with detail and precise analysis; the other to handle the broad scope, complex with political and economic implications. There is no reason to suggest that the roles should have been reversed or that one ability is superior to the other. And yet, there is often a lack of understanding and appreciation on the part of the analyst and decision maker about the role that each plays in the decision-making process. The result is often frustration on the part of both. The analyst views the decision maker as lacking intellectual rigor and depending far too much on intuition; the decision maker views the analyst as narrow and blind to the broad implication of a problem.[8]

A significant portion of a manager's time must be devoted to making decisions. In fact, most planning and organizing activities require making key decisions regarding strategy and allocation of resources, and most control activities depend upon decisions concerning corrective actions once plans no longer seem practical. Yet what we find is that many CEOs fail to take action. They tend to procrastinate. This indecisiveness impedes the decision-making process, which, in many cases, leads to non-action or action taken too late. Then the question is why these chieftains hesitate to make decisions. Why do they tend to be indecisive?

A number of factors contribute to such conduct. Procrastinators often have a difficult time with problem determination, due to their inability to assess the issues. CEOs often try to avoid conflict or unpleasant issues instead of meeting them head on. Taking a side in a controversial debate is so distasteful to an indecisive CEO that he or she refuses to decide at all. This

CEO tends to vacillate between issues in order to avoid choosing a side that may displease employees, shareholders, or the board of directors, which are not the only interests that the manager must balance. He or she must worry about other stakeholders' interests. Let's examine the following chart:

Some of the Stakeholders in the Business Environment

The indecisive manager reasons that displeasing even one of these stakeholders may mean paying an unbearable price—his or her career! To properly sustain itself, the corporation must give appropriate attention to all those who hold a stake in its performance. If we add to the list other factors and forces, such as environmental, legal, economic, political, technological, and demographic, the decision-making process is further complicated. Other considerations may include the impact on the company's products, market prices, business ethics, profits and losses, capital, the employees, and competitors' positions. Thus, we begin to understand the real or imagined pressures on the CEO in his or her quest to make a proper decision in a timely manner. Many CEOs react by either "freezing," and in reality doing nothing, or by analyzing the situation to the point where it becomes paralysis by analysis.

Some may argue that making no decision is in fact a decision. That argument may satisfy the philosopher or the theoretician, but it certainly does not satisfy the practitioner. As Norman Vincent Peale said, "If you put off everything till you're sure of it, you'll get nothing done." CEOs can't put off things that need to be done. Shaky bridges don't long endure. CEOs must be the "repairers of bridges."

Paralysis Through Analysis: Lost in the Information Flow

In order to truly understand and appreciate the problems faced by many CEOs as they attempt to make qualitative decisions, we need to briefly examine the inputs for decision making by a CEO. To illustrate the point, let's look at decision making in the 1940s and the 1990s. These two periods were chosen because significant advances occurred technologically and otherwise. The birth of the computer was followed by its dramatic development. Computing capacity that cost a million dollars in the 1940s costs only a few dollars in the 1990s and is thousands of times faster. During this period, management science proved to be a powerful decision-making approach in a wide variety of managerial contexts—the quantitative approach to decision making. The emergence and use of management information systems in decision making and the automation of information processing have paralleled automation of manufacturing.

To understand why many managers are indecisive, we need to understand both the inputs necessary for making a sound decision and the steps in the decision-making process. Let's briefly examine two theories of decision making: the classical theory and the "administrative" theory. The classical theory of decision making assumes that decisions are directed toward a single, unchanging goal and that rational decisions can be reached to meet that goal. To a large extent, these assumptions were derived from the theory of the "economic" individual. Economic individuals are assumed to know all alternatives available in a given situation and the consequences of each. It is further assumed that they behave rationally; that is, they are able to order their preferences according to their own hierarchies of values, and they always seek to maximize some desired goal.[9]

Classical theory has, however, come under serious criticism from modern management theorists and behavioral scientists. They criticize classical theory for assuring that once the imbalance has been resolved by an appropriate decision, the matter is settled once and for all. They agree that the more organizational members are united and guided by common, stable, and well-defined goals, the more likely it is that the organization will be effective and its members satisfied; however, modern theorists argue that goal stability and consequences can never be fully realized, due to both environmental changes and individual differences.[10]

As a result of a significant amount of research, some believe that decisions are aimed at a sequential rather than a simultaneous resolution of conflict. Each decision must "strike a balance among so many conflicting values, objectives, and criteria that it will always be suboptimal from any single viewpoint. Every decision or choice affecting the whole enterprise has negative consequences for some of the parts."[11] Thus, each resolution of conflict creates other conflict in terms of developments in the environment over which decision makers have little or no control. In effect, decision makers must precariously make their own way through an unending series of imbalances toward a constantly redefined goal. The result is continuous rejection, clarification, redefinition, and alteration of goals.[12]

Some argue that such sporadic and erratic decision making may in the long run produce better results than decisions aimed at stable and clearly defined goals, most of which are only vaguely understood anyway. In their view, progress may actually be impeded by the kind of centralized and rational decision making prescribed by classical theory.[13] Instead, they favor a view that has been termed a "quasi-resolution" of conflict and believe this to be characteristic of most organizational decision making.[14] The quasi-resolution model is based upon circularity; that is, there is no ideal end goal toward which decisions should be rationally directed; rather, there is a continual evolution. Since the future is unknown, uncertain, and too complex for human beings to grasp, people will probably make better decisions if they ignore some aspects of a problem and deal primarily with the more tangible and predictable aspects of it. In time, a creative synthesis may be possible.

In 1936, Chester Bernard said that three objectives had to be pursued in decision making: (1) to ascertain the truth, (2) to determine a course of action, and (3) to persuade. Although Bernard laid the groundwork for a process that could help business executives reach decisions, the idea was ignored. Little attention was paid to the decision-making process developed by Irwin D.J. Bross when it was first published in 1953. He described three stages as critical to the process: (1) responding to conditions in the environment, (2) determining mutually exclusive courses of action, and (3) selecting a course of action to achieve a specific purpose.[15]

The theories of Bernard and Bross might have remained in relative obscurity if *Fortune* magazine had not published an article in 1955 pointing out that chief executives from some of the largest and most important companies in the world used no deliberate process to arrive at their decisions.[16] The author of the article, John McDonald, raised a very serious question: Was business decision making an unconscious and intuitive art form, or could a person be taught a conscious, rational, and systematic process for making business decisions?

In 1956, Peter Drucker wrote an article entitled "How to Make a Business Decision" in which he stated that decision making is a rational and systematic process and that its organization is a definite sequence of steps, each of them, in turn, rational and systematic. He listed the steps in the process as: (1) defining the problem, (2) defining expectations, (3) developing alternative solutions, and (4) knowing what to do with the decision after it has been reached.[17]

In 1965, Herbert A. Simon stated that the decision-making process consists of three steps: (1) the intelligence phase—finding conditions calling for a decision; (2) the design phase—inventing, developing, and analyzing possible courses of action; and (3) the choice phase—selecting a course of action. He felt that there were problems with the economic theory of decision making. Its assumptions were not valid in actual happenings. He also felt that the values issue in decision making should be left to the decision maker. He saw two important differences between the artificial "economic" individual and his true-to-life decision-making "administrative" individual.

First, he rejected the notion that people can be fully informed about anything, arguing that since consequences lie in the future, it is impossible for any person to know all potential alternatives and to anticipate all potential results. In actual practice, only a few alternatives can be known, and future values can only be anticipated as projections of the imagination. Because of this physical limitation upon the administrator's ability, Simon advanced the principle of bounded rationality. This principle states that when the limits to rationality are viewed from the individual's standpoint, they fall into three categories: He is limited by his unconscious skills, habits, and reflexes; his values and conceptions of purpose, which may diverge from the organizational goals; and the extent of his knowledge and information. The individual can be rational in terms of the organization's goals only to the extent that he is able to pursue a particular course of action, he has a correct conception of the goal of the action, and he is correctly informed about the conditions surrounding his action. Within the boundaries laid down by these factors, his choices are rational—goal oriented.

According to the administrative theory of decision making, "choice is always exercised with respect to a limited, approximate, simplified 'model' of the real situation." In place of the concept of "objective rationality," Simon offered the concept of "subjective rationality," which depends on the individual's personal values and unique modes of perceiving, learning, and thinking. Whereas objective rationality is in fact the correct behavior for maximizing given values in a given situation, subjective rationality maximizes attainment relative to the actual knowledge of the individual. Accordingly, people would be considered subjectively rational if they attempted to maximize an end, even if the attempt failed or was inappropriate. Rationality, then, can only be defined within the unique frame of reference or "psychological set" of the decision maker.

Second, according to Simon, the administrative individual satisfices rather than optimizes when making most decisions. "Satisficing" means that when individuals are confronted with a situation where a decision must be made, they begin by searching for possible alternatives and for information concerning the consequences of each alternative. This search continues only until an alternative is found that meets a subjective minimum standard with respect to the things being sought. In other words, rather than continuing the search until an optimum alternative is located, individuals discontinue their search as soon as one is found that is satisfactory. The economic individual's goal of searching the haystack for the sharpest needle is replaced by the more modest objective of finding one sharp enough to sew with. Only in exceptional cases is one concerned with the discovery of optimum alternatives.[18]

Since managerial decisions are made about future events, they are made on the basis of incomplete information. Consequently, they involve risks. The possibility always exists that a good decision will have undesirable consequences. It is obvious from this discussion that even if managers want to make the best decisions for the organization, without putting their careers ahead of the organization, there is plenty of opportunity for something to go wrong. Thus, the manager feels safer by doing nothing and, therefore, doesn't decide. Couple that with the manager's fear for his or her career and we have an explanation and a perceived justification for being indecisive.

The foregoing discussion points out some of the critical factors which affect decisions, as well as some of the inputs for decision making. Close examination reveals that there really has been very little, if any, change in them during the last fifty years. However, during that time, the computer has entered the field of decision making. Management information systems, management science, and operations research have also entered the picture. They certainly aid the decision maker in making the "proper" decision, but they have not replaced the individual in making "unstructured" decisions. Richard Anderson asks the question: "Do computers leave room for judgment?" More specifically, he asks, "Is there a place for judgment decisions in a computer-dominated media world?"[19] His unequivocal answer is "yes." Furthermore, he says, the judgment area may have been widened and deepened by the very computer which has appeared to threaten it. He goes on to say:

> Yes, we are heavily influenced by the computer. And I must confess that I often find myself in the same position described by B.B. King, the great American blues singer. In one of his mournful ballads, he recounts his suspicion that his lady is sharing her favors with another man. The lyrics detail one piece of evidence after another and finally add up to Mr. King's colorful description of his plight: "I think I'm gettin' more help than I really need." Computers can give a man that kind of feeling, too.[20]

Computers help decision makers use data. Much more data are available through the use of computers. That certainly helps the decision maker, but in most instances, the data must be converted into information before they can be used by the decision maker. What does information mean? Even though the terms data and information are often used interchangeably, they refer to two distinct concepts. Data are language, mathematical, or other symbolic surrogates, which are generally agreed upon to represent people, objects, events, and concepts. Information is the result of modeling, formatting, organizing, or converting data in a way that increases the level of knowledge of the recipient. Using these definitions, data are viewed as being objective by nature, whereas information is subjective and exists only relevant to a recipient.[21] The following example serves to point out this difference:

> ...To demonstrate a point...let's consider the implications to various people of a train whistle penetrating the evening dusk. To the saboteur crouching in a culvert, it might signify the failure of his mission because the whistle indicates that the train has already passed over his detonating charge without causing an explosion. To the playboy, it might presage the imminent arrival of the transgressed husband.
> ...To the lonely wife, it means the return of her traveling husband. To the man with his foot caught in the switch down the track, it pre-shadows doom.

...In brief, the nature and significance of any information is fundamentally and primarily a function of the attitudes, situations, and relevant responsibilities with respect thereto of the people involved with it.[22]

While data and information are separate concepts, they are distinctly related; information is produced from data. To use manufacturing terminology, data are the raw materials from which the finished good—information—is produced. Data are transformed into information through infusion of purposeful intelligence, so that it (information) communicates knowledge to help the user arrive at decisions for proper execution of the functions in the management process. In other words, information is data that have been culled, analyzed, interpreted, and presented on a selective basis in a format that aids the understanding of a situation and fosters making better decisions (than without it). However, because management must perform many different functions, information at one level of usage may only be data at another level.[23]

When there were no computers, many managers hand-picked the data and carefully and painstakingly analyzed it. They knew exactly where it came from and what it meant. They had knowledge and used it. They followed Confucius's advice: "The essence of knowledge is, having it, to use it." They could convert the data into information to be used for making decisions. The point is that they really knew what they had. With the computer, the decision maker generally has much more data and information, but the problem is that sometimes he or she doesn't understand what the information really means. The decision maker didn't collect the raw data, didn't decide what or how much data were needed to obtain the information necessary to make the decision, and doesn't know what other factors were combined with the data to form the information to be used in making the crucial decision. Consequently, managers who are unfamiliar with computers may be suspicious of them, sometimes to the point of not trusting them.

Some would go even further than what President Reagan said about the Russians' nuclear weapons: "trust but verify." If they are not able to verify, they don't trust either. That being the case, they are afraid to make decisions which need to be based on information obtained through the use of computers. They don't want to risk their careers by relying on something they don't understand. Yet they are afraid to ignore the computer-aided information and make decisions without it—because that information could make the difference. The risk is too great, so they just don't decide.

Even managers who are comfortable with computers know that the human element cannot be completely eliminated in reaching the "proper" decision. They search for the appropriate mix and find solace in not deciding.

There is no question that computers and man can work together. The question is how they work together. The answer begins by the user, the decision maker, knowing the limitations of both. Norbert Wiener put it well when he said:

> Render unto man the things that are man's and unto the computer the things which are the computer's. This would seem the intelligent policy to adopt when we employ men and computers together in common undertakings.[24]

CEOs are being engulfed by an information explosion. Obviously, more information can be helpful, but only if it is understood by the *ultimate* user and is used properly. If it is not understood and properly used, it can have detrimental effects.

The new advances in management science as a result of the "information explosion" must be analyzed carefully in order to determine their value in decision making. Just because it is new doesn't necessarily mean that it is better. Conversely, we shouldn't hang onto something that is old and rationalize that it is good because it has stood the test of time. The times are changing, and CEOs must be on the cutting edge. Dean Inge reflected on this when he said: "There are two kinds of fools. One says, 'That is old, therefore it is good.' The other says, 'This is new, therefore it is better.'"[25]

Management must be sure that its information requirements are clearly understood and the techniques employed fit its intended purpose. Stafford Beer used a Charlie Brown cartoon (see next page) to illustrate what happens when a tool, no matter how powerful or elegant, does not fit the need of the user.[26]

CEOs must be careful not to confuse having a lot of facts with having the right facts in decision making. More is not necessarily better. The right facts are needed. In *What They Don't Teach You at Harvard Business School*, Mark McCormack writes that when Ford Motor Company managers interview an applicant for a managerial-level position, they note whether the potential employee puts salt and pepper on his or her food before tasting it. The theory is that such a person is likely to make a decision before knowing all the facts.[27]

In his analysis of the story, McCormack says he hopes it is not true "first because I don't think it has anything to do with decision making—I know some excellent decision makers who happen to like their food very spicy—and second, because one of the biggest problems people have with decision making is a desire to know too *many* facts, their theory being if you have enough facts the decision will make itself."[28]

A Tool Not Fitting the User's Needs
(Peanuts reprinted by permission of United Features Syndicate, Inc.)

The people he respects the most in business "are all instant decision makers. They don't need to know every 'knowable fact first'. They accept that they are going to make their share of wrong decisions and are self-confident enough to know that most of the time they are going to make the right one." He continues by stating, "A reputation as a good decision maker is usually based as much on how quickly and definitely that person decides as it is on the results."[29] There is such a thing as paralysis by analysis.

Tremendous technological advances have been made in the last fifty years or, more specifically, in the last fifteen years. However, no analytical tool is so sophisticated that it can totally replace the judgment skills of the administrator. Judgment is a central activity of decision making, and the act of making value judgments is within the domain of the administrator, not the techniques employed. Even though science is very powerful, it is not powerful enough to force a CEO to believe what he or she does not want to believe.

A CEO can make a great decision or come up with a great solution, but if the decision cannot be properly implemented, it is little more than an abstraction. Consequently, a good decision can be hurt by poor implementation. It can even be argued that implementation may be more important than coming up with the "proper" solution or decision. This causes a big problem for CEOs. They may have control over coming up with the proper decision, but they know that they will not be able to implement it alone. They have to call on subordinates for help. Whether subordinates would help or undermine the CEO is often outside of the CEO's immediate control. The CEO's relationship with subordinates is crucial. This is where the CEO's delegation skills come in. A CEO who is a good delegator can accomplish his or her mission. The CEO can delegate but still retain enough control to influence the implementation process. This allows the CEO to participate in both making the decision and implementing it. The CEO who is unsure of his or her relationship with subordinates who will be involved in implementing a decision may decide to delay the decision, fearing it would not be properly implemented, which is another example of indecisiveness.

Coping with Bigness—Bureaucracy

Prior to the 1970s, many employees rose to the top of their organizations primarily on the basis of their performance in previous jobs in the organization, regardless of whether their jobs were technical or general in nature. The reasoning was that employees who did a good job should be rewarded. Promotion was the reward for a job well done and for being loyal. Performance was viewed as proper justification for advancement. For some who were promoted to the top, the move was good, but for others, the result was quite different. They may have done well in their "technical" jobs as accountants, engineers, nurses, lawyers, chemists, or biologists. They understood and were in tune with what was happening in their fields. Many attended conferences and seminars which gave them insight into the latest happenings in their area. Thus, when technical decisions needed to be made, they felt comfortable getting involved. Indeed, they helped their supervisors to make more intelligent decisions. Their promotions were seen as a win–win situation.

However, with the stroke of a pen, many were placed in a different position without adequate training. Now they had to become generalists. All of a sudden, the nurse found it difficult to translate her effective bedside skills, for which she had been promoted, into managerial skills. In many instances, her well-developed technical skills didn't translate into conceptual skills. Neither did the engineer's technical skills translate into managerial skills. The same was true of the skilled accountant and the brilliant researcher. Neither was ready to make those tough managerial decisions. As a result, they made plenty of mistakes. Some were mistakes of commission, where wrong actions were taken, while others were mistakes of omission, where no action was taken and the status quo was contentedly embraced amid a changing environment. They just weren't ready for the limelight! They weren't ready to manage. Yet they were put in that position, and Wall Street was watching their every move.

Are such moves proper for either the organization or the employee? Occasionally, they are acceptable, but in the majority of cases, they are not. In some instances, the size and bureaucracy of the organization mask the effects, and it takes time for such moves to be recognized for what they are—failures. These moves are damaging to both the organization and the individuals who are moved. The Peter Principle sets in, and there is very little that can be done. To make matters worse, professional careers are bruised, some beyond repair.

What was overlooked by those who were doing the promoting is the fact that managing is not a completely instinctive process. It isn't something that can be done without academic or practical training. "Technical" professionals were promoted to take over roles as "generalists" without any preparation. They were, in fact, being asked to decide complex and sensitive issues without any training in general decision making. They may have been brilliant in their specialties, but it takes more to properly fill their new roles in their organizations. How would Einstein, for example, have performed as president of Exxon or General Motors?

Against that background, consider the agony many new CEOs have to endure when called upon to make complex decisions that are interwoven with other decisions which demand an understanding of the entire organizational process. They are not asked to just make decisions. Anyone can do that. Their real task is to make qualitative decisions. Because of their lack of knowledge of the complexities of the organization and their fear that their decisions may be wrong, and may have adverse consequences for their careers, they feel that the safest thing to do, under the circumstances, is to do nothing, and so they become indecisive. The situation is further complicated when the CEO is not an effective delegator. When a decision is needed to address a problem, failure to do so hurts the organization and eventually may jeopardize the manager's career. In time, managers who commit the fatal sin of indecision fall from grace. While this scenario is quite common, often it does not immediately surface, and many managers escape, at least for a while, the consequences. Sooner or later, however, they pay dearly for their inaction. Many times, the cost is their jobs.

The "DaD" Principle—Delegate and Disappear

Some managers are unwilling to make a decision because they fear the consequences, and so they do nothing. Others turn to consultants, and still others delegate. Some managers, about 15 to 30%, do a good job of delegating. The majority of those who delegate, either for the right purpose or because they want somebody else to make an unpopular decision, are ineffective delegators. Some even think they can delegate not only the work but also the responsibility and accountability. Overall, their attempts to delegate are not only done for the wrong reasons but are ineffective, as evidenced by our survey.

Our panel members were asked whether they "feel that delegation is *effectively* used in organizations." A sample of the responses follows.

University business deans:

- As a general rule delegation at the top of the organization is done for all the wrong reasons.
- No, unfortunately, many CEOs do not know how to delegate effectively.
- No, too many managers are afraid to delegate and/or are unable to do it effectively.
- No, often used to place blame—should be used more for rewards and to solve problems.
- No, but it certainly should be.
- In general no. Some use it as a way to avoid responsibility.
- No. Empowerment isn't used either.
- No. Not effectively enough!
- Very often it is not.
- Most managers equate delegation with dumping on subordinates.
- Not across the board, but improving with trend to flatten organizations.
- No. People have not been trained to delegate effectively.
- Better than many parts of the world, but can be improved.
- Not unless authority goes along with the delegation.

- ■ To a degree, but in public sector organizations, the accountability leg is not adhered to very often.
- ■ We have a mixed bag. Generally (say 70% of cases) yes.

University business professors:

- ■ No, too many CEOs delegate ineffectively. They delegate for all the wrong reasons.
- ■ No, for the most part it only receives lip service.
- ■ Usually it is not used effectively.
- ■ Most CEOs don't really understand the real meaning of delegation. They don't understand its power. Consequently, the use by many is ineffective.
- ■ Overall, probably no.
- ■ No, need to learn to delegate better.
- ■ No, many times there is just lip service.
- ■ No, because the decision maker lacks necessary control he/she is afraid to delegate.
- ■ No, there needs to be more delegation.
- ■ I believe that delegation is an antiquated term. I think of empowerment as a more useful concept today. I believe that more organizations and managers are realizing the power of empowerment.
- ■ It is unfortunate that managers don't really understand this powerful technique they have which could, if effectively used, do wonders for them and their organizations.

CEOs:

- ■ No, but it's improving.
- ■ Not as well as it could.
- ■ It varies. Some use it very effectively.
- ■ In some organizations, but still have a way to go.
- ■ Delegation becomes much more effective when the firm is organized in a way to fully employ it. If a firm is hierarchically oriented and tries to just decree delegation, it will fail.

Union presidents:

- ■ No! There is great fear of empowering subordinates.
- ■ Should be—usually it's to hide from responsibility.
- ■ Sometimes.

Business news editors:

- No.
- No and the result is inactivity and one stalled project after another.
- Varies with organizations.
- Rarely.
- Sometimes.

Obviously, there is more to delegation than telling someone to do something. Anyone can delegate. The key question is whether managers can delegate *effectively*. Studies show that 70 to 85% of managers are not effective delegators. Many don't really understand the true meaning of delegation, and those who do can't do it properly. Coupled with that is the fact that some insecure managers who understand delegation and could properly delegate are afraid to do so because they see the delegatees as a threat to their careers.

When used effectively, delegation can be a strong and effective tool for the manager. Unfortunately, some managers use delegation for the wrong reason; they use it in a somewhat deceptive way, to avoid making unpopular or risky decisions for which they can't predict the consequences. By having someone else decide, the manager can avoid criticism of unpopular or unsuccessful decisions. On the other hand, if the decision is a good one, it doesn't take long for the manager to claim the credit. Unfortunately, this deception sometimes works, but when it is discovered and exposed, the manager's career with the organization may be cut short. This is another way for the manager to avoid his or her responsibility to decide. Again, indecision is alive and well.

The Craze for Consultants

Do organizations really need consultants? How do they fit into an organization? The answers to these questions often depend on the circumstances. In some instances, they are complex. Consultants are needed in certain instances, particularly in areas where they have special expertise or when the organization needs something immediately. When time is of the essence, an organization may miss an opportunity by taking the time to train its own people. An organization needs to grab an opportunity when it knocks. Victor

Hugo said, "There is nothing stronger than all armies of the world: and that is an idea whose time has come." Consultants may be able to help an organization identify and put into motion those ideas which may be tailor-made for that particular organization. They can help with those technical problems that can make or break the organization. In today's business environment, speed is important. If an organization is to remain or become successful, it needs to keep up the pace. However, keeping up the pace, making those critical and crucial decisions, doesn't mean an organization is excused from paying close attention to detail. As Benjamin Franklin said, "...for want of a nail the shoe was lost; for want of a shoe the horse was lost."

On the other hand, when consultants are used by CEOs as a way to avoid making tough decisions themselves, one begins to question the wisdom. As the president and CEO of a Fortune 500 company said, "Many executives today don't have the guts to make a key decision, so they opt for consultants. If the decision is wrong, the executive can blame the consultant." The executive can say, "It was the consultant who advised me to do or act as I did—it wasn't my fault. As a matter of fact, I was against such action from the outset, but I deferred my better judgment to the consultant's." Yet, the same executive would not hesitate to reap the benefits—to claim the glory—if the result was favorable. And it would be icing on the cake if the action also helped the manager's career. After all, it was the executive's strategy to hire the consultant. Is such a strategy fair? The answer to that question must be based on whether the decision was grounded in deception, especially when the executive has committed the organization to additional expense to make a decision that he or she should have made. Is it done? You bet. Do managers get away with it? Sadly, the answer is often "yes." Is the risk high? For the "marginal" or "incompetent" manager, not really, because he or she will not be around for long anyway!

The preceding comments should not be interpreted as meaning that hiring consultants indicates poor managerial judgment or that consultants are used to avoid making decisions. On the contrary, consultants can be and indeed are often useful and productive, as well as necessary, for organizations. The real issue is whether executives use consultants for technical or other legitimate advice to help them make qualitative decisions. Proper use of consultants is good and sound management strategy. The problem occurs when executives use consultants to make the unpopular decisions they don't want to make themselves. It is a way for managers to avoid getting blood on their hands. There is a huge market for consulting. In 1993, for example, AT&T

spent $347.1 million on "consulting and research services." To overcome suspicion and skepticism, consultants are increasingly working side by side with managers to analyze operations, draft recommendations, and implement changes. The days when the outside SWAT team worked in isolation, drafting a report and then leaving, are over.[30]

Some managers make decisions by making an implicit choice among alternatives and then continue to gather data until the implicit choice is confirmed. As Peter Drucker puts it:

> To get the facts first is impossible. There are no facts unless one has a criterion of relevance...everyone is too prone to...look for the facts that fit the conclusion they have already reached...opinions come first...one does not argue them; one tests them.[31]

It is important to remember that to err is human, and professional managers are human. When executives make decisions that prove to be wrong, they should not have to face a firing squad. The question that needs to be asked is whether the manager acted properly. Remember that Babe Ruth hit 714 home runs, but he also struck out 1,330 times!

As Pizza Hut CEO Steve Reinewind told Tom Peters, "People here don't get shot for taking risks." For example, Pizza Hut marketing director John Lauck got stuck with $5 million in sunglasses when a sales promotion tied to the launch of *Back to the Future, Part 2* misfired badly. The result? Lauck was later promoted.[32]

Chief executive Wayne Calloway of PepsiCo said:

> Our business is built on two foundations: one is integrity; and the other is, get results. If you do those two things around here, you are very successful. We don't care how old you are, what race you are, what school you went to. What's important is integrity and results. And everybody would agree on results. But the integrity part is that in order to get people to take risks, in order to get people to change, you have to have a nurturing and a trusting environment. We do encourage risks, and if you blow it, you blow it. We don't fire you, and we don't shoot the wounded. We don't even put you in the penalty box.
>
> On the other hand, if you keep making a lot of dumb mistakes, we would probably suggest that maybe there's a better place for you to work. But if you're going to get results in the long term, you've got to have integrity—openness, honesty with your customers, suppliers,

and associates, and even with your competitors. All of that has to be part of it.

All of our associates have to feel that this is their business, that they are the steward of these assets, wherever they might be.[33]

In their book *Leaders*, Warren Bennis and Burt Nanus relate how Tom Watson, Sr., IBM's founder, handled a mistake made by an employee. A promising junior executive was involved in a risky venture and managed to lose over $10 million in the gamble. When Watson called the nervous executive into his office, the young man blurted out, "I guess you want my resignation." Watson said, "You can't be serious. We've just spent $10 million educating you!"[34]

The consequences of the fatal sin of indecisiveness are extensive and varied. Conflict arises between management levels due to frustration. This often results in turnover in the management ranks, which is costly to a company in terms of lost experience. Indecisiveness results in lack of direction. Corporations without direction tend to lose their competitive edge quickly. Clients lose faith, and market share is lost. Product innovation and technological advances often depend upon quick decisions to be first to enter a market. Such windows of opportunity are only open for a short time. The ultimate financial impact of this sin is poor returns and failing stock prices. Indecisiveness can also have legal ramifications. Issues related to safety, the environment, or governmental compliance can result in significant penalties if not resolved immediately. Such problems can damage a corporation's reputation, which is not easily repaired. In turn, the CEO's reputation is damaged, which may lead to the CEO's departure from the organization.

Notes

1. J.W. Gardner, *No Easy Victories* (New York: Harper and Row, 1968).
2. Lee Iacocca, with William Novak, *Iacocca, An Autobiography* (New York: Bantam Books, 1984), p. 50.
3. Bernard M. Bass, *Organizational Decision Making* (Homewood, IL: Richard D. Irwin, 1983), p. 5; citing Milan Zeleny, "Descriptive Decision Making and Its Application," *Applications of Management Science*, Vol. 1, 1981, p. 327.
4. Ibid.; citing K.R. MacCrimmon, "Managerial Decision Making." In J.W. McGuire, *Contemporary Management* (Upper Saddle River, NJ: Prentice-Hall, 1974), p. 446.
5. Ibid.; citing H. Mintzberg, Duru Raisingham, and André Théorét, "The Structure of 'Unstructured' Decision Processes," *Administrative Science Quarterly*, Volume 21, 1976, pp. 250–51.

6. Lawrence Barton, *Crisis in Organizations: Managing and Communicating in the Heat of Chaos* (Cincinnati: South-Western Publishing Co., 1993), pp. 21–22.
7. Ibid. at p. 22: citing Theodore H. White, *In Search of History: A Personal Adventure* (New York: Harper & Row, 1978), p. 496.
8. Raymond M. Wilmotte and G. Gail Crotte, "Bridging the Gap Between Analysis and Decision Makers," *Management Review*, January 1979, pp. 24–26.
9. Louis E. Boone and Donald D. Bowen, *The Great Writings in Management and Organizations Behavior,* 2nd edition (New York: McGraw Hill, 1987).
10. Ibid.
11. R.J. Katz, *Management of the Total Enterprise* (Upper Saddle River, NJ: Prentice-Hall, 1970).
12. A.O. Hirschman and C.D. Lindblom, "Economic Development, Research and Development, Policy Making: Some Converging Theories," *Behavioral Science*, Volume 7, 1962, pp. 211–22.
13. Ibid.
14. R.M. Cyert and J.G. March, *A Behavioral Theory of the Firm* (Upper Saddle River, NJ: Prentice-Hall, 1963).
15. Earnest R. Archer, "How to Make a Business Decision: An Analysis of Theory and Practice," *Management Review*, February 1980, pp. 54–61.
16. Ibid.
17. Peter Drucker, "How to Make a Business Decision," *Nation's Business,* April 1956, pp. 38+.
18. Herbert A. Simon, *Administrative Behavior: A Study of Decision-Making Processes in Administrative Organization*, 3rd edition (New York: The Free Press, 1976); Irving L. Janis and Leon Mann, *Decision Making: A Psychological Analysis of Conflict, Choice, and Commitment* (New York: The Free Press, 1979); Kit Grindley, *Systematics: A New Approach to Systems Analysis* (New York: PBI Books, 1975); Alvar Elbing, *Behavioral Decisions in Organizations* (Glenview, IL: Scott, Foresman and Company, 1978).
19. Richard C. Anderson, "Do Computers Leave Room for Judgement," *Advertising Age*, January 14, 1980, pp. 48–50.
20. Ibid.
21. David Katch, "What Is Management Information System," *Infosystems*, Volume 25, June 1978, p. 94; C. West Churchman, *The Systems Approach and Its Enemies* (New York: Basic Book, 1979).
22. John G. Burch, Jr., Felix C. Strater, and Gary Grudnitski, *Information Systems: Theory and Practice,* 2nd edition (New York: John Wiley and Sons, 1970); Edward D. Dwyer, "Some Observations on Management Information Systems," *American Management Association*, 1961, pp. 16–17.
23. Robert G. Murdick and Joel E. Ross, *Introduction to Management Information Systems* (Upper Saddle River, NJ: Prentice-Hall, 1977).
24. Sherman C. Blumenthal, *Management Information Systems: A Framework for Planning and Development* (Upper Saddle River, NJ: Prentice-Hall, 1969).

25. Herbert G. Hicks and C. Ray Gullett, *Organizations: Theory and Behavior* (New York: McGraw-Hill, 1975).
26. Stafford Beer, *Management Science: The Business Use of Operations* (Chicago: Aldus Books, Ferguson Publishing, 1967).
27. Mark H. McCormack, *What They Don't Teach You at Harvard Business School* (New York: Bantam Books, 1984), p. 231.
28. Ibid.
29. Ibid.
30. Blumenthal (note 24).
31. Ibid.
32. Anonymous, "A Different Brand of Leader," *Chief Executive*, July–August 1991, p. 46.
33. Ibid., p. 48.
34. Warren Bennis and Burt Nanus, *Leaders: The Strategies for Taking Charge* (New York: Harper Perennial, 1985), p. 76.

CHAPTER 10

Sin #5   Blurred Focus: The Fuzzy Vision

Vision is the art of seeing things invisible.
  —Jonathan Swift

*If you don't know where you're going, you might end up some-
where else.*
  —Casey Stengel

*The important thing in life is to have a great aim and to possess
the aptitude and the perseverance to attain it.*
  —Johann Wolfgang von Goethe

Restructuring without vision is called "paving the cow path."
  —Tom Peters

*Everything depends on execution, having just a vision is no
solution.*
  —Stephen Sondheim

Dig a well before you are thirsty.
  —Chinese proverb

The "Corporate Eyes"

The chief executive officer creates, establishes, and conveys the vision of an
organization; continuously modifies the strategy; and then organizes resources
to accomplish the strategy in an ethical and decisive manner. That's how it
should work, but is that how it works in practice? When a list of the characteristics of CEOs is compiled, high on the list one finds the word "visionary." Does it belong there? The answer, of course, is an unequivocal "yes."
As a matter of fact, many would argue that it should be first on the list and
certainly not less than second.

The reason is obvious. A company with a brilliant CEO who has vast resources at his or her disposal but who lacks vision will, at best, limp along aimlessly, and the CEO will spend his or her tenure with the company putting out fires. A CEO without a clear vision or with a blurred focus or a fuzzy vision ends up managing crises instead of the company. Crises, of course, are those major, unpredictable events that have potentially negative results for the organization and its employees, products/services, financial condition, and reputation. Crises are unexpected happenings that pose threats, ranging from moderate to catastrophic, to the organization's future. If a crisis occurs, obviously, it must be managed. Crises are generally counterproductive and destructive. In almost all cases, they can be prevented if the CEO takes the proper precautions, the first of which is vision. The CEO has to be alert to changing conditions and set up contingency plans for dealing with them. The CEO needs the vision, the aspiration, and the action plans to lead the company to its destination. It is part of the down payment for a better and focused company.

To lead with vision means knowing exactly where one is going (where one needs to take the organization), knowing precisely how to get there, and knowing what needs to be done after getting there. To that end, a CEO needs both vision and insight. Vision and insight must blend together to accomplish the mission.

A firm's leaders, particularly its CEO, must create a vision statement. A primary goal for the CEO is to unite the people in the organization into a responsible community. When a CEO has a clear vision that is both coherent and credible, it serves as a source of power. Practically stated, the "leader's power is the capacity to translate a vision and supporting values into reality and sustain them."[1] The CEO's insight into the future can mean the difference between success and failure for the organization.

The leader inspires confidence in his or her followers and essentially pulls rather than pushes the followers on. Joseph V. Quigley points out that it is the leader's responsibility to communicate vision and values throughout the organization. He terms this "vision rollout." It is based, he states, "on the understanding that the work of the leadership group will be meaningless unless those leaders passed on their vision effectively to their people."[2] He defines vision as:

> ...the most fundamental statement of its (the corporation's) values, aspirations and goals. It is an appeal of its members' *hearts* and *minds*. It represents a clear understanding of where the organization is *today* and where it wants to be *tomorrow*, and offers a road map of how to get there. A firm's vision is *the foundation of its*

culture. It must be simple, understandable, and desirable, and it must motivate the firm's members.[3]

Vision, of course, is more than sight. As Helen Keller said, "The greatest tragedy in life is people who have sight but no vision." History books are full of examples of people who were great visionaries as well as people whose vision was blurred. Myopia caused not only the downfall of the latter, but also the demise of their families, their organizations, and their nations. Speaking of John D. Rockefeller, his successor at Standard Oil of New Jersey and former vice president of Standard Oil Company said: "…he could see further ahead than anybody and then see around the corner." Henry Kissinger was quoted in *In Search of Excellence* as saying:

> The task of the leader is to get his people from where they are to where they have not been. The public does not fully understand the world into which it is going. Leaders must invoke an alchemy of great vision. Those leaders who do not are ultimately judged failures, even though they may be popular at the moment.[4]

It has been said that a man is limited not so much by his knowledge/tools as by his vision. Sam Walton said: "I had no vision of the scope of what I would start. But I always had confidence that as long as we did our work well and were good to our customers, there would be no limit to us."[5] Even though he said he had no vision of the scope of what he was starting, he certainly had a clear vision of the end result. He had a conviction about what it was that needed to be done. Sometimes convictions do not have immediate results. A vision is a point on the horizon in the future. Consequently, our aim—our focus—has to be on the future, without neglecting the present.

Let's take a look at two franchises started in the 1950s: McDonald's and Burger Chef. Where are the two today? What made the difference in their future? Was it the products they sold? The answer is a simple "no"; both sold the same products. Was it timing? No, both were started at about the same time. Was it location? Again, no. Not only were they located in the same cities, but often they were within view of each other. What, then, made the difference? The real answer is their strategy. It was their CEOs' vision—managing for the present versus managing for the future, unwise expansion versus proper expansion. It was the clear vision versus the blurry vision. Did Ray Kroc's vision have anything to do with McDonald's success? Kenneth Lobich says that Ray Kroc pictured his empire long before it existed, and he saw how to get there. That led him to create the company's motto: "Quality, service, cleanliness, and value." He kept repeating it up and down the organization. If the job of a leader is to create a vision, what precisely was the vision of Burger Chef's CEO? Was it a clear or blurry vision? It is important that there be managerial alertness in the organization. The organization must be attuned to not only competitive changes but also to emerging social and environmental pressures.

What happened to the railroads? The title of Theodore Levitt's classic article, "Marketing Myopia,"[6] sets the stage for the explanation. What about People Express? Did its demise have anything to do with its CEO's vision and resulting strategy? Did it have something to do with Donald Burr's philosophy: "Grow, grow, grow. Don't worry about profits, they'll come later." Is that what happened? Did the profits come later? For how long? Why? What was People Express' future? Would the results have been different if there had been a clear vision—if the focus had been right? What about the Edsel, STP, and the World Football League? What went wrong? Why? What has been Montgomery Ward's focus in the last ten years? Could blurred vision have contributed to its present condition? What about Woolworth's vision? Clear or blurred?

The symptoms of the sin of blurred vision includes micro-managing the organization; having a narrow scope, focus, and direction; having short-sightedness and lack of customer focus; and demanding total control of business decisions. Some resulting problems include hesitation and overcautiousness, failure to plan for the future, failure to involve other decision makers, and the inability to adapt corporate strategy to the marketplace. If these problems are not corrected, the results will be high employee turnover, a diminished customer base, loss of trust (from both customers and employees), lack of accountability, and an inability to respond to changing market conditions. Eventually, the CEO will be forced to make bad financial decisions, which will drive the company into bankruptcy or out of business.

Do U.S. managers have a fuzzy vision? Here are the responses of our panel:

**Managers today, generally, have a
"fuzzy vision" regarding their organizations' future.**

Survey Panel	Disagree Strongly	Disagree	Neither Agree Nor Disagree	Agree	Agree Strongly
University business deans	2%	30%	13%	45%	10%
University business professors	2%	22%	15%	48%	13%
CEOs	12%	38%	13%	31%	6%
Union presidents	11%	11%	11%	33%	34%
Business news editors	8%	23%	15%	54%	0%

Not many of us would agree that these responses give a good picture of managerial competence. Why do many managers have a fuzzy vision? Can it be corrected? Are there clearer lenses out there, in the corporate sector, to help managers focus better? How can they be acquired? Why aren't they being acquired?

Myopia: "Tunnel Vision" Syndrome— Loss of Peripheral Vision

In "Market Myopia," Theodore Levitt states that "in every case, the reason growth is threatened, slow, or stopped is not because the market is saturated. It is because there has been a failure of management. The failure is at the top. The executives responsible for it, in the last analysis, are those who deal with broad aims and policies."[7] It would appear that the very essence of leadership is having a clear vision. It needs to be as clear as possible in terms of the various activities of the organization. The clearer the better. The vision has to be coherent and credible and has to be communicated throughout the organization in order to unite and focus the members of the organization toward achieving the specified goals. In order for the CEO to communicate the corporate vision and values throughout the organization, it is essential for the CEO to have a clear definition of what the vision is and properly use it to achieve the mission of the organization. If there is no vision or if the vision is fuzzy, the organization will suffer and may even fail. What the damage will be and how quickly it will set in are often closely related to the CEO's lack of organizational vision.

In principle, fine-tuning a vision may not be an awesome task. The problem is the obstacles encountered in trying to put the vision into practice. Managers often find themselves in a stranglehold, where they are forced to implement short-term goals that will satisfy the various stakeholders of the organization. Yet many managers feel that such short-term goals are incompatible with the long-term goals of the organization.

Many managers do understand the importance of the company's vision. They understand that a firm's vision is the foundation of its culture—the foundation of the organization. It is the compass, or road map, that enables the organization to move from where it is today to where it wants to be in the future! Many managers are capable of fine-tuning the vision. They are capable of setting well-defined and clear goals for the corporation. The problem is that they are preoccupied by immediate organizational pressures. The perceived or actual need to achieve short-term results usually ends up cluttering the CEO's vision. Time constraints also enter the picture.

As a result, the focus turns to the short-term rather than the long-term objectives. When that happens, the vision automatically becomes blurred. Myopia sets in and attention turns to the bottom line. How will the balance sheet look next quarter or at the end of the year? The days when managers could tighten their belts and look down the road five or ten years before enjoying big profits are gone. If today's managers can't show a successful bottom line within a year or two, Wall Street reacts and the organization's stakeholders begin to take action, and the CEO's "honeymoon" comes to a shaky and turbulent end.

It is not difficult to understand why a CEO's vision turns into "tunnel" vision. The focus is on the bottom line and the CEO acts accordingly, which causes serious problems in terms of peripheral vision. Without peripheral vision, there can be no clear vision; there can only be a fuzzy vision. With a fuzzy vision, an organization cannot endure for long, although some organizations may be able to limp along for a while if they are well established or if their products are unique. However, a fuzzy vision does not contribute to an organization's long-term success and it certainly doesn't contribute to the CEO's longevity with the organization. Unfortunately, once the fatal managerial sin of "blurred vision" sets in, it is usually compounded as managers try to use a band-aid approach. They stay where they are, seeing it as a safe harbor or even believing that it is working. As Will Rogers said: "Even if you think you are on the right track, you'll be run over if you just sit there." A CEO's efforts must be directed toward achieving the company's goal and mission, and the vision has to be focused on the future. According to Peter Drucker, "The best way to predict the future is to create it." As Jong-Hyon Chey, chairman of the Sunk Yong Group, said, "We are not awaiting the 21st century, we intend to shape it."

Many managers seem content with the present. Their vision is both short-sighted and tunnel focused—and lacks peripheral vision. They spend most of their time figuring out what happened, why it happened, and on damage control. Their time would have been better spent deciding: (1) what is needed in the future to carry on the corporate mission, (2) what might prevent the organization from accomplishing its stated mission, and (3) what could be done to prevent something that might interfere with the organization achieving its mission. They spend too much time on Monday morning quarterbacking instead of Friday morning strategy planning. A well-defined strategy will help define the structure that is needed to accomplish the organization's goal, but management often fails to focus and does not spend the necessary time on its core business.

Even when they begin to focus, many executives focus on the wrong things. The primary focus for many is on their careers. Unfortunately, focusing on individual career goals many times does not help the organization reach its destination. Other executives become complacent, which often does not lead the organization to where it needs to go. "When conformity is the creed, mediocrity is the result!" Also, "If you are going the wrong way, it doesn't help to speed up. You need to turn around and ask for directions."

Sometimes blurred vision is due partly to the fact that those who prepare the plans are not those who implement them. Consequently, there is lack of understanding about what and how things must be done to reach the stated goal. A plan without the right planning and execution is like having the perfect violin without a master violinist to play it. Many CEOs spend a lot of time talking about and preparing plans but spend very little time actually planning and executing plans. Often, plans just sit there and wither. Some CEOs don't know when and how to proceed to the next step. An axiom attributed to the Pentagon gives some meaning to this dilemma: "There are two phases to any program—too soon to tell and too late to kill." President Dwight D. Eisenhower said, "Plans are nothing, planning is everything."

Unfortunately, many executives with limited vision take planning for granted once the plans are ready. They think anyone can guide their plans down the road. What they forget is that not all roads are straight; there are curves and hills. Without vision, the deliverer and the implementer of the plans will have a bumpy and often unsafe ride. The CEO, the navigator of the plans, must be able to use his or her vision to implement or help others properly implement the plans. It is like a traveler driving a car down an unfamiliar road at night. To see down the road, the traveler may have to turn on the bright lights. The same is true for converting plans into planning. The focus is different for the short term than it is for the long term. For long-term plans, the vision should normally be brighter and more peripheral. "Long-range planning does not deal with future decisions," says, Peter Drucker, "but with the future of present decisions." CEOs must be able to see the fit of their products into the future. Danish physicist and Nobel Laureate Niels Bohr was quoted as saying: "It is very hard to predict, especially the future."

Seeing Through the Clouds

It is the job of a leader to create a vision that is to be reached at some point in the future. That point can be five, ten, or even twenty years into the future.

In order to create a vision, a leader has to concentrate on the future. It is difficult at best to predict what will take place years ahead, even when one hones in on the many variables that can affect the future. That task becomes all the more difficult when the person who must create and implement the vision is preoccupied with things he or she sees as more important to the organization or to his or her own career. Managers with tunnel vision focus on their careers rather than their organizations and may see organizational goals as obstacles to reaching the ladders they need to climb to get where they want to go. They see the organization, the system, and the employees as objects to be utilized—to help them in their climb. As a result, it is difficult for such managers to see the organization's mission. It is hard for them to see the vision through the haze. It is important that the vision be properly shaped. It has to be shared and understood from top to bottom. Managers can't manage something that they don't understand. Therefore, it is important to ask the following questions: What kind of organization do we want to be? What values are important to us? What will the organization be like for our customers and for us when we achieve our vision? What place does each person in our organization have in this vision?

Once these and other related questions are answered, and the proper strategy has been determined, then it is the duty of the leader to guide the organization toward its destiny. This, of course, requires the right strategic planning, detailing how the organization is to reach its mission. Consider Motorola's position on the subject: "To purposefully plan the future course of the corporation by preparing written strategies for each business, as contrasted to reacting to situations; and to measure our performance against these plans, with the ability to properly modify plans when appropriate."

The Status Quo: Conservative on Risk Taking

An old man was asked, "Have you witnessed a lot of change?" "Yes," said the old man, "and I was against it all." One of the obstacles to a clear vision is that many CEOs are afraid to take risks, risks which some of them perceive as possibly having detrimental effects on their careers. As a result, they tend to take what they perceive as a safer road—staying with the present order of things. Even if the status quo proves not to be a proper course of action, they think that it will be easier to justify something that has been in place and accepted for some time than to justify a new idea which may prove to be wrong. Obviously, there is danger in such thinking. There has to be a balance between maintaining what exists and expanding into new horizons. The visionary CEO must carefully analyze the alternatives and pick that which is the best. As Peter Drucker argues, a decision is a choice between alternatives but rarely a choice between right and wrong. CEOs generally should be cautious in their approach to the unknown but should not let the chance of risk paralyze them and keep them from accomplishing their mission. They can't let Pogo's words come true in their quest to govern: "We have met the enemy and he is us."

CEOs sometimes try to do too much, which often causes their efforts to become unfocused. Research has shown that there are as many as 300 initiatives going on at the same time in a company, with up to 40% of managers' time taken up by one or another of them. That being the case, it becomes obvious why some embrace the status quo over such initiatives, and it is apparent why the vision becomes fuzzy. Obviously, executives should not do something different just for the sake of being different, but where would we be if our policy were to cling to the status quo? We need to try to accomplish what we think is possible and perhaps more. As General Colin Powell writes in *My American Journey*, "Leadership is the art of accomplishing more than the science of management says is possible."[8]

A myopic attitude, a status quo philosophy, allowed foreign competition to take over many industries once dominated by American companies. The 1970s and early 1980s were times of great prosperity and profit for a number of industries, including automobiles, heavy equipment, and other manufacturing-type industries. There was little competition; a business could produce just about anything and consumers would buy it. Then, in the late 1980s and early 1990s, those industries had a rude awakening. Competitors such as Honda, Toyota, Nissan, and Komatsu were able to gain considerable market share with higher quality (at least perceived) and lower priced merchandise. The "pounding" by the competition was severe. It was more than some American CEOs could take, and it meant their demise. For others, the wounds were deep but treatable, and for still others, it was just what the doctor prescribed—a jolt that woke them up from a deep sleep. The impact was so severe that it opened their eyes and made them focus on the future. Just look at the IBMs and General Motors of the world: they may have found the status quo easy and comfortable in the past, but they found out it is no longer acceptable. They needed swift change to stay competitive. They were awakened to the realization that success does not guarantee continued success or freedom from adversity. Success, we have been told, is a journey, not a destination.

The future calls for a new order of things for business. Creativity, speed, vision, technology, and excellence in leadership will be the new CEO's banner. Managers need to fully awaken to what is happening globally. They need to adjust to the new reality and stop yelling protectionism. They have to accept the changed world as it is or propose, and be able to effectuate, different realistic and workable changes. They should also expect more changes in the world environment and must be ready for them. New products that in the past took five years to develop and introduce into the marketplace will take less than a year in the future. Companies that are not ready to respond will become "has-beens." The bottom line is that we cannot commit ourselves any longer to the status quo. It might have been the proper course in the past, but it is not the proper strategy for the future.

"Punch the Clock": The Adversarial Mentality

It certainly can be validly argued that there is a very definite correlation between trust and morale. As trust decreases in an organization, the morale of the employees decreases proportionally and oftentimes more. As morale decreases, so does productivity, in the short term as well as the long term. Unquestionably, the productivity and trust of employees are reduced when they are told that they are not trusted. One new CEO attended a gathering of company employees his first day at the job. His first words to them were: "I am your new CEO. I don't know you; consequently, I can't trust you, but you have to trust me because I am your CEO." You can guess how that relationship ended up. One can only wonder what his first words were to the employees of his new organization the following year, assuming someone hired him.

There are ways other than words to reduce trust in organizations. Acts or deeds can also accomplish that. A frequently used technique is to have employees punch a time clock. What message does that send? It says: "I want to make sure that you work the required hours. To make sure you do, I am using the clock as my witness." If management doesn't trust the employees, what does that say about the organization? The CEO has to set the standard for the organization regarding trust. Sure, there are cases in organizations where verification of employee behavior or conduct is necessary, but they are few. Our employees are generally the people we depend on to make our high-quality products.

When employees finish their work, they shouldn't have to wait around just to punch the clock. Organizations need to be set up with employees in mind. Employees should look forward to coming to work. How many employees can say that they can't wait for Monday morning so they can go to work?

At Motorola, an employee honor system exists in lieu of a time clock and the company has had a profit-sharing system for thirty-five years. A sign at Lincoln Electric tells employees that they cannot enter the premises more than forty-five minutes early. Why do they want to get there early? Humane treatment of employees coupled with incentive plans can take care of much more than a time clock.

In summary, the manager who has a blurred focus—who has a fuzzy vision—not only commits a fatal managerial sin that hastens his or her demise but also brings down others in the organization and sometimes even the entire organization. There is no compelling reason why a CEO must commit such a sin. Planning, training, and caring can help prevent it. CEOs who are not able to plan, train, and care shouldn't be there in the first place.

Notes

1. Reprinted from *Business Horizons,* Joseph V. Quigley, "Vision: How Leaders Develop It, Share It, and Sustain It," Sept.–Oct. 1994, p. 39 by the Foundation for the School of Business at Indiana University. Used with permission.
2. Ibid., p. 40.
3. Ibid., p. 39.
4. Thomas J. Peters and Robert H. Waterman, Jr., *In Search of Excellence: Lessons from America's Best-Run Companies* (New York: Harper & Row, 1980), p. 282.
5. Vance H. Trimble, *Sam Walton: The Inside Story of America's Richest Man* (New York: A Dutton Signet, a division of Penguin Books, USA, Inc., 1990), p. 121.
6. Theodore Levitt, "Marketing Myopia," *Harvard Business Review*, Sept.–Oct. 1975, pp. 1–12.
7. Ibid.
8. Colin Powell, *My American Journey* (New York: Random House, 1995), p. 264.

CHAPTER 11

Sin #6   Employees Perceived as an Expense, Not an Investment

It doesn't take a hero to order men into battle. It takes a hero to be one of those men who goes into battle.
—Gen. H. Norman Schwarzkopf

What firmly unites the company is infinitely more important than that which divides it.

There's only one class and that's "We the people."

Everyone needs to know and feel that he is needed.
—Jan Carlyon

Leaders don't inflict pain, they bear pain.
—Max DePree

Hire people who are better than you are, then leave them to get on with it...Look for people who will aim for the remarkable, who will not settle for the routine.
—David Ogilvy

It is not the employer who pays wages—he only handles the money. It is the customer who pays the wages.
—Henry Ford

What's in a Name?

Father Demetri Kangelaris, a Greek Orthodox priest, started a sermon by relating an incident which occurred when he was nine years old and living in Israel. One day, he and his mother were riding a bus. He noticed that an older lady, who was holding onto a strap for support, had a tattoo on her arm. This tattoo wasn't like the ones he had seen before. He asked his mother why this lady had a tattoo with a bunch of numbers. His mother, fearing the lady would hear the conversation, told him to be quiet.

Later, she explained to him that the lady had been in a concentration camp and that the tattoo was the number assigned to her. She was known by that number rather than by her name. He wanted to know why someone would refer to a person by a number instead of his or her name. His mother explained that that was a way of keeping track of people as well as dehumanizing and impersonalizing them. Taking away someone's name, she said, was a way of stripping a person of his or her dignity and pride.

Certainly the horrors of the Holocaust cannot be compared to employee treatment today, but lack of personalization exists, to some extent. Some organizations think of their employees as numbers and not people. One CEO said that not only did he not know the names of his employees, he didn't even know those close to his office. He said he didn't want to become attached to them, so he could fire them if he had to. In contrast, Sam Walton not only knew the names of his employees but also knew the names of their families. The CEO of *your* organization may know the names of the employees, but ask a couple of friends about their organizations. You may be surprised by what you find out about how some employees are treated.

Most managers appreciate their employees and treat them professionally. However, some managers treat their employees as objects to be utilized, as machines to be used. Even though we have come a long way in this area, some organizations are far from being where they should be. Consider Texaco's recent $176.1 million settlement of a racial discrimination lawsuit. Following the settlement, Texaco's chairman and chief executive officer said, "With this litigation behind us, we can now move forward on our broader, urgent mission to make Texaco a model of workplace opportunity for all men and women." Two questions need to be asked: Why did the company have to wait so long? How will employees interpret that statement? Elaine Burke, founder and president of EBI Training Services Corp., says, "Intellectually companies mean it when they talk about empowering workers. But in practice, it is hard for them to accept the second half of the empowerment equation—which is the concept of paying them more." The reason given is, "There is no real way for companies to quantify human resources—workers—as assets, so workers come up as expense on the balance sheet."[1]

It is easy to lose sight of a person's makeup, background, and self-worth if he or she is seen as just a number rather than as an individual with a name.

This is true whether the number is assigned to an individual at a concentration camp, a prison, or a corporation. If you wanted to lay off someone or refuse someone a promotion or a raise, would it be easier if she were referred to as 000-60-1313 instead of Miss Pamela Brightstar? Would you rather your boss referred to you by your name or your social security number? Yes, there is a lot behind the question: What's in a name?

A manager who treats employees as expendable parts of a machine rather than as company investments displays the primary symptom of this managerial sin. By looking at employees as financial liabilities and focusing on the bottom line, managers who develop this sin lack the people skills necessary to deal with employees. Any manager who ignores employees and uses a "slash-and-burn" approach to cut expenses (such as employee salaries and benefits) risks destroying employee morale and incentive, which leads to poor company performance.

To find out where business is today in this area, we solicited the help of our panel of experts:

Managers, in general, perceive their employees as an expense to the organization rather than as an investment.

Survey Panel	Disagree Strongly	Disagree	Neither Agree Nor Disagree	Agree	Agree Strongly
University business deans	3%	31%	16%	41%	9%
University business professors	4%	20%	16%	44%	16%
CEOs	25%	50%	13%	12%	0%
Union presidents	0%	0%	11%	22%	67%
Business news editors	0%	31%	31%	38%	0%

An alarming 60% of university business professors and 89% of union presidents either agreed or strongly agreed with the statement. So much for the concept of the organization as one big happy family. So much for the employees really trusting and respecting managers and managers trusting and respecting the employees.

That doesn't mean that many CEOs don't appreciate or are unaware of their employees' value to the organization. They do. Our concern is with those who don't. Consider the following comments:

■ Rene McPherson of Dana Corporation was quoted in *In Search of Excellence* as saying: "The philosophy comes first. Almost every executive agrees that people are the most important asset.

Yet almost none really lives it. The good manager knows or should know that the good organization knows that it wins when everyone wins."[2]

▪ It has been said that Thomas "Tip" O'Neill, Jr. always put the little people first. He never forgot that behind every statistic is a person and that government exists to serve people. Judging from his re-elections, it would appear that "the little people" didn't forget him either.

▪ Reginald Jones, former CEO of General Electric, said he spent more time with the human resources department than with the other departments.

▪ Phil Knight, CEO of Nike, said that when it comes to capital or people, people always come first.

▪ Ford Motor Company's mission states: "Our people are the source of our strength. They provide our corporate intelligence and determine our reputation and vitality. Involvement and team-work are our human values."

▪ J.C. Penney remarked: "People are the principal asset of any company, whether it makes things to sell, sells things made by other people, or supplies intangible services." One of the principles adopted by J.C. Penney in 1913 as part of the Penney Idea was: "To reward men and women in our organization through participation in what the business produces."

▪ Management at ALCOA introduced a compensation plan that helped put workers, executives, and shareholders on more common ground. According to the plan, hourly workers should not have to depend on variable compensation for their standard of living. On the other hand, they should not be cut out of the rewards when their efforts produce substantial rewards.

▪ The board of directors at Ben & Jerry's implemented a 5-to-1 salary ratio because of a belief that:
  1. Everyone who works at Ben & Jerry's is a major contributor to the success of the company.
  2. Corporate America overpays top management and under-pays entry-level employees.
  3. Corporations should attempt to reduce wealth discrepancies in the distribution of wealth.
  4. The board of directors of Ben & Jerry's recognizes that their compensation is linked to others in the company and that they benefit as others benefit.

Every person in the organization should have a reason for being there. When that is not the case, the person is probably unproductive and useless to the organization. During Napoleon's reign, one country that feared it would be invaded placed a soldier at the top of a mountain as a lookout. He was instructed to blow his bugle when he saw Napoleon approaching. Many years after Napoleon's death, there was still a soldier at the top of that mountain looking for him! What a waste! Such situations occur more often than they should. The good news is that they can be prevented.

Each person has to be carefully picked and placed in the proper position. Anything less should be unacceptable. Walter B. Wriston of Citicorp was quoted as saying: "Unless you have good people in the right spots, there's absolutely nothing you can do to save anything. If you have the right people in the right spots, there is almost nothing you can do to screw it up." Plato said: "More will be accomplished, and better, and with more ease, if every man does what he is best fitted to do, and nothing else."

If managers take the time to properly place employees where they belong, it stands to reason that there will be greater focus on the employees and, consequently, greater recognition of their importance and value to the organization. Hence, it will be easier to view employees as assets rather than expenses. This will enable a corporation to listen to not only the voice of its customers but also to the voice of its employees. By better knowing their employees, managers can help their employees reach their full potential. This will allow the organization and its managers to get closer to each other and closer to success. As Norman Vincent Peale said: "The man who lives for himself is a failure; the man who lives for others has achieved true success."

Expense versus Investment

Are employees in the corporate sector perceived and often treated as an expense or an investment? Do you agree with our panel's results? Should an employee's pay be based on his or her position, value, or contribution to the organization? As an example, let's consider two government employees. Both are promoted to GS-11 at the same time, but their experience, training, and education are quite different. One has much more training and experience than the other, yet under the current system their pay would be exactly the same. Should we pay the person or the position? What about in the private sector? Should the next president of General Motors, IBM, or General Electric be paid the same as the current president? Do his or her qualifications make a difference? What about past performance at previous jobs?

Many organizations today are feeling the pressure, whether real or imagined, to cut costs. They think that they are accomplishing something if they can replace an experienced employee at a higher salary with someone who will work for less pay. It is similar to what some schools are doing when they replace a teacher who has a master's degree with a teacher who has only a bachelor's degree for the sole purpose of saving money.

Some companies pay less attention to the cost of a new computer system than to the cost of the operator. They will hire an operator who will work for less money instead of a more experienced operator who commands a higher salary but can also better utilize the potential of the new computer system. Obviously, paying more money does not necessarily mean better results, but often it does, just as a more expensive stock can pay many times the dividends of a less expensive stock.

Employees must be treated as assets, as investments. Nothing less should be acceptable. That makes sense not only from the humanitarian or moral side of the equation but also from the overall business side. The right person should be matched with the right job, not only initially but continuously. That means planning an employee's future in the organization. An employee who was placed in the proper job when he or she was hired may have outgrown that job a year later. A good manager must recognize that and proceed accordingly. Once placed in an organization, many employees are, for all practical purposes, forgotten until someone "dares" to speak out. The sad thing is that such indifference hurts not only the employee but the organization. It is the responsibility of managers to get the best employees for their organizations and to place them in the right slots. But the manager's job is not over at that point. It is equally important for managers to continue the orderly and timely advancement of their employees.

It is essential that everyone in the organization work together toward a common goal, to ensure that the organization not only survives but meets its stated mission in the years to come. It is important that everyone in the organization realize the importance of such words as productivity, efficiency, and quality. As Jack Welch, chief executive officer of General Electric Company, says, "Managing better means managing less. The old 2-by-4 style of management is dead…We don't have a prayer of winning or surviving without a self-confident work force that comes to work every day searching for a way to succeed. We need to empower the worker and encourage open communication and the sharing of ideas."[3] He adds, "American corporations managed their way into the worst of all possible worlds. We made our workers bored, sullen, and silent. American workers put in their time and go home. Our challenge is to tap into their intellect and creativity. People with

10–30 years service have never been asked their opinion about anything. Suddenly, they felt some worth." Welch related how one long-time employee put it: "For 20 years you've paid me for my arms and legs. You could have had my brain for nothing." He continued by saying, "Ignoring a worker's ideas would be like turning Ted Williams into a relief pitcher or having Picasso paint the white lines on Route 128 without getting their feedback."[4]

Every employee should be carefully selected, just as each stock in an investment portfolio is carefully chosen. Every employee should be part of the corporate family. While that may be the case in some organizations, in other organizations employees are numbers—objects to be utilized and manipulated. Motorola stresses that the organization is a "family" with humane and democratic values, where no one can be fired without approval from the top. Employees are on a first-name basis, no matter what their levels. Sam Walton believed that employees should think like partners; that's why he called them "associates."

There must be respect for each individual as well as concern for the dignity and rights of each person in the organization at all times instead of just when it is convenient or expedient to do so. Respect for the individual employee should not mean respect for the employee only as long as it benefits the company. Managers need to take time to talk to and understand their employees. They need to realize that the employees are the most important resource in the organization. Generally, employees want to know that the company cares about them and will invest in them. If they are convinced of that, most will work harder to make the company successful. The company should not insist on conformity and dedication to a single master. Employees should not be placed in the position of having to compromise their personal beliefs and integrity to fit the company's image.

When asked whether or not it is the duty of managers to develop their subordinates to their potential, the overwhelming response of our panel was "yes."

It is the duty of managers to develop their subordinates to their potential.

Survey Panel	Disagree Strongly	Disagree	Neither Agree Nor Disagree	Agree	Agree Strongly
University business deans	0%	2%	5%	46%	47%
University business professors	2%	2%	2%	52%	42%
CEOs	0%	0%	0%	44%	56%
Union presidents	0%	0%	0%	56%	44%
Business news editors	0%	8%	23%	54%	15%

In practice, however, the evidence is very mixed. Many progressive companies are very good at developing their employees and are constantly aware of the needs of their employees. After all, by adhering to that philosophy, the organization also benefits. It is truly a win–win situation. If employee performance appraisals are accurately done and used, the job of developing employees becomes much easier and is much more accurate and realistic. Unfortunately, as our survey shows, organizations often view performance appraisal as a formality rather than for its intended purpose.

Generally, employee performance appraisals are used more for formality rather than for a meaningful and constructive purpose.

Survey Panel	Disagree Strongly	Disagree	Neither Agree Nor Disagree	Agree	Agree Strongly
University business deans	0%	16%	8%	60%	16%
University business professors	2%	11%	11%	49%	27%
CEOs	0%	37%	6%	44%	13%
Union presidents	0%	0%	0%	67%	33%
Business news editors	0%	31%	23%	31%	15%

Business schools teach the importance of guiding employees in their jobs and helping them improve their weaknesses. One opportunity to provide such help is the performance appraisal. Yet, many managers forego the opportunity and view the appraisal as a formality.

The Union: Ally or Enemy?

Conflict can be a serious problem in any organization. It might not bring about the demise of an organization, but it certainly can hurt performance and result in the loss of many good employees. All conflict is not bad. Conflict has both a positive and a negative side. A perennial issue in many organizations is the actual or perceived conflict between management and labor unions. In the United States, approximately 15% of the work force belongs to and is represented by a union. This number is considerably higher in other countries. For instance, in Japan, Germany, Great Britain, and Canada, typically 30 to 40% of the labor force belongs to a union. The existence of a union in an organization adds another variable in our search to explain and predict employee behavior. Unions have been found to be an important contributor to employee perceptions, attitudes, and behavior. The informal norms that union cohesiveness fosters can encourage or discourage high productivity, organizational commitment, and morale.

The issue here is not the value of unions but rather their impact on the organization. Undeniably, how management and labor treat each other plays an important role in the success of the organization. As we approach this issue, we need to ask whether the interests of labor, management, and the customer are the same. If the answer is "yes," then why is there friction? Are there any winners? How about losers? What differentiates labor from management? Is it ability or motive? Aren't labor and management on the same team? If either is inefficient, does the other suffer? Let's take a look at our panel's responses:

Organizations would function better
if they stopped referring to their employees as either "labor" or
"management," but instead refer to all of them by one name, i.e., "associates."

Survey Panel	Disagree Strongly	Disagree	Neither Agree Nor Disagree	Agree	Agree Strongly
University business deans	2%	21%	29%	44%	4%
University business professors	2%	25%	18%	46%	9%
CEOs	6%	19%	38%	31%	6%
Union presidents	22%	34%	22%	11%	11%
Business news editors	8%	33%	17%	42%	0%

Aren't all the people in an organization employees, including the CEO? Aren't they all working for the same cause—toward the same end? Why differentiate between them? Why refer to each other as "we" and "they"? In the book *Sam Walton: The Inside Story of America's Richest Man*, the author relates the following story:

> ...a union attempted to organize two Wal-Marts in Missouri. Sam sought help from a respected labor lawyer named John E. Tate and found him a down-to-earth realist. As Tate described the episode to *Fortune*: "I told him: You can approach this one of two ways. Hold people down, and pay me or some other lawyer to make it work. Or devote time and attention to proving to people that you care."
>
> Sam listened and decided to take the latter approach. Within a short time, Sam was undertaking such management seminars as "We Care," and concocting attractive and meaningful profit-sharing

schemes, as well as a variety of incentive bonuses, all stressing his sincerity in selling his "family" concept. Sam was impressed by the lawyer and in 1988 added Tate to this corporate staff as executive vice-president for professional services.[5]

Perhaps Sam Walton was able to defuse the labor–management problem, and as of today only one store in Windsor, Ontario has a union representing workers. All other attempts to unionize have failed. But how are other U.S. organizations coping with and handling it? We asked our panel to shed some light in this area:

Organizations are doing a good job in managing management–labor disputes.

Survey Panel	Disagree Strongly	Disagree	Neither Agree Nor Disagree	Agree	Agree Strongly
University business deans	5%	34%	34%	27%	0%
University business professors	4%	27%	36%	33%	0%
CEOs	0%	0%	44%	56%	0%
Union presidents	67%	33%	0%	0%	0%
Business news editors	8%	46%	38%	8%	0%

It is obvious from the responses that union presidents certainly have serious concerns about how management is handling one of its responsibilities—managing labor–management disputes. Over one-half of the business news editors also disagree with the statement. What is the message here? Is the news good for organizations and their employees?

A related statement was also posed to the panel:

The *ultimate* responsibility to settle labor–management disputes lies with management.

Survey Panel	Disagree Strongly	Disagree	Neither Agree Nor Disagree	Agree	Agree Strongly
University business deans	5%	34%	17%	38%	6%
University business professors	7%	44%	11%	34%	4%
CEOs	19%	31%	13%	37%	0%
Union presidents	34%	0%	22%	22%	22%
Business editors	0%	46%	0%	54%	0%

It is the duty of management to manage. When there is a problem that can be solved, it is management's responsibility to solve, or manage, it. Can that statement be disputed? Should it be disputed? Who should have responsibility for handling labor–management disputes? Let there be no mistake: the CEO has the ultimate responsibility to manage disputes. If a dispute is not managed and continues to cause problems in the organization, the CEO has to take the "blame." The CEO cannot try to escape that responsibility by taking the position that the fault lies with the union. That may be the case, but it is not the solution. It is the responsibility of the CEO to take the necessary action to "solve" the problem. Anything less is unacceptable. There must be cooperation between labor and management. Both need to work together in the same way that the members of an athletic team pull together to win a game. In unity there is strength. After all, everyone should be working for the same goal. By doing that, there is institutional power.

Many CEOs are very good in solving these disputes. Properly solving them means more than just getting employees back to work or having them sign a contract. It means settling the dispute without leaving any permanent wounds. It is important not to lose sight of the fact that work must continue after the dispute is settled, and the company must be able to produce goods that are not only of high quality but competitive. In settling a dispute, management cannot exploit either its employees or its customers. There is life for the corporation after the dispute is settled, and it is management's responsibility to position the organization to meet future challenges. That, of course, cannot be accomplished if some employees are left wounded and unhappy following the settlement.

Many U.S. companies and institutions have no broad, explicit structure for dealing with employee concerns and no non-union appeal channel other than the traditional chain of command. When they are unable to resolve disputes with their supervisors, employees at all levels are expected to either drop difficult problems or take them up the line if they dare.

Senator Orrin Hatch, labor's archrival on Capitol Hill for nearly two decades, was quoted as saying: "There are always going to be people who take advantage of workers. Unions even that out, to their credit. We need them to level the field between labor and management. If you didn't have unions, it would be very difficult for even enlightened employers to not take advantage of workers on wages and working conditions, because of [competition from] rivals. I'm among the first to say I believe in unions."[6] Hatch still opposes organized labor at nearly every turn, but when pressed, even he concedes a point that is a growing concern to economists, administration officials, and some executives: free-market economies need healthy unions. They offer "a system of checks and balances," as former Labor Secretary

George P. Shultz put it, by making managers focus on employees as well as on profits and shareholders.

The concern of Shultz and others is that the balance has shifted significantly. In the 1950s and early 1960s, as much as 35% of the U.S. labor force was represented by unions. Between 1983 and 1993, union membership has fallen 6% to 16.6 million, or 15.8% of the work force—the lowest since the Great Depression. Subtract government employees, and unions represent a mere 11% of private-industry workers.[7] The recent figures according to the Department of Labor indicate that it is now down to 14.9%. However, former Labor Secretary Robert Reich points out that workers' unease over corporate downsizing and job security may revive the nation's unions. To highlight this, imagine what would happen if Congress enacted a law outlawing all union activity in the United States. How would organizations react? Perhaps the new order of business in some organizations would be lower wages and poorer working conditions. Many organizations treat employees decently not necessarily because it is better from a management standpoint but rather because of fear of punishment or penalties. Do some of those CEOs believe in what Aristotle said: "I do without being commanded what others do because of the fear of the law." Isn't this consistent with the management philosophy that happy employees are better employees?

The arguments advanced for or against unions, as well as their philosophy and purpose for existence, have long been around and will continue to be for some time. It is safe to conclude that unions will continue to exist, although it is unclear whether they will be stronger or weaker. Having said that, let's briefly explore how organizations are handling or managing labor–management disputes. There is plenty of evidence to suggest that such disputes are not being handled well. They seem to persist, and in some instances, there seems to be no finality. They are not being managed. Each side blames the problem on the other.

One thing is certain. The task of managing labor–management disputes falls, as it should, on management. It is the responsibility of management to manage the affairs of the organization. Labor–management disputes are affairs of the organization; consequently, they must be managed by managers, but that is not happening in many organizations. In some organizations, the labor–management disputes are played out like children's games. The unions blame management, and management blames the unions for the disputes. In many cases, that's as far as it goes. Debate and conflict can be healthy, and both are inevitable as well as necessary. However, they must be managed. The key word is *managed*. Anything less is unacceptable.

Management must exercise its power and influence to resolve conflict when and where it exists. At a certain point, finality becomes important, and conflict and debate are no longer healthy. At that time, management must finalize the outcome. Sometimes that takes courage. Many managers are afraid to act because they fear controversy. They view controversy as bad for their careers, and they certainly don't want to do anything to hurt their careers. So what happens? Often they hide behind smoke screens, such as keeping a low profile to avoid firing someone and thus exposing the company to a lawsuit. They justify that argument by pointing out that we are living in a litigious society, and any action taken by management could result in a lawsuit. Generally, however, that doesn't happen, but if someone does bring suit, so be it. Companies should not let themselves be blackmailed by fear of lawsuits. Management must assess the situation and then act responsibly and decisively.

There needs to be unity in organizations. The relationship between management and unions/employees must be one of cooperation and mutual respect. Both must recognize that they are really on the same side. CEOs and employees are not adversaries. How can a company be competitive and successful in an atmosphere of hatred and disagreement or antagonism and mutual suspicion? Everyone in the organization must work together in order for the organization to succeed. Together, everyone achieves more. Success here means more than showing a profit. It means maximizing the wealth of the organization. Japanese labor unions work very closely with management. Each side is cognizant of the fact that its fate is tied to the other's success.

Can we realistically expect a company whose employees are not united to produce products that can compete against those of a company whose employees are united and whose culture dictates such unity? It is critical that the people in charge of negotiating disputes be knowledgeable in technical areas and the law, but they also need a good understanding of management. It is important to remember that after a dispute is settled, the individuals involved—both labor and management—must work together toward the successful accomplishment of the corporate goals. Labor disputes should be viewed and handled not as adversarial situations but rather as misunderstandings or conflicts that need to be mutually resolved.

It is important to avoid a "we–they" attitude after a dispute is over. Negotiators sometimes consciously or unconsciously tend to foster such attitudes. The outcome has to allow the organization to accomplish its goals. It also has to promote a win–win attitude. Consider the major league baseball strike. Who won? Who lost? What was accomplished? Could the controversy have been avoided? Were the right parties handling the dispute? Could the strike have been settled earlier? How? What lessons did we learn? What about the public's perception of the dispute? How could the situation have been handled differently? We may be doing some Monday morning quarterbacking here, but that's okay because incidents repeat themselves. If we can learn from previous incidents and handle them better in the future, doesn't everybody win? Speaking about the baseball strike, President Jimmy Carter said during an interview on "Larry King Live": "The desire to find a solution needs to be there to reach a settlement." Was there a real desire to reach a mutually agreeable settlement? What about the United Parcel Service (UPS)/Teamsters strike? Was the strike predictable? Unavoidable? Who will be the winners and who will be the losers?

Management must remember that the union is not the enemy; it represents the company's employees and is an integral part of the organization. The organization's products are the result of the joint efforts of all the people in the organization. By working together, the organization has a better chance to succeed. After all, an unprofitable organization means that everyone loses. The principles of people management are simple: care, consideration, and kindness build a highly motivated work force, and absolute commitment to quality products takes care of the bottom line. Mary Kay Ash proved and continues to prove that a company can thrive in a competitive business environment by managing by the Golden Rule. If we believe in the dignity of labor, we must pay working people well for their time and effort. How can anything counter to that make sense or be tolerated?

It is important to be realistic in terms of what works and what doesn't work for employees. What worked twenty years ago may not work today. What was not tolerated twenty years ago may be tolerated today. For example, office romances were once taboo, but of 200 CEOs polled, 79% said they aren't a company's concern as long as people are discreet. Twenty-one percent said that office romances inevitably result in problems for a company, but 75% disagreed.[8] One poll asked, "Do you think that having married couples working at the same company is good or bad for productivity?" The results were: good, 8%; bad, 16%; doesn't matter, 63%; and not sure, 13%.[9] We need to be open-minded and periodically clean out our mental closets, throwing away old and unworkable ideas that have been proven to be wrong or no longer applicable and replacing them with workable ones.

Cooperation, not competition, between union and management is what is needed in the workplace. For example, there have been a number of brief wildcat strikes at Caterpillar and hostility inside the plants. UAW members were told by a union official to "check your brain at the door; don't volunteer for anything" to protest the company's treatment of them.[10] If the employees were to follow that advice, where would the company end up?

We know the importance of trust in organizations, yet we see it disregarded in various forms. One example is computer monitoring. In some instances, it has been associated with spying or lack of trust. Consider the titles of some recent articles in the business press: "Big Brother Is Counting Your Keystrokes," "How Companies Spy on Employees," "Employee Performance Monitoring...or Meddling?," "The Dark Side of Computing," "The Boss That Never Blinks." These articles capture the primary way in which computer monitoring has been used in the workplace—as a surveillance technique to control employee behavior. Eavesdropping is not acceptable behavior outside the workplace, so it is not hard to understand why electronic eavesdropping in the workplace elicits negative reactions.[11] "Computer monitoring should not be seen as a way of gathering information about workers, per se, but rather as one part of a production and quality strategy that provides needed information to a diverse team of workers. In its most powerful and effective form, computer monitoring is the use of computers to collect, process, and provide feedback information about work with the intent of improving performance and developing employees. Unfortunately, computer monitoring has also been used to punish employees."[12]

Viewing employees as assets is dictated by management theory, by logic, and by common sense. What is a company's most valuable asset? It has to be intellectual capital. Where does intellectual capital come from? It comes from the employees. Consequently, intellectual capital has value. How much value? Can it be measured? The answer is "yes," if management cares to do so. Value as price can be determined. A cynic, said Oscar Wilde, knows the price of everything and the value of nothing. If so, then many managers are cynics. They know their costs but not what their work is worth.[13] Thomas Housel, who was responsible for reengineering at Pacific Bell and later a research director for Telecon Italia (the Italian phone company), says, "Reengineering ought to increase value, not just cut costs—and especially not cut costs at the expense of value. Without a salable output, we had no way of knowing if we increased value or of figuring a return on investment."[14] This analysis should be applied to our employees. After all, assets which translate into investments have returns that can be measured. John Locke said: "Labor makes the far greatest part of the value of things."

It is important that CEOs strive to create a working environment where everyone works together and where there are no barriers. The workplace should be a fun place, a place employees look forward to going to every working day. Some people get uptight as soon as you mention that the workplace should be a fun place. They interpret a fun workplace as a place where there is no order and a place where there is less dignity and respect for rules. Does a fun workplace have to mean less order and respect? As a matter of fact, generally the opposite is true. There is no compelling reason why people in organizations can't have fun as long as it is tasteful and orderly. It fosters openness, happiness, togetherness, and increases productivity. Herb Keller was asked: "Why is it so important to have fun at work?"

> It's very liberating, and it's stimulating. Robert Frost said, "Isn't it a shame that people's minds work furiously until they get to work." My philosophy is that if you have an environment that's fun to work in, your mind doesn't stop working furiously—as a matter of fact, you might even anticipate coming to work. Work may seem pretty good compared to a lot of other things you have to do in life. So we take the competition seriously, but not ourselves, and I think that's helpful to use in terms of competing.[15]

There has to be trust in the workplace. That doesn't mean just telling employees that the CEO and the management team are nice people who wouldn't do anything to hurt the employees and consequently they should be trusted. It takes more than that. Trust must be earned. It must be earned through past deeds and acts. Sometimes it is difficult to earn the necessary trust. Nevertheless, there is no compromise. Management must gain that trust no matter what, or the company will suffer. The following example illustrates how management's past dealings can affect trust.

> The employees in the technology division did not believe that senior management was telling them the truth because of a recent history of reorganizations, large work force reductions and the belief that further reorganizations were likely. Moreover, before the most recent reorganization, the company had denied rumors that reductions in work force would occur until hours before the announcement was made. The combination of historical evidence and a lack of trust made every statement issued by senior management suspect.[16]

It is obvious from the foregoing discussion that treating employees any other way than as an asset or as an investment is counterproductive, to say the least. It hurts the employees, the organization, other stakeholders, and certainly the CEO. The amount of damage it causes varies depending on the circumstances. Is it fatal? The answer is "it depends," but it can be fatal for the CEO's career in that organization and can even be fatal for the organization.

The good news is that this fatal managerial sin is easy to prevent. Furthermore, preventing it translates into good things for all the stakeholders in the organization. Wins can happen without losses—a win–win–win–win situation. That being the case, it is all the more frustrating when a CEO fails in this area. As one writer sums it up:

> Workers must no longer be considered as cost factors to be "compressed" or "rationalized" but as allies to be won. Conversely, managers must stop seeing themselves as the only people fit to think, to decide, and to manage. Although the pursuit of profit is a legitimate objective, it must not become the only factor to be considered and must stop being perceived as a short-term goal to be reached for the sole benefit of managers and shareholders. Instead profit should be regarded as the result of collective efforts of all parties, and it should be administered accordingly. The rates and applications of profits should therefore be decided in common by all stakeholders (managers, shareholders, and workers alike).[17]

Ultimately, it is the responsibility of each CEO to make sure that each person in the organization performs at his or her best at all times. The CEO must realize that each individual is unique and must be treated as such. The uniqueness of each organization's employees—its people—can be summarized in the following quotation:

> The only thing that cannot be duplicated by another company or organization is the commitment, competence, and enthusiasm of the people![18]

Notes

1. Michael A. Verespej, "Pay-for-Skills—It's Time Has Come," *Industry Week*, June 15, 1992, p. 26. (Reprinted with permission from *Industry Week*. Copyright Penton Publishing, Inc., Cleveland, Ohio.)
2. Thomas J. Peters and Robert H. Waterman, Jr., *In Search of Excellence: Lessons from America's Best-Run Companies* (New York: Harper and Row, 1982).
3. Bill Brotherton, "GE Employees, Management Work-Out Together to Make a Better Company," *Daily Evening Item*, November 15, 1991.

4. Ibid.

5. Vance H. Trimble, *Sam Walton: The Inside Story of America's Richest Man* (New York: A Dutton Signet, a division of Penguin Books, USA, Inc., 1990), p. 229.

6. Aaron Bernstein, "Why America Needs Unions But Not the Kind It Has Now," *Business Week*, May 23, 1994, p. 70.

7. Ibid.

8. Shelly Reese, "Office Romances Gaining Acceptance," *USA Today*, September 15, 1994, Section B.

9. Anne B. Fisher, "Is Love in the Air at Your Office? A Slew of Social Trends Are Converging to Encourage Romance at Work as Never Before. Surprising New Research Shows That This May Be Good for Productivity," *Fortune*, October 3, 1994, p. 139.

10. "We Did It…We Made Them Competitors. For Some, the Strike at Caterpillar Has Become a Stand for Their Contribution to American Dream," *Quad-City Times,* July 4, 1994, p. 7A.

11. Terri L. Griffith, "Teaching Big Brother to Be a Team Player: Computer Monitoring and Quality," *Academy of Management Executive*, Volume 7, Number 1, 1993, p. 73.

12. Ibid.

13. Thomas A. Stewart, "Your Company's Most Valuable Asset: Intellectual Capital," *Fortune,* October 3, 1994, p. 69.

14. Ibid.

15. Jim Sexton, "The Zany Captain of Southwest," *Best of Business Quarterly*, Fall 1990, p. 10.

16. Beverly Goldberg, "Manage Change—Not the Chaos Caused by Change," *Management Review*, November 1992, p. 41.

17. Omar Aktous, "Management Theories of Organizations in the 1990s: Toward Critical, Radical Humanism," *Academy of Management Review*, July 1992, p. 426.

18. Ken Blanchard, *Mission Possible: Creating a World Class Organization* (New York: McGraw-Hill, 1997), p. 44.

CHAPTER 12

Sin #7   Managing Unchecked: Lack of Real Accountability

It is wonderful how preposterously the affairs of the world are managed. We assemble parliaments and councils to have the benefit of collective wisdom, but we necessarily have, at the same time, the inconvenience of their collected passions, prejudices and private interests.
—Benjamin Franklin

We make a living by what we get; we make a life by what we give.
—Winston Churchill

The question, "Who ought to be the boss?" is like asking, "Who ought to be the tenor in the quartet?" Obviously, the man who can sing tenor.
—Henry Ford

We choose directors for all the wrong reasons.

Complete authority with no responsibility is anarchy and chaos.

Irresponsibility Due to Lack of Accountability

Perhaps the managerial sin most frequently committed by CEOs is their failure to account for their actions. Some CEOs commit this sin so frequently that it is their standard way of doing business. Whether this irresponsibility due to lack of accountability negatively affects the organization and the careers of the CEOs is primarily a matter of degree of irresponsibility. However, lack of accountability can cause fatalities. There is no question that the lack of accountability of a number of CEOs has slowly but surely brought about their demise. Lack of accountability is surely a fatal managerial sin.

Lack of accountability can result from two closely connected circumstances. First, it can come about from a CEO's failure to accept responsibility for the actions of the organization. The CEO has the power over decision making, yet passes the buck when things run astray. The "scapegoats" for this type of CEO can include employees, competitors, government regulations, market conditions, and the economy, to name a few. When a board of directors tolerates this type of behavior, the CEO is not accountable for the activities of the organization.

Second, it results from a weak board of directors that does not have control over the CEO. The CEO has too much power over decision making, and no one effectively checks his or her authority. The CEO is generally out of control and does not really focus on the rights and demands of the various stakeholders. Organizations that have strong CEOs who lack accountability do not have a system of checks and balances in place to control the decision-making process.

Who Watches the Managers? Careful in Getting Rid of the Disturbers of the Peace!

"I was so successful and powerful," says Donald Burr, former CEO of People Express, "that no one could suggest to me that I was wrong. My picture was on the front cover of magazines. I was making millions, so who on the board was going to tell me that I was doing things wrong?" He continues, "Beware of CEOs who are very powerful." There can't be much disagreement as to whether people at the top of organizations have power, but sometimes they have too much power. They are chieftains—almost like little kings of their organizations. When they speak, others listen—whether they want to or not.

Let there be no misunderstanding that CEOs need to have power. Obviously, without power, it would be almost impossible for them to effectively lead their organizations. But should such power have checks? Without checks, there is no real accountability. Thus, the real issue is whether CEOs in corporate America are accountable. If they are, to whom? If not, why not? To whom should they be accountable? The first step in accountability is properly monitoring actions. Are actions of managers being monitored? Here's what our panel had to say:

The actions of managers are being well monitored.

Survey Panel	Disagree Strongly	Disagree	Neither Agree Nor Disagree	Agree	Agree Strongly
University business deans	5%	50%	17%	27%	1%
University business professors	22%	40%	14%	22%	2%
CEOs	0%	19%	31%	44%	6%
Union presidents	45%	33%	11%	11%	0%
Business news editors	15%	46%	8%	31%	0%

Take a close look at the responses of the union presidents, deans, and professors. What about the board of directors? What precisely is their function regarding accountability? Are the boards of directors effectively "minding the store"? Are they in control of what is going on in their organizations? Can they be, given the present makeup?

The panel also responded to a closely related statement:

Generally, there is a lack of "real" accountability by the chief executive officers.

Survey Panel	Disagree Strongly	Disagree	Neither Agree Nor Disagree	Agree	Agree Strongly
University business deans	7%	35%	13%	32%	13%
University business professors	7%	21%	4%	45%	23%
CEOs	50%	25%	13%	12%	0%
Union presidents	0%	22%	11%	0%	67%
Business news editors	15%	15%	8%	46%	16%

If, indeed, CEOs are not effectively monitored (and there is not much evidence to think otherwise), why not? Is it because they have too much power and the boards fear them? Is it because they are able to hide their actions or inactions? Do they report only those actions that put them in a favorable light? In many cases, the answers to these questions are equivocally "yes." Sixty-eight percent of the university business professors and 62% of business news editors either agreed or strongly agreed with the above statement. If those responses accurately represent the present state of affairs in corporate America, what is the message that is being conveyed? Should there be any reason for concern? Are our corporations headed in the right direction?

Returning to the issue of the CEO's power, the panel was asked to respond to the following statement:

Chief executive officers have too much power.

Survey Panel	Disagree Strongly	Disagree	Neither Agree Nor Disagree	Agree	Agree Strongly
University business deans	5%	46%	30%	12%	7%
University business professors	5%	33%	27%	29%	6%
CEOs	25%	69%	0%	6%	0%
Union presidents	0%	0%	22%	22%	56%
Business news editors	0%	31%	38%	31%	0%

It appears the responses are somewhat mixed. When the CEOs' responses are compared with those of union presidents, we notice two fairly strong opposing opinions. The responses of the university business professors and business news editors are more divided. Overall, the results are not what they ought to be. Here again, the situation can be corrected by implementing the proper checks and balances. After all, there are checks and balances in other areas, such as state and federal governments. Isn't the executive branch "checked and balanced" by the legislative and judicial branches? When checks and balances are used properly, the result can be

"Naturally, I can't take all the credit. I have a wonderful support group."

(*Harvard Business Review*, November–December 1994.
Permission granted by Leo Collum, cartoonist.)

positive, healthy, and productive. It allows for more thought-provoking discussion and effective decision making.

To Whom Are Managers Accountable?

When asked to whom CEOs are accountable, people tend to point the finger in a number of directions. Included in the list are the board of directors, stockholders, employees, customers, the public, and a number of other stakeholders. When asked how effective as overseers these stakeholders are, the answers are mixed at best. The prevailing view, however, is that none of these stakeholders are effective overseers; none of them really do a good job of holding managers accountable.

In this section, the focus of our discussion is primarily on the effectiveness of the board of directors in monitoring, guiding, and directing the CEO. After all, it is the legal responsibility of the board to manage the affairs of the corporation. Let's begin by examining the responses of our panel to several related statements. Here is what the panel had to say regarding the effectiveness of the board of directors:

U.S. organizations are governed by strong and effective boards of directors.

Survey Panel	Disagree Strongly	Disagree	Neither Agree Nor Disagree	Agree	Agree Strongly
University business deans	15%	47%	20%	18%	0%
University business professors	18%	62%	13%	5%	2%
CEOs	6%	19%	44%	31%	0%
Union presidents	45%	44%	11%	0%	0%
Business news editors	8%	61%	31%	0%	0%

The responses don't really paint a positive picture of U.S. corporate boards. Indeed, the picture is bleak at best. Yet, boards are legally entrusted with the responsibility to manage corporations. In effect, they are, or at least should be, the guardians of the stockholders' investments. They should see that the stockholders are well protected—that their money is secure and invested well. In addition, other stakeholders rely on the board. They expect and hope that their organizations would be managed by the best and brightest. Are they? Do the panel's responses warrant such a conclusion? If not, what are we doing about it? What should we be doing? Who needs to take the lead to correct the situation?

In order to get a clear picture of the situation, the panel was asked to respond to another statement:

In "reality" corporate boards of directors are "rubber stamps" for the presidents and/or chief executive officers of organizations.

Survey Panel	Disagree Strongly	Disagree	Neither Agree Nor Disagree	Agree	Agree Strongly
University business deans	2%	32%	21%	39%	6%
University business professors	5%	15%	17%	54%	9%
CEOs	19%	38%	25%	6%	12%
Union presidents	0%	0%	11%	56%	33%
Business news editors	0%	15%	39%	31%	15%

Again, the picture of corporate boards is not too complimentary. In fact, rightfully or wrongfully, the perception here is sad. The tragedy is that many of the directors are intelligent and hard-working people who certainly can do a very good job, if they choose to do so—but do they? Let's look at whether we can realistically expect them to do more. How often do they meet? For how long? What other obligations do they have? Can they realistically accomplish all that is needed to run an effective organization in that short period of time? Given the present setup, isn't the most that we can really expect the board to do is select a good CEO who can effectively manage the corporation? But even if that were the case, there are still other problems. For openers, let's ask who, in practice, not in theory, chooses whom. Does the board choose the CEO or does the CEO choose the board of directors? Because of its importance, and to make sure that the panel had sufficient opportunity to reflect on the previous statement, on another section of the survey the panel was asked to respond to the following statement:

Generally, whatever recommendation management makes, the board of directors approve.

Survey Panel	Disagree Strongly	Disagree	Neither Agree Nor Disagree	Agree	Agree Strongly
University business deans	2%	27%	19%	48%	4%
University business professors	5%	13%	7%	73%	2%
CEOs	19%	25%	19%	37%	0%
Union presidents	0%	22%	11%	56%	11%
Business news editors	0%	15%	31%	54%	0%

Here again, the results are fairly consistent. In light of the results, it is fair to ask what is really happening in our corporations. Are boards insensitive to the plea for more accountability? Is there apathy out there? Board members are generally smart and competent individuals. Why don't they take their legal and ethical duty more seriously? Are they afraid that they may upset or interfere with the status quo? Do they realize how much the stakeholders depend on them to keep things in proper perspective and to avoid the cloud of suspicion? What is needed to turn this situation around? Is it fair to say that what is needed is to rethink the corporate structure? Should the present setup and makeup of boards of directors become a thing of the past? Is it time for an overhaul of the system? If it is, who should be responsible to start the ball rolling? Do you find the responses of the panel alarming? Are they really a wake-up call? Do we need more evidence before we act? If so, what kind of evidence do we need? Is it available? Where do we find it?

Most would agree that many problems arise when there is lack of accountability on the part of the CEO. Lack of accountability gives the CEO more control of the organization. With more control comes more power to make "unchecked" decisions. In turn, that means the organization will generally move in the direction the CEO dictates. If the CEO happens to place more emphasis on his or her own career than on the welfare of the organization, the result will be less protection and less regard for the various stakeholders' interests.

Most would also agree that no one is above the law. Everyone should have some accountability. After all, management is about accountability. Most CEOs would say that they are accountable. If the question were should CEOs be accountable, the answer would be an unequivocal "yes." But the question is if they really are accountable and to whom they are accountable. Legally, the answer to the latter question is clear. They are accountable to the board. They take their marching orders from the board. The board has the ultimate responsibility to manage the company and is legally given the power to manage. However, often that is not the case in practice. The board doesn't really manage the company. At best, the board turns that power over to the CEO. That in itself would not be so bad if the board at least spent the necessary time to monitor the actions of the CEO. It would not be so bad if the board took the time to see that the new "possessor" of power exercised it rightfully. Who is the trustee of the power? Isn't the board the true trustee of the power?

Given the present corporate structure, it is not easy for corporate boards to accomplish what is legally expected of them. Perhaps that explains why in 1993 roughly 300 U.S. companies were hit with 713 claims against directors and officers—23% more than in 1988. Furthermore, companies with more than $1 billion in assets experienced a greater jump, with claims up 53% since 1987. At the heart of these and other actions is the belief that some directors are simply too cozy with management to be independent, either because of personal loyalties or reliance on company-related business.[1] When members of the board are friends, clients, or confidants of management or are lawyers representing competitors, the result is often conflict of interest.

In an article entitled "The Best and Worst Boards," the author states:

> They settle into high-backed chairs around burnished mahogany conference tables. And what they say and do is often an enigma to anyone outside those closed doors. They are the directors in the boardroom, a collection of names, egos, and experience that serves as the critical link between a public company's owners—its share-holders—and management.
>
> That, at least, is the theory. In practice, too many boards have been mere "ornaments on a corporate Christmas tree" as a landmark study of boards by Harvard business school professor Myles Mace put it—decorative and decorous baubles, with no real purpose.[2]

The article, which is subtitled "Our New Report Card on Corporate Governance," delves into this area and not only defines what a good board is but also through surveys and interviews rank some of the best and worst boards. The article points out that:

> Somehow, directors forgot—if they ever new—that they were in the boardroom to act on behalf of shareholders and oversee that collection of hired hands known as management. Directors watched idly at one seemingly invincible corporation after another—from Eastman Kodak and General Motors to IBM, Sears Roebuck, and Westinghouse Electric—as their companies faltered and declined. Only when the directors were prodded by investors and activists, only after their companies and CEOs were publicly pilloried, were many finally goaded into action—what some call "governance by embarrassment."[3]

Since boards are legally entrusted with the responsibility of managing corporations and since we know what has been taking place in corporate America, it is appropriate to ask: What is wrong with our corporate boards and what is needed to remedy any wrongs that presently exist? Rightfully or not, whenever an organization is judged a failure, whether for failure to reach financial goals or for falling short of society's expectations, the critics turn to the board and ask: "Where was the board?" To answer that question, we begin by looking at the makeup of corporate boards. Most would agree that the majority of board members are intelligent, sincere, honest, and capable men and women who are able to make good and, in many instances, very good business decisions. If given the proper corporate structure and circumstances, the affairs of the organization could be in good and capable hands. However, from what we see, read, and know, it would generally appear that things are not what they ought to be. There has recently been some movement toward improvement in this area, but we are still far from being where we should be. Since the mid-1980s, criticism of boards has increased in both volume and stridency.

Is such criticism fair and warranted? Is it justified based on their misdeeds or are the misdeeds corporate misdeeds that are attributable to other members of the organization? If it is indeed fair to place the blame for corporate and CEOs' failures on the boards, then we must look into why they failed. Why they failed is important to the stakeholders. The answer can help us improve, shape, and direct what will happen in the future.

If we were to delve into this area, we would conclude that the way corporate boards are presently set up is not appropriate. The way boards are structured and expected to operate does not measure up to present corporate demands. The question here is not whether boards were set up to properly function in the past; rather, the question is whether they are properly set up now. The past is not the real issue; the present is. Therefore, our discussion will focus on the present state of affairs.

The present way of choosing board members, their structure, and the way they are expected to operate places them in a vulnerable situation and sets them up for potential problems and possible failure. The present system is at best weak, ineffective, and inefficient. What saves organizations from disaster, in many instances, is the fact that they do well in spite of their boards. That could be the result of good products, good people, good timing, or even good luck, but imagine what organizations could accomplish if they had the right guidance from the right boards. More organizations could be unstoppable giants. Perhaps there would be more Campbell Soups or General Electrics!

Before turning to the makeup of corporate boards and the way they are asked to function, let's consider whether they can realistically be expected to manage their organizations. What are boards specifically being asked to do when they are legally charged with the responsibility of managing the organization? Does managing the organization equate with letting the CEO run the show? Management textbooks state that the key responsibilities of the board of directors are: (1) to review the organization's financial statement, (2) to ensure that the organization is on track in setting and accomplishing its objectives, and (3) to oversee the orderly succession of management. Undeniably, all three responsibilities are proper and are part of the agenda of anyone who is given overall responsibility to manage, but is that all there is to managing, and can the board realistically accomplish all its duties within the allotted business time?

How often do boards meet and for how long? How prepared are the board members for those meetings? Can board members realistically, not theoretically, be expected to make objective decisions on all the issues they face? Can board members who are company executives be expected to be objective in their decision making on matters that are supported by the CEO? What happens after the meeting when they go back to work for their boss, the CEO? Is it fair to put them in that position? In view of the time they spend preparing for meetings and the amount of compensation that some receive, can board members realistically be expected to tackle all the complex issues that need to be addressed in the period of time that is allotted? In theory, they can ask for more time for meetings, and occasionally they do, but because of who they are, they are likely to have other pressing matters. Do they put those matters on the back burner?

Who really monitors the boards? Who assesses their performance? Who checks to see if they are managing properly? These questions need to be answered before there are crises in organizations. Monitoring and checking should take place before crises set in. The media has been able to penetrate almost every aspect of life, including the public and private behaviors of individuals. Yet, when it comes to corporate boardrooms, the press has not been able to penetrate its walls until a crisis arises. This is not to advocate that the media be allowed in the boardroom but rather to point out that there is lack of monitoring of the board. In *The Corporate Board*, the authors state:

> In the newspapers, in business circles, and on the cocktail circuit, board failures and scandals elicit scorn, anger, and some righteous indignation. "Sadly," John Harvey-Jones writes, "it is perfectly possible for boards of directors to meet regularly and never discuss any creative business at all." Yet, by and large, few people focus on board performance, or board effectiveness, until there is a crisis.[4]

Commenting on the lack of media scrutiny of the boardroom, one manager said: "Perhaps, there is an easy answer for that. Maybe the media knows that nothing of importance is being discussed or is taking place at those board meetings!" That is a frightening thought, but, unfortunately, there may be some truth in this comment.

Can boards that meet infrequently and for short periods of time realistically be expected to manage the affairs of organizations with so many complex problems? The answer is clear—they often cannot. In essence, they become reactive and less proactive. Is that enough? Are they properly meeting their legal responsibility? Generally, no. Can they do more? Yes, given the opportunity, but that opportunity often is not available under the present structure. What happens in most instances is that the board delegates most of its functions to the executive management group.

Writing about the showdown, that is, his firing, at Ford Motor Company, Lee Iacocca states in his autobiography:

> But what about the board? These guys were the illustrious guardians of the Ford Motor Company. They were supposed to constitute the system of checks and balances to prevent the flagrant abuse of power by top management. But it seemed to me their attitude was: "As long as we're taken care of, we'll follow the leader."
>
> When Henry ordered the board to choose between himself and me, why did they let him fire the guy they had such great faith in? They may not have been able to prevent it, but at least some of them could have resigned in protest. Nobody did. Not one person said: "This is a disgrace. This guy is making us a couple of billion a year and you're firing him? Then, I'm leaving too."[5]

It is important to defend what is right—what is needed for the company to prosper. There must be a view from the top, but the view must be clear, honest, and impeccable. The board has to be both knowledgeable and wise. Dr. Jonas Salk said, "I am a perennial optimist. We certainly have the knowledge. The question is whether we have the wisdom." The CEO cannot be allowed to take over and dictate what the board should do. President Clinton said, "The well connected and the well protected can work the system."

What about the makeup of the board? Are the right people on the board? Are all stakeholders properly represented? Should they be? For example, should employees who belong to the union be represented on the board? Should the president of the union be on the board? Wouldn't the board benefit from his or her views? Addressing this matter, Lee Iacocca writes:

> Even before the union had made any concession, I invited Doug Fraser to sit on our board of directors. Despite what the press has reported, Fraser's appointment was not part of a package deal with the union.
>
> ...It's true that the union had been asking for labor representation on the board for many years. But it had become a kind of ritual. I don't think they ever expected to get it. I put Doug Fraser on our board because I knew he could make a special contribution. He's smart, he's politically savvy, and he says what he thinks.
>
> ...When I brought Doug Fraser onto the board, the business community went wild. They said: "You can't do that! You're putting the fox into the henhouse. You've lost your mind."
>
> I said: "Wait a minute. Why is it all right to have bankers on the board when you owe them millions, but not a worker? Why is it all right to have suppliers on the board? Isn't that a conflict of interest?"
>
> Until then no representative of labor had ever sat on the board of a major American corporation. But it is pretty standard in Europe. And in Japan they do it all the time. So what's the problem? It's that the average American CEO is a prisoner of ideology. He wants to be pure. He still believes that labor has to be the natural, mortal enemy of the manager....
>
> It wasn't only management types who opposed the Fraser move. Plenty of union guys were against it, too. They were afraid that Fraser's being on the board might compromise their leadership's ability to extract the last drop of blood out of the turnip. All their lives they've had the attitude of get all you can because management will never do anything for the good of the worker unless it's extracted with violence or bloodshed.
>
> For this kind of thinking to change, you need to have reasonable men who can discuss the concept of sharing profits only when we have some to share and wage increases when we have improved productivity. Maybe that's a concept whose time has not yet come. But it will have to come, because if we continue to slug it out and fight each other for a bigger piece of the pie when all the while that pie is getting smaller, the Japanese will continue to have us for lunch.
>
> When I was at Ford, labor and management saw each other only every three years when it came time to negotiate a new contract.

And every three years you'd walk into the room with a chip on your shoulder. You wouldn't know the guy and you'd immediately think: "I don't like him, he's the enemy." It's like meeting at a bridge and trading spies. You hate the other side, even though the exchange is a good thing.[6]

Other countries, such as Germany, have allowed the practice of employee representation on the board. In the United States, however, that practice is seldom followed. Even though workers own a majority of stock in 1,000 to 1,500 companies, union and non-union employee representatives sit on boards in only about 250, mainly small, companies.

In addition to the above-mentioned potential shortcomings of boards, the presence of certain individuals on the board of directors raises the issue of conflict of interest. Whether the conflict is real or imagined may not be clear in some instances. What is clear, however, is that it has the potential to cause corporate harm. The conflict may arise from several fronts or relationships. For example, a director or his or her company may also be acting as a consultant to the company. The New York Stock Exchange does not consider directors to be independent if they simultaneously act as advisors, consultants, or lawyers for a company on an ongoing basis.[7] Yet many organizations pay no attention to that. Responding to the growing debate regarding the role of directors, American Express has become one of the first major corporations to prohibit board members from acting as consultants for the company.

Forcing such action is not easy. Individual stockholders do not own enough stock to have the necessary clout. It usually takes large institutional holders to exert enough pressure to change the makeup of the board. This type of pressure does bring results, as evidenced by the resignation of a number of directors from W.R. Grace. The effect, however, of such pressure on the overall health of the organization is not always clear.

The good news is that the trend appears to be that companies are adding more directors from outside the organization. The bad news is that the majority of organizations still have a long way to go. Many are not meeting the standards proposed by those (i.e., the American Law Institute) who advocate that all corporations be required to have outside directors form a majority of the membership of their boards of directors. The Teachers Insurance & Annuity Association's College Retirement Equities Fund recommends not only that boards be made up of a majority of independent directors but that key committees have only unaffiliated "outsiders." Some argue loudly that there are no "real watchdogs" in this area. The regulators and the regulations are minimal at best. For example, the Securities and Exchange Commission requires corporations whose stock is listed on the New York Stock Exchange to have at least two outside directors. How effective is that? Are two outsiders sufficient? What about family ties, business links, and long-standing friendships? What about corporations whose boards consist of a significant number of current or former executives? Is it proper for the CEO or its vice chairman to sit on the board's nominating committee? It is proper for directors to sit on five or even ten boards? Do they have the time and the proper expertise to do the right job on all of the boards they sit?

The message that is being sent should be carefully scrutinized. The public, at least in theory if not in reality, is given legal assurance that corporations are being managed by their boards of directors. Consequently, the public, primarily the individual stockholders and creditors and not necessarily the institutional stockholders or creditors, perceives the board as a sophisticated group of individuals whose primary focus and responsibility are the organization. They see the board's mission as assuring the success of the organization and assume that board members will devote the necessary time to accomplish that mission. They feel that nothing less is acceptable. But is that what is happening? It is obvious what a good director can do for an organization if he or she asks the right questions and gives the proper advice.

Consider what happened when the CEO of a utility company went before a rate commission and asked for a rate increase. To justify the increase, he presented certain facts that he felt were relevant. Based on the presentation and relying on the perceived integrity of the CEO, the commission was prepared to grant the increase without asking the appropriate management questions: Was there a real need in the company for the current twenty vice presidents? Did the company really need all the employees and/or equipment that it had? If not, were those numbers included in the facts presented to justify the rate increase? Misconception is exactly what happens in many cases if we simply rely on the person presenting the facts instead of delving into the facts. The question is: What facts? The answer is: Anything short of all the pertinent facts is unacceptable. Sir Arthur Doyle is quoted as saying: "It is capital to theorize before one has data." In other words, one begins to trust facts to suit theories instead of theories to suit facts. Directors need all the relevant and necessary facts to make the right decisions in matters that affect the future of the organization. In addition to having all the facts, they must analyze them and properly understand them. That is the only way they can make proper decisions. That is their responsibility. It is what they are being paid to do. Many stakeholders rely on them, and it is their responsibility to find ways to improve their performance. For if they don't, someone else will! (For an example of a compensation package for directors, see Appendix 2.)

Public Director—Is It Time for One?

Some argue that corporations exist to serve society, and society should, therefore, be represented on boards of directors. Consequently, at least one board member should be selected by some group other than the stockholders. Such a suggestion was advanced by Robert Townsend, former chairman of Avis Rent A Car, in *Up the Organization*.[8] Should a public director be a requirement? Would it help or harm corporations? This concern was posed to the panel.

Corporations should be required to have a "public director"
(to be selected by some group other than the stockholders) on their boards.

Survey Panel	Disagree Strongly	Disagree	Neither Agree Nor Disagree	Agree	Agree Strongly
University business deans	19%	28%	23%	24%	6%
University business professors	20%	33%	16%	26%	5%
CEOs	69%	13%	0%	12%	6%
Union presidents	0%	11%	33%	45%	11%
Business news editors	0%	38%	46%	8%	8%

Do we need at least one public overseer on each board of directors? What positive and negative outcomes might result from taking such action?

Roadblocks to Removing Incompetents: Paralysis Through Analysis Syndrome— The Legal Hurdle, The Political Hurdle

What happens if the CEO and/or chairman of the board does not meet the demands of the organization? What if the person in charge is not the right person for the organization? In theory, the answer should be simple. Most of them do not have long-term contracts, so they can be removed at will. The problem arises when the CEO resists the ouster. If the CEO does not voluntarily leave, the organization is faced with a practical rather than a legal question. The CEO's friends are probably on the board, many because the CEO helped put them there. Is the controversy that results when the CEO is ousted worth it to them? What about their careers? What happens to those who vote to oust the CEO? Will they be vulnerable to repercussions from their own boards, which are comprised of other CEOs? Often, the practical problems and obstacles faced by those who are asked to replace the CEO are more difficult than the legal issues. If not for these obstacles, how many CEOs would have been replaced in the last five years?

This, of course, is not to minimize the legal implications, which are time consuming and expensive. Many contracts with CEOs, even though they contain provisions for removal of the CEO under certain conditions, are tied to monetary costs that make them practically unenforceable. The threat (perceived or real) of being removed by the court generally results in a CEO's "resignation." It really hurts a corporation when the CEO is removed. An additional consideration is where the ousted CEO ends up. Will he or she be hired by a competitor? If so, what are the potential consequences for the corporation? If removal of a CEO is necessary, how will the board members view their role in such a situation? What are their roles, both in theory and in reality?

One CEO is of the opinion that the board serves only in an advisory capacity. And that's precisely how he used his board. He felt that he could accept or reject the board's advice. He summed it up by stating, "The board chooses the president and then supports the hell out of him." Should a board support a CEO who is not doing a good job? Is the board being disloyal if it fails to support the CEO to the end? Does the CEO's lack of accountability become a serious managerial sin? Where does the CEO's accountability begin? Many would argue that, if presently there is any accountability by CEOs, it begins not with the directors but rather with the investors (stockholders). Stockholders are finally speaking out because of the poor performance record of some companies. If that is true, and there is plenty of evidence to support such an assertion, then can we really say that a corporation and its CEO are only as strong as the board of directors?

Stockholder revolts and concerns on the part of the general public regarding accountability of boards and CEOs in general serve as a band-aid. They are at best reactive actions rather than a proactive management approach. They are problem driven rather than vision led. It is time to rethink our current ways of managing organizations. We need to get down to basics. It is time to make some tough decisions that may change the way organizations are being operated and put them on the right course for the future. The board structure may have served organizations well in the past, but times are rapidly changing, and it is important that organizations position themselves to keep up. Anything less is asking for trouble—big trouble. It puts an organization at risk, perhaps even leading to its demise. CEOs will be presiding over the downfall, especially those who don't jump ship right before the boat sinks. Some may do just that, and some may even try to sell off or merge their organizations while negotiating a "sweetheart deal" for themselves. That certainly sounds like a fatal managerial sin.

The Test of Fairness—Managerial Compensation Packages: How Much Is Too Much?

The preceding discussion demonstrates that accountability in the corporate sector is not what it should be. Consequently, when accountability is missing, it is easier for many CEOs to focus more on themselves than on their organizations. A natural area on which to focus is compensation for their services. Let's begin the discussion regarding this area by examining the responses of our panel of experts regarding CEO compensation.

The relation of managerial compensation packages to the compensation for the rest of the employees in the organization can be described as "equitable."

Survey Panel	Disagree Strongly	Disagree	Neither Agree Nor Disagree	Agree	Agree Strongly
University business deans	30%	47%	10%	12%	1%
University business professors	30%	48%	11%	7%	4%
CEOs	12%	13%	19%	56%	0%
Union presidents	78%	22%	0%	0%	0%
Business news editors	31%	31%	15%	23%	0%

The responses are not too encouraging. Except for the CEOs, the panel's responses clearly indicate that compensation in corporations is far from equitable. What are corporations doing to remedy such inequities? What are stockholders doing about the perceived and/or real inequities? What should they be doing? Is this issue over- or underplayed by the press? Is there just a lot of talk and very little action? Do the stockholders and creditors just talk the talk, or do they walk the walk? In order to gain a more in-depth understanding of this issue, the panel was asked an open-ended question. "Generally, do you feel that managers' compensation packages are out of line?"

University business deans:

- Too high.
- Yes, chief/senior executives are paid too much because there is little accountability.
- Middle, no; top, yes.
- Yes. It's disgraceful that we lead the world in the ratio of CEO to lowest worker's compensation.
- Compensation that is five to six times more than average employee wages is "obscene."
- Yes. Travelers, Pratt/Whitney, for example, are outrageous.
- Too high in relation to their subordinates.
- Yes, see no reason for pay above $1 million a year.
- No. The market sets the salaries—most CEOs make less than mediocre professional athletes.
- Their value is determined by the market.
- Yes. Managers deserve more than labor but the differential has gotten way out of line compared to their real worth and contribution.
- In some cases it is not only high, it is obscene. How can some of these people justify their salary and fight against the minimum wage? Do they have any idea what an employee earns, if he gets the minimum wage? Do they ever think how these employees pay their bills? Do they really care?

University business professors:

- Out of line with what? They take a lot of risk and incur a lot of stress. This deserves good compensation.
- When one compares their pay with the pay of the U.S. president and other employees in their organization, it is easy to see the inequity.
- No, we live and operate in a capitalistic economy/social system. Let managers be compensated based on their perceived worth.
- Way out of line. Too many managers of firms that are doing poorly are being rewarded handsomely.
- Many are underpaid.

- Only for top management.
- Yes, the amounts have altered the framework of organizations.
- No, it is a function of supply and demand, with shareholders' oversight.
- No. There are some excesses—but reward for creating profits is central to a free market.

CEOs and chairmen of boards:

- Yes. Many are too high.
- No.
- Yes, there should be a requirement for personal investment, not options.
- CEOs yes, managers generally not.
- They are at and near the top.

Union presidents:

- No, only CEOs.
- Yes.
- Very much so. It is vulgar.

Business news editors:

- Yes.
- No, except at the top.
- Not if their organizations succeed.
- Absolutely.
- No, greater responsibility demands greater compensation.

There is a continuing uproar over pay packages for top executives in American corporations. Is their compensation equitable? Can it be justified? Is there evidence that huge bonuses and other financial incentives motivate top executives to do better work? Are top executives compensated in ways that serve the best long-term interest of business? Are executives who are paid millions of dollars robbing their organizations of the wealth that should be shared with the workers and other stakeholders or recycled back into the company for future investment and expansion?

The prevailing question regarding compensation is: How much is too much? Is the gap between pay for the CEO and pay for others in the organization widening? How much do CEOs really make? What should CEOs make? Should there be a cap on how much they can make? What is a CEO worth—35 times the salary of the average worker in the corporation? A thousand times? Do managers distribute corporate profits equitably? Are managerial compensation packages in line with compensation packages for the rest of the organization's stakeholders? Is there something wrong with the principle that the wealth of an organization should be proportionately shared and enjoyed by those who helped create it? Are corporations really paying CEOs for performance? If not, what are they being paid for? Are CEOs measuring up to their pay? What about golden parachutes? What about coffin parachutes? Is determining the CEO's pay the responsibility of the board? Are boards properly structured and equipped to make such decisions?

How much compensation is too much for a CEO? A number of years ago, a million dollars a year seemed unimaginable. Then $10 million. Then $50 million plus a bonus. Then $100 million. It has been predicted that by the year 2001, there will be a CEO whose total compensation package for one year will be $1 billion plus. Odds are, this prediction will become a reality.

Compensation for American executives seems to be heading out of control. The effects of these soaring levels of pay on the various stakeholders of corporations can no longer be ignored. And as Joani Nelson Hochler, the author of "What's Your Boss Worth? 35 Times Your Salary? 1,000 Times? The Work Force Gets Angry," writes:

> And it's by no means just union leaders and "leftists" who are angry about soaring executive pay. The fury has gone mainstream: Increasingly, it's coming from middle managers, mid- and small-sized company managers, compensation and productivity experts, front-line workers, even stockholders. It's coming from capitalistic and patriotic folks who basically believe in the American dream, but who have come to feel that executives betray their loyalty and trust by gobbling up increasingly bigger and juicier shares of the American pie.
>
> The ever-widening gap between CEOs and their workers is causing resentment and the loss of a true middle class. We've become a nation of industrial slaves, and the CEOs are the masters of the plantation.
>
> The average CEO of a large U.S. company makes 35 times (and, in several cases, 1,000 times) as much as the average U.S. manufacturing employee. In Japan the ratio is only 15 to 1 and in Europe 20 to 1.
>
> In Japan the average CEO of a large firm makes about $352,000 in pay, benefits, and perks. Compare this with the mind-boggling

figures recently revealed in U.S. proxy statements. Total 1989 re-muneration—including salary, bonus, stock options, restricted shares and other long-term incentive opportunities—of the average CEO in one of the nation's 100 largest companies rose 20 percent in 1989 to a staggering $3.3 million. The average CEO in these firms took home in base salary and bonuses alone $1.4 million, up 11 percent from 1988.

The pay issue is "a terribly important problem in a global economy where our own productivity is so severely marred." In much the same way that companies' environmental awareness has become a criterion for consumer purchases, people will increasingly buy a particular product based on whether they believe the manufacturer's work force is happy.

For example, the 1982 and 1984 flaps over G.M.'s executives taking millions in bonuses for themselves after winning billions in union concessions "persuaded many people never to buy a GM car again. They saw a company, whose workers were so ticked off that they were going to produce lousy cars."[9]

Another author, Graef S. Crystal, opines:

…As a believer in a free market, how can I criticize a CEO's pay package, no matter how large it is, provided it was forged in arm's length negotiations between him and his board?

But when I look at how much other valuable employees of the corporation get paid for their work, and at the compensation scales for top executives in other countries, how can I not find fault with the amounts some CEOs are earning?

In a recent study of British executive compensation scales, I found that the typical American company pays its CEO two and a half times more in salary and bonus than he would have earned in the U.K. Were stock options and restricted stock considered as well, the gap could widen to five times or more.[10]

According to a *Business Week* editorial entitled "Executive Pay: It Doesn't Add Up":

The figures for executive pay are simply astonishing. The average CEO in Business Week's 43rd annual compensation survey pulled down a record $3.8 million in 1992, up more than 50% from last year. To get into 1992's Top 10 a chief executive had to make more that $22.8 million. For all the talk of boards of directors cracking down on excesses, for all the prodding of activist shareholders, for all the disclosure rules passed by the Securities & Exchange Commission, CEO pay continues to climb to ridiculous heights. Just how many tens of millions of dollars are needed to motivate CEOs to do their jobs properly?...

The issue, of course, isn't simply the stratospheric numbers but the linkage of pay to performance. Many CEOs deliver great value to their shareholders. But many others fall short—very short. A few continue to take home huge sums while their companies decline. More often, CEOs can point to a decent rise in return on equity, but the growth in their own pay far exceeds their company's performance.

What is troubling is the disparity between CEO pay and what everyone else in the country earns for their work. At a time when the incomes of 90% of corporate employees are barely growing as work loads get heavier every day and job security is a constant concern, these multi million-dollar windfalls are more than unseemly: They are arrogant. They imply that no one else but the CEO is responsible for the good performance of the company—not the team of workers, the salespeople, the managers, or the support staff. It is insulting to workers who are told they are critical members of a team only to see one individual walk away with a disproportionate share of the rewards.

The gap between the executive suite and the shop has widened to the point where the average American CEO makes an incredible 157 times what a factory worker gets and 66 times what an engineer takes home. And the gap has been getting progressively worse. Back in 1960, when U.S. economic power was at its height, CEOs pulled down an average $190,000. That was 41 times a factory worker's average income and only 19 times what an engineer made....

If corporate America doesn't show some restraint on executive compensation, a populist wave may soon push politicians to take a crack at it.[11]

The authors of another study, Harrison Rainie with Margaret Loftus and Mark Dadden, state:

A new study for *U.S. News* by compensation expert Graef Crystal of the 500 biggest firms in the country shows that the average CEO's compensation package of salary, bonuses and stock grants was $4.06 million in 1995, up 16 percent from 1994. That's 197 times higher than the salary of the average American worker in 1995, which grew just 2.8 percent as corporate profits rose 14.8 percent. The CEO-to-worker differential was 41 to 1 between 1973 and 1975.

Especially galling is the fact that these pay scales are not based on a rational market, compared with, say, big-league baseball, where logic usually prevails: the best pitchers and hitters command the highest salaries. Instead, Crystal found that pay varied so wildly from firm to firm that over 70 percent of the differences in CEO pay are unexplainable—they bear no relation to the rationality of markets. Top performers often had low pay, while lesser performers sometimes had Croesus-level compensation. "Most of it is simple piggery; they grabbed what they could." Crystal says, "Generally, with some very honorable exceptions, these guys have no shame."[12]

To highlight this, in November 1996, citing delivery improvements and a year-end profit, the U.S. Postal Service announced that it would award bonuses to some 63,000 workers. So far so good! But the bonuses will average $12,500 for executives, $3,900 for large facility supervisors and postmasters, and $1,600 for administrative workers and supervisors. The total planned is $169 million. Are we forgetting anyone? What provision has been made for the other employees? Should they receive something—a little bonus? Were any of the improvements and the resulting profit attributable to them?

To complicate and frustrate the discussion, we read articles whose titles read: "Coke's Chairman Defends $86 Million Pay and Bonus,"[13] "Kodak's CEO Got $1.7 Million Bonus in 1994 Despite Below-Target Profit,"[14] "Ford Chairman's '94 Pay Doubled to $8 Million,"[15] "GM President Collects Cool $6.1 Million,"[16] "Raise the Minimum Wage: How Can Anyone Oppose It?...How Can a Family Live on That? A Family Can't,"[17] and "Ben & Jerry's Debates Cap."[18] These articles add fuel to the already heated discussion, which, obviously, does not boost the popularity of CEOs. Included in such conversation is Disney CEO Michael Eisner's 1993 profit of more than $127 million after exercising stock options. How does that compare with an employee who makes minimum wage? How does it compare with the salary of the president of the United States—the person whose responsibility and power are awesome, to say the least. How is such an amount perceived by the employees in that or in other organizations? Eisner may have done a lot for Disney, such as creating wealth for stockholders, but was the contribution by other employees minimal? To add insult to injury, while CEOs are receiving huge increases, the average employee's "bonus" is in the form of a reduction in benefits because corporations have to watch the bottom line. Furthermore, we shouldn't overlook the total severance package of over $90 million to Michael Ovitz, who had been with Disney for less than two years. One asks: Who are the winners and who are the losers here? Need we say more?

In an article entitled "Executive Severance Agreements: Benefit or Burglary?"[19] the authors state:

> While executive compensation in general has been subject of critical attention—executive severance agreements continue to have the potential to be far more embarrassing for America at large, the specific corporation, and any executive involved....
>
> ...excesses...are not common to all corporations. A key issue, however, is the large exposure through media attention that is often attendant to such incidents. As Peter Drucker stated in the slightly different context of those few with unusually large executive compensation packages: "Its members are highly visible. And they offend the sense of justice of many, indeed of the majority of management people themselves."
>
> ...Thomas M. Wyman, former chairman of CBS, received a severance payment of $11.4 million. Michael Vailland, chairman of Schlumberger, received $6.2 million; John R. Miller, president of Standard Oil, collected $5.6 million on his departure. Each of these separations has a troubling aspect in common: Each was either "ousted by the board," "resigned under pressure" or "was forced to resign"...
>
> After a headline-generating sequence of events, Frank Lorenzo received $30.5 million for his departure from Eastern Airlines. Notably, the common stock of Eastern held by Lorenzo at the time was valued at less than $5 a share. Even so, Mr. Lorenzo's departure package requested a payment of $14 per share. While Lorenzo's severance package was contentious, one director noted that "the scheme was the only way to get Lorenzo out."
>
> In a similar incident, Robert A. Schoellhorn, long-time CEO and chairman of Abbott Laboratories, was essentially relieved of command by his board. Mr. Schoellhorn's severance package was estimated to have been between $4.8 and $10.6 million. Abbott's board of directors "had hoped that Schoellhorn would agree to retire as chairman and as director if he got a generous send-off...."

Given these examples, it is not surprising that criticism for such separation payments has been unrelenting: Big exit packages often mean management gets "rewarded for failure." That's very hard to swallow...It's pure greed.

...American bosses are rarely fired when they manage badly but are usually give golden handshakes..."So, even though the corporation may stall or crash, the chief executive is equipped with his golden parachute and is thereby guaranteed to land safely and comfortably."[20]

As stated in a May 1997 article entitled "CEOs are Rewarded Despite Layoffs":

Chief executives of big companies are continually being rewarded with fat compensation for laying off more employees, according to a study...and apparently even some CEOs think it's outrageous practice.

The Institute of Policy Studies, a liberal research group, said it has found the same trend for four consecutive years: Wall Street rewards CEOs for making layoffs by pushing up stock prices, which are the basis for the biggest component of CEO compensation—stock options. The new survey, done with Boston-based United for a Fair Economy, found that pay for CEOs at the 30 corporations with the biggest layoffs last year rose an average 67.3 percent—compared with 54 percent for CEOs at the top 365 American corporations.

"Such excessive pay should garner even less respect when the beneficiary is a leading job-slasher," the study said.

More surprisingly, CEOs apparently agree.

A new Business Week Harris poll shows that top executives at the nation's largest corporations believe the current executive pay system is out of control.

Almost half the 400 senior executives surveyed said they think CEO pay at big companies has surpassed acceptable limits. Fifty-six percent said top managers should take salary cuts if their companies post poor results—and 88 percent said those managers should lose all or most of their bonuses. Among what the Institute for Policy Studies dubbed the "layoff leaders" and their total direct compensation—including salary, bonus and long-term compensation—in 1996 were:

- Lockheed Martin CEO Norman Augustine: $23 million, 3,100 layoffs...
- Allied Signal Inc. CEO Lawrence Bossidy: $11.8 million, 3,250 layoffs...

The study said 459,000 U.S. workers were laid off in the last three months of 1996, a 2 percent increase from the same period a year earlier.[22]

Spread Wealth Wide and Deep: Salaries of the CEO and the Employees

If the top people in the organization need a bonus to motivate them to perform, isn't it logical to assume that employees at other levels of the organization need the same to motivate them to become more productive?

A Yankelovich poll asked Japanese and American workers whether they would benefit if their company did well. While 93% of Japanese workers said they would, only 9% of Americans said they would. Why? Because the average semi-annual profit distribution bonus for a Japanese employee (of a large export-oriented firm) is 25% of his or her paycheck, and in slightly above-average years it runs 40%. In the United States, where Procter & Gamble introduced the profit/bonus distribution program 100 years ago, less than 20% of the work force is part of such a program.[21] Let's look at what our panel had to say about organizations sharing their wealth.

The wealth of the organization should be
proportionately shared and enjoyed by those who have helped make it happen.

Survey Panel	Disagree Strongly	Disagree	Neither Agree Nor Disagree	Agree	Agree Strongly
University business deans	4%	15%	15%	50%	16%
University business professors	2%	9%	13%	61%	15%
CEOs	0%	13%	25%	56%	6%
Union presidents	0%	0%	0%	44%	56%
Business news editors	0%	23%	0%	62%	15%

Why shouldn't raises be given proportionally to all those who contributed to the success of the organization? That does not mean that everyone should receive equal pay, but it does mean that employees should receive bonuses proportionate to their contribution. The greater an employee's input toward achieving the organization's profit, the greater the bonus he or she should receive.

There is no compelling reason why an organization should give big raises in a year when it makes a big profit. That can even be counterproductive. What would happen if the organization makes very little profit or has a loss the next year? Should the organization reduce salaries? A better approach would be to give a cost of living increase and anything over that as a bonus. If the organization does well the next year, the same scenario can be repeated. If, on the other hand, the organization has low profits or negative earnings, no bonuses are given. Doesn't it make sense to tie increases to performance?

Thomas J. Watson, Jr., former chairman of IBM, writes in *Father, Son and Co.*:

> When I joined IBM many years later, the company was famous for high pay, generous benefits, and the intense devotion of the employees to Dad. But back at the beginning, when there was hardly any money, Dad gained their loyalty with words.
>
> My father loved to recall his and Flint's [Charles R. Flint, the founder of what was to become IBM. In those days Flint was known as the hottest financier on Wall Street] discussion of compensation on the day Flint offered him the job. He said to Flint, "I want a gentleman's salary, so that I can support my family. And I want a percentage of the profits that remain after the stockholders get their dividends." Flint went right to the heart of it and said, "I understand. You want a peck of the corn you harvest." When Flint presented this arrangement to the other directors, they were incredulous because it was hard to imagine that there would ever be surplus profits to divvy up. But by the time I was in college, a version of the formula they agreed to would make Dad the highest paid man in America.[23]

In an article on compensation, Michael A. Verespej writes:

> The traditional pay system ignores the productivity, efficiency, and value that workers add to the organization and flies in the face of empowerment as well.
>
> It's time for business to throw out the old way of paying people and find new ways to compensate workers and new yardsticks to measure their performance.

It's not just the CEO compensation system that's broken. That generates the most attention because U.S. CEOs earn nearly twice as much as their counterparts worldwide. But there are just as many—if not more—inequities in the worker and management ranks.

The current hierarchical approach to compensation, in which the preponderance of pay is sucked up by people at the top, makes it hard to pay the workers at the bottom who actually make the product or provide the customer service...

...We need CEOs to have the philosophy that until I pay my people a just pay, I shouldn't be paid myself...

...Intellectually, companies mean it when they talk about empowering workers. But, in practice, it is hard for them to accept the second half of the empowerment equation—which is the concept of paying them more.

Why? There is no real way for companies to quantify human resources—workers as assets—so workers come up as an expense on the balance sheet.[24]

The members of the panel were asked the following question: "Should a manager's compensation package have a direct relation to the average wage earned by other employees (e.g., X times the average wage of the lowest paid employee in the organization)?" Here are some of the responses:

University business deans:

- The relationship should be primarily based proportionately on each person's contribution toward the wealth of the organization.
- Wages should have a real relationship to performance. Artificial relationships should be avoided.
- Yes. Some proportionally based on productivity.
- Not direct, but there should be a balance, a reasonableness.
- It would appear only reasonable to expect some relationship.
- There should be some relationship.
- That is the Japanese tradition. The U.S. tradition is to let the market determine the package in most cases.
- Yes, and it should be in line with the rest of the world.
- I would prefer it this way if I were the leader.
- Not a bad benchmark but best approach is to link net present value added to organization.
- Not a bad idea.

- Good place to start.
- Not necessarily—but something other than the excesses we witness is needed.
- Yes, a smaller multiple from top to bottom would be beneficial.
- Yes. Some figure such as a range of 25 to 40 times average wage.
- Would be a useful gauge.
- No. It didn't work at Ben & Jerry's after the company reached the $150 million earnings level.
- No, this would be too destructive.
- In a general sense, yes.
- No, linked to performance of company but with a cap.
- Good idea worth considering.
- This is a good guideline.

University business professors:

- I think a valid case can be made for such a viewpoint.
- Absolutely not! That's a crazy idea because the value to the organization cannot be measured that way.
- Yes, in general, while recognizing that in Europe and Japan, culture, tax laws, etc. dictate lower CEO salaries.
- Yes, should not be allowed to get out of proportion.
- No, it should be based on "general" performance of the overall organization.
- No way...Ben & Jerry's is having trouble with this.
- In general, yes.
- No, it should be tied to production and contribution.
- That might be a start or perhaps a limit. But primarily it should be a reflection of how well the firm does.
- Yes, but it should not be required.
- Yes, but not by a strict formula, but rather in terms of reasonableness.
- That has some appeal—but there should definitely be a relationship between compensation package, managerial performance and organizational success.
- That is another example of the "flavor of the month" consultant axioms. There should be a relationship which is fair.
- Some relationship would be helpful.
- No. Different skills and requirements. It's like comparing apples to oranges.

- Employees' annual compensation should definitely have some relationship to the annual net profit/wealth of the organization.

CEOs and chairmen of the board:

- No. This is an overintellectualized argument which has no relationship to productivity and accountability.
- Base pay should. Incentive pay should not.
- No. Compensation should track with value. In this regard, there are no significant "caps."
- Maybe not lowest but some relation to the median plus long-term performance requirement.

Union presidents:

- Yes.
- Perhaps profit instead.

Business news editors:

- No, he/she makes risky decisions that could affect job stability and should be rewarded.
- Compensation should be in line with what others are making— not the outrageous sums paid to some of the bigger corporate bosses.

What is the real purpose of golden parachutes? Who is intended to benefit from them? Who actually benefits from them? The panel was asked to respond to the following statement:

In actuality "golden parachutes" are generally designed for the benefit of managers rather than for their organizations.

Survey Panel	Disagree Strongly	Disagree	Neither Agree Nor Disagree	Agree	Agree Strongly
University business deans	0%	6%	9%	53%	32%
University business professors	2%	4%	5%	53%	36%
CEOs	0%	25%	0%	69%	6%
Union presidents	0%	0%	11%	22%	67%
Business news editors	0%	0%	15%	39%	46%

Again, the responses clearly demonstrate that, at least in the panel's opinion, managers, with the consent of the board of directors, are more interested in their own welfare than in the overall interest of the organization. So, what is the answer? Should the practice of giving golden parachutes be stopped? In the long run, would the organizational interest be better served with or without golden parachutes?

Capping the CEO's Salary

It has been argued that there should be a "cap" on the CEO's compensation. Some claim that a cap would help the corporation, the stakeholders, and would help keep the CEO's compensation in line with that of other employees. It would also help keep the CEO from committing the managerial sin of lack of accountability. Can organizations realistically predict the worth of the CEO to the organization? Do organizations pay the person in the position or do they pay for the position regardless of who occupies it? There is, of course, a precedent for a cap; there is a cap, as well as a minimum (which happen to be one and the same) for the salary for the president of the United States, and there are caps for the salaries of the governors. Are we better served because of these caps? Here are the responses of the panel to the following statement:

There should be a "cap" on managers' compensation.

Survey Panel	Disagree Strongly	Disagree	Neither Agree Nor Disagree	Agree	Agree Strongly
University business deans	16%	38%	12%	19%	15%
University business professors	27%	33%	7%	24%	9%
CEOs	44%	44%	6%	6%	0%
Union presidents	0%	11%	0%	33%	56%
Business news editors	0%	54%	16%	15%	15%

Caps are troublesome. How do we set them in advance? Would there be exceptions? If the people making compensation decisions are honest, equitable, conscientious, and visionaries, the task may be better managed by them; we can rely on their better judgment. However, the argument that caps are accountability measures also needs to be examined. While there are some merits associated with salary caps, there are also some drawbacks.

The CEO's Annual Press Conference

In our quest to get a better understanding of the CEO's role in the organization, several related statements were posed to the panel for their response. Here is how the panel responded to the following statement:

Chief executive officers should be required to hold annual "press conferences."

Survey Panel	Disagree Strongly	Disagree	Neither Agree Nor Disagree	Agree	Agree Strongly
University business deans	11%	43%	24%	20%	2%
University business professors	5%	39%	24%	30%	2%
CEOs	25%	19%	19%	37%	0%
Union presidents	0%	11%	34%	33%	22%
Business news editors	8%	39%	15%	38%	0%

The idea of the CEO's press conference was advanced by Robert Townsend in *Up the Organization*.[25] The question that needs to be asked is whether press conferences help or hinder organizations and their stakeholders. What is the real reason for having press conferences? Society has some interest in organizations. Corporations exist because society sanctions their existence. That being the case, shouldn't society have the right to ask those in charge what is going on in their organizations? How useful are press conferences held by governors or the president of the United States? Confidentiality may be an issue, but it can be handled similarly as other (i.e., governors) have handled the issue. Governors and presidents seem to handle the issue of confidentiality pretty well, and so could CEOs if they were required to hold an annual press conference. To some extent, they do that at shareholders' meetings. A press conference would be, in effect, an extension; instead of facing the stockholders, CEOs would be facing the media and the general public.

Limiting the CEO's Term in Office

Is limiting the term of office for the CEO a good or bad practice for the organization? There is much talk about term limits in the political arena. We limit the term in office of the president and most governors. Many people advocate term limits for legislators. Would that be productive? The panel was asked to comment on this issue.

Limiting the term in office for managers is a sound business strategy.

Survey Panel	Disagree Strongly	Disagree	Neither Agree Nor Disagree	Agree	Agree Strongly
University business deans	11%	58%	17%	13%	1%
University business professors	25%	43%	17%	11%	4%
CEOs	31%	44%	13%	12%	0%
Union presidents	11%	22%	45%	11%	11%
Business news editors	0%	31%	31%	31%	7%

The results aren't surprising, in view of public opinion on predetermined limits. An effective board could be capable of controlling the term of the CEO. However, that again raises the question whether boards of directors are effective. A related question is whether the board members' term in office should be limited.

Sabbaticals for Managers

An interesting issue is surfacing in the United States: Do employees view their priority of work and their personal responsibilities somewhat backwards? Do people live to work or work to live? Some would argue that we work our best years, and when we finally retire we are given a watch, which many can't even focus on! By that time, our children are grown, and we have missed the opportunity to spend time with them. The irony is that we could have had both. For example, what if we worked for six years and then were given six months off? Although this idea may seem somewhat unprecedented, it is only because of choice and not for any compelling reason. It can be done if we choose to do so. Some organizations are doing it. Such a practice is followed by many universities. The panel members were asked for their response.

Sabbaticals for managers should be a part of corporate policy.

Survey Panel	Disagree Strongly	Disagree	Neither Agree Nor Disagree	Agree	Agree Strongly
University business deans	3%	17%	14%	56%	10%
University business professors	4%	14%	14%	55%	13%
CEOs	6%	50%	25%	19%	0%
Union presidents	0%	11%	45%	22%	22%
Business news editors	8%	8%	15%	46%	23%

Sabbaticals can be a win–win situation. The employee benefits, and so does the organization in the long run. Sabbaticals can work as an accountability check. The person who fills in for the CEO when he or she is on sabbatical may be able to uncover any impropriety that may exist. Furthermore, the CEO can return reenergized and retooled, having had time to rethink and reflect on priorities. It would also give someone else the opportunity to gain experience in a different job. After all, what happens when the CEO gets sick? Is there someone who can replace him or her? A sabbatical may help answer that question.

Quarterly Raises—An Idea to Explore

Just before raises are announced, employees seem to get excited, reenergized, and more productive. The question, then, is why most organizations only give annual raises. Why not give quarterly raises? The primary justification seems to be that's the way it's always been done. Surely, that is not a compelling reason for not adopting such a policy. Past policies should be reviewed and continued if still appropriate, but they should not be continued just because they were used and were successful in the past. They should not continue to be used just because they have withstood the test of time. The past is history, and while we can learn from history, we should apply that knowledge to future decisions. Managers must have an eye to the future and make decisions that will properly position their organizations to meet the challenges of the future. While quarterly raises may be small, they would be given more often and can be supplemented by bonuses. Here is what the panel had to say about that:

I would favor "quarterly" raises for employees (similarly to the way quarterly dividends are paid) instead of the traditional yearly raises.

Survey Panel	Disagree Strongly	Disagree	Neither Agree Nor Disagree	Agree	Agree Strongly
University business deans	17%	35%	18%	27%	3%
University business professors	9%	47%	16%	24%	4%
CEOs	56%	38%	6%	0%	0%
Union presidents	11%	22%	22%	34%	11%
Business news editors	8%	23%	15%	46%	8%

Stockholders are paid quarterly dividends. Why not give employees quarterly raises? In order to pay dividends, the books need to be checked and balanced; consequently, the work to determine if raises are in order would be practically done. If employees get more excited and more productive just before raises are determined, quarterly raises would get employees excited and more productive not just once during the year but as many as four times.

Across-the-Board Raises—Are They Equitable and Effective?

Another issue that must be briefly addressed is across-the-board raises. Generally, salary increases in most organizations are given across the board. Employees are given a percentage increase instead of individualized increases. Many CEOs, backed by their human resource managers, try to justify that practice by viewing such a system as more equitable. But are across-the-board raises really more equitable? They may be easier to administer, but that does not mean they are more equitable? We asked our panel's opinion regarding this issue.

Across-the-board salary increases may be easy to administer but are *less effective* than individualized increases.

Survey Panel	Disagree Strongly	Disagree	Neither Agree Nor Disagree	Agree	Agree Strongly
University business deans	0%	4%	4%	55%	37%
University business professors	0%	5%	6%	42%	47%
CEOs	0%	0%	13%	37%	50%
Union presidents	22%	11%	23%	22%	22%
Business news editors	0%	0%	0%	92%	8%

In view of the responses, one would think corporations would be more responsive to such a dictate. However, that generally is not the case. The easier way seems to be preferred over the more effective way. Why would organizations maintain something that is less effective? Perhaps the answer is simple: it is much easier to administer and less controversial. It is less controversial because the CEO or human resources manager does not have to explain to an employee why he or she received less than a coworker, especially if the CEO or manager has not taken sufficient time to really know the employee's abilities and contribution to the organization. Is that fair? Is it good for the organization? Does it increase employee morale?

Summary

"Eternal vigilance," said John Philpot Curran, an Irish lawyer and statesman—a champion of Irish liberties, "is the price of liberty." CEOs must be accountable for their actions. There is no compromise here; nothing less than full accountability should be tolerated. Lack of accountability is definitely one of the seven fatal managerial sins. Failing to account for one's actions will sooner or later be brought to the attention of others in or outside of the organization. When lack of accountability is discovered, there will be repercussions. Some CEOs will exit their organizations voluntarily before they are discovered, while others will leave involuntarily. Some will get their just reward—their wages for their managerial sins, which could mean the end of their careers with their organizations.

A strong CEO should not need someone else to hold him or her accountable; a strong CEO should hold himself or herself accountable. Not only is it honorable to do so, the CEO is duty bound to do so. When the CEO holds himself or herself accountable, he or she, as well as the other stakeholders, win. When that is not the case, the CEO hurts himself or herself, the organization, and the other stakeholders. With all the other problems a CEO faces, he or she certainly can't afford to be self-destructive. A CEO should follow the first rule of winning in sports—don't beat yourself.

Notes

1. Linda Himelstein, Stephen Baker, Ronald Grover, and Robert D. Hof, "Board Rooms: The Ties That Bind?" *Business Week*, May 2, 1994, pp. 111–12.
2. John A. Byrne, "The Best and Worst Boards: Our New Report Card on Corporate Governance," *Business Week*, November 25, 1996, p. 82.
3. Ibid.
4. Ada Demb and Friedrich Newbauer, *The Corporate Board* (New York: Oxford University Press, 1992), p. 161; citing John Harvey-Jones, *Making It Happen* (London: Collins, 1988), p. 162.
5. Lee Iacocca and William Novak, *Iacocca: An Autobiography* (New York: Bantam Books, a division of Bantam Doubleday Publishing Group, Inc., 1984), p. 131.

6. Ibid., pp. 236–37.
7. Himelstein et al. (note 1), p. 113.
8. Robert Townsend, *Up the Organization* (New York: Knopf Publisher, 1970).
9. Joani Nelson-Horchler, "What's Your Boss Worth? 35 Times Your Salary? 1,000 Times? The Work Force Gets Angry," *Washington Post*, August 5, 1990; the article is excerpted from *Industry Week,* ©1990, Penton Publishing, Inc.
10. Graef S. Crystal, "At the Top: An Explosion of Pay Packages," *The New York Times Magazine (The Business World)*, December 3, 1989, p. 25.
11. Editorial, "Executive Pay: It Doesn't Add Up," *Business Week*, April 26, 1993, p. 122.
12. Harrison Rainie with Margaret Loftus and Mark Dadden, "The State of Greed," *U.S. News & World Report,* June 17, 1996, p. 63.
13. Jerry Schwartz, "Coke's Chairman Defends $86 Million Pay and Bonus," *The New York Times*, May 15, 1988, p. 4.
14. Wendy Bounds, "Kodak's CEO Got $1.7 Million Bonus in 1994 Despite Below Target Profit," *Wall Street Journal*, March 13, 1994, p. A6.
15. Oscar Suris, "Ford Chairman's '94 Pay Doubled to $8 Million," *Wall Street Journal*, April 7, 1995, p. A4.
16. "GM President Collects Cool $6.1 Million," *Quad-City Times*, April 11, 1995, p. 7A.
17. Michael Gartner, "Raise the Minimum Wage: How Can Anyone Oppose It? Wages of $4.25 an Hour Equal $170 a Week, or $8,840 a Year. How Can a Family Live on That? A Family Can't," *USA Today*, January 10, 1995, p. 11A.
18. "Ben & Jerry's Debates Cap," *Quad City Times,* June 27, 1994, p. 7A.
19. Dan R. Dalton, Catherine M. Daily, and Idolene F. Kesner, "Executive Severance Agreements: Benefit or Burglary?" *Academy of Management Executives*, Volume 7, Number 4, 1993, p. 69.
20. Ibid., pp. 74–89.
21. Alex Gibney, "In Search of Thomas J. Peters," *Best of Business Quarterly,* p. 10.
22. "CEOs are Rewarded Despite Layoffs," *Quad-City Times*, May 2, 1997, p. 7A (Associated Press Article used with permission).
23. Thomas J. Watson, Jr. and Peter Petre, *Father, Son & Co.: My Life at IBM and Beyond* (New York: Bantam Books, 1990), p. 15.
24. Michael A. Verespej, "Pay-for-Skills: Its Time Has Come," *Industry Week*, June 15, 1992, pp. 22–26. (Reprinted with permission from *Industry Week.* Copyright Penton Publishing, Inc., Cleveland, OH.)
25. Townsend (note 8).

PART IV

The Road to Greatness: A Summation, Not a Closing Argument

CHAPTER 13

A Wake-Up Call and a Call for Action: A Realistic, Not Idealistic, Approach to Managing

In any organization there are the ropes to skip and the ropes to know.
—R. Retti & G. Funkhouser

A manager develops people. Through the way he manages, he makes it easy or difficult for them to develop themselves. He directs people or misdirects them. He brings out what is in them or he stifles them.
—Peter Drucker

We are now strategically positioned to capture the wealth of opportunities that exist for us.
—Dexter Corp. '90

Nearly anyone can stand adversity, but if you want to test a man's character give him power.
—Abraham Lincoln

The Road to "Greatness"

As I began to write each of the seven chapters dealing with the seven sins, I paused to consider whether what I was about to discuss should be termed a fatal sin or, as someone suggested, a fatal disease. My conclusion was the same each time—all seven should be termed a sin rather than a disease. It was obvious to me from the outset, and later confirmed by my research, that these misdeeds—these acts, attitudes, and behaviors of practicing CEOs which can bring about their downfall—were generally caused not by accident but by intent. They weren't inherited or involuntarily transmitted by someone, but rather they were thought out, planned, nurtured, and "voluntarily" put into practice by the CEOs themselves.

To that extent, I found solace in writing this book because it is a book of analysis, reflection, and hope. It is a book of hope because the analysis and reflection reveal that there are avenues and ways for correction. It is encouraging that practically all of these sins are preventable—if the CEO chooses to do so. The decision to follow the straight road is the CEO's. However, to do that effectively, the CEO has to be convinced that, in the long run, not committing these sins is far better for him or her and for the organization. Hopefully, the CEO will take the better road in his or her corporate journey. The better road may be "bumpier" at the outset, it may be longer, and perhaps it may be lonelier and less traveled, but in the long run that road will lead the CEO to a better future—to a better destination, to the "pot of gold." It is the road to "greatness"—and it is the road to "goodness." It is the road to excellence! The end must be reached in the right way. And the end must be right. For as we know, there is no right way to do a wrong thing. Cicero said, "Let us regard this as settled: what is morally wrong can never be advantageous, even when it enables you to make some gain that you believe to be to your advantage. The mere act of believing that some wrongful course of action constitutes an advantage is pernicious." CEOs need to be certain that their means are as good and noble as their ends, because the ends do not always justify the means. And when you get there, your conscience must be clear. As Norman Vincent Peale said, "There is no pillow as soft as a clear conscience."

CEOs need to understand and accept the fact that, as someone said: "Running a successful and ethical business is not like a sprint, it is like a marathon." Firms that perform better financially over time are those with a commitment to ethical behavior. Just as nations cannot succeed by following the Carthegian creed, neither can organizations. Polybious, the Greek philosopher, summarized a nation's decline in a single sentence: "At Carthage, nothing which results in profit is regarded as disgraceful." He could have substituted the word organization in place of Carthage and the statement would still be true. CEOs must put their careers and the organizational goals in line with ethical expectations of the corporate stakeholders, including society as a whole. That with which they are entrusted cannot be taken lightly. Much has been given to them, and much is expected of them. To put it in a biblical context, in Luke 12:28, we read: "From everyone to whom much has been given, much will be required; and from the one to whom much has been entrusted, even more will be demanded." CEOs have to stand up and champion that which is right. Edmund Burke said, "All that is necessary for the forces of evil to win in the world is for enough good men to do nothing." We should not tolerate conduct that damages one's character and integrity for material gain. German theologian Dietrich Bonhoeffer said:

> They came after the Gypsies
>   I said nothing because I wasn't a Gypsie.
> Then they came after the Jews
>   I said nothing because I wasn't a Jew.
> Then they came after the Catholics
>   and I said nothing—I wasn't Catholic.
> Then they came after me and there was nobody left.

A CEO has to be careful not to be content and find comfort in pursuing projects solely because they are safe for the organization. Being safe does not necessarily mean being good for the organization. Nor does it mean that something is right for the organization. What needs to be asked is whether it meets the mission and goals of the organization. As John A. Shedd, an American educator, put it, "A ship in harbor is safe, but that is not what ships are built for." We can add to that the admonition to physicians: "Above all do no harm." If the right people are in place and are properly managed, organizations will generally prosper. William Ouchi states that the secret to Japanese success is not their technology but rather the way the employees are managed. He describes it as "a style that focuses on a strong company philosophy, a distinct corporate culture, long-range staff development, and consensus decision-making."[1]

A corporation acts through its agents, and the "chief" agent is the CEO. He or she represents the corporation. The CEO's corporate acts and deeds, including his or her managerial sins, not only reflect on the corporation but bind the corporation. His or her image is the image of the corporation. The CEO must autograph his or her work with excellence, dignity, and honesty, for that work is a reflection of not only the CEO but also the corporation.

In the 1800s, a Colorado judge wrestled with a case which involved a railroad company. The judge reached two conclusions. First, he found that the company had used every trick in the book so it could rig its rates to swindle the poor farmers and other settlers in the area. The second conclusion he reached was that there was no actual violation of the law, and consequently he couldn't do anything about the situation. Faced with these two conclusions, he ended the trial by complaining, "A corporation ain't got a soul to curse or a backside to kick, and it damn well oughta have both." Henry David Thoreau said, "It is truly enough said that a corporation has no conscience; but a corporation of conscientious men is a corporation with a conscience."

Having detailed the acts, attitudes, and behaviors that are associated with the fatal managerial sins, we need to briefly focus on ways to help CEOs refrain from committing them. Proper steps must be taken by those who have committed one or more of these sins—the sinners who are looking for the road to "goodness" for the road to "greatness," who are in pursuit of excellence." They need guidance to get out of the fast lane—the lane of greed, selfishness, mistrust, fuzzy vision, indecisiveness, shortsightedness, questionable commitment, and managing unchecked. We need serious people to lead because there are serious problems that need to be solved.

Even though there are plenty of books on good managerial practices, it would be remiss on my part if, after detailing the sins, no provision was made to help the sinners. It is important that managers are steered away from creating for themselves an environment or a situation where the seeds of these sins, if they happen to fall on fertile ground, will grow rapidly and flourish. There needs to be a more proactive than reactive management philosophy. Often, a little care can prevent the real harm. Managers should not allow those little sins to spread and grow to the point where they become deadly. Mediocrity should not take over excellence. It has been said that the enemy of "best" is "good." CEOs are duty bound to resist mediocrity from taking over excellence. They must pursue excellence, and once excellence is achieved, they should strongly resist any attempt by the forces of "good" to tether excellence. John D. Rockefeller said: "Good management consists in showing average people how to do the work of superior people."

Focused on Excellence—Is Excellence in Management Performance Within Reach?

Corporate America has been blessed with many CEOs who have performed and who are performing excellently. As a matter of fact, for some of them, excellence is just the beginning. For them the "wow!" is not next. They are at the "wow!" They have been able to get there and stay there. They did not fall prey to the seven fatal managerial sins. They were able to avoid them. That is not to say that some weren't tempted, but their strength, their confidence, their commitment and knowledge enabled them to resist the temptation. That is good news; these managerial sins can be avoided by practically all CEOs who are committed to the true mission of their organizations—but they certainly are not unavoidable. As discussed herein, in the end, the real forces or the actions that bring them about are not external but rather are internal. They are intentional violations. And in practically all cases, the CEO knows better—knows that he or she is committing them; they are premeditated. That is why some find it hard to forget and to forgive.

There is often danger when the CEO tries to rationalize the activity which brings about the conduct that results in one or more of these sins. However, even after one of these sins is committed, the CEO generally has the opportunity to correct or reverse the improper action. Obviously, these sins are not new; they have been around much too long. We have seen the consequences that result from committing them. There is no compelling reason for management to get involved in or to fall prey to these sins. Like other kinds of sins, they are temptations, they are self-centered, they are quick fixes, and they are deadly. They must be resisted and avoided. There are plenty of managers who, if given the opportunity, could lead the nation's organizations in an honorable manner. Our task is to find them and persuade them to lead.

CEOs have to take charge of both their personal lives and their corporations. They can and must take the necessary action to correct what may actually be or may be perceived to be off the right course. If they stray, they can correct the situation if they act quickly and sincerely, but that may require paying the necessary penance. If no corrective action is taken, the result can almost be predicted: "What you soweth you shall reap." The wage of managerial sin is corporate death. The unfortunate thing, however, is that the fatal blow often is not only a fatal blow to the CEO's career but a mortal blow to the organization. It can bring about the end of an organization before its time. It can result in a wasted corporate life.

Business has been around since the beginning of mankind. Millions have gotten behind the helm to lead and manage. Some performed that task poorly, some were mediocre, and some were excellent. A lot has been learned by managers from managers about managing through the years. Managers have had the opportunity to witness the trials and tribulations of the past. They have seen the good and bad and have learned from both. Many of us are convinced that we have the knowledge and tools to manage properly. Excellence in management performance is within the reach of CEOs, but they need to look for, find, adopt, nurture, and execute the principles learned. They can then sit back and reap the benefits. Their wages would be the "real success" that follows. Striving for excellence is a continuous process. It is contagious. There is no stopping it. A work of art is never finished, and management has the elements of both science and art.

It is important for the CEO to know, understand, and believe in what he or she is expected to do. It has been said that the world steps aside to let any man pass if he knows where he is going. But to do that, a CEO needs to know himself. He needs to examine his life. "The unexamined life," said Socrates, "is not worth living."

In the past fifty years, many management theories have been advanced by management writers, theorists, professors, consultants, practitioners, and gurus. Many of them have helped to shape both organizations and their management philosophies. Other theories have come and gone. Some had substance, and those CEOs who employed them were rewarded handsomely. Others had questionable value at best; they rewarded only those who articulated and taught them at seminars. For example, management has been influenced by such theories as management-by-objectives, job enrichment, job enlargement, quality circles, matrix structures, total quality management, empowerment, reengineering, and the like. All of them made some impact on the practice of management. Their merits or shortcomings will not be discussed here, as there are plenty of books that contain in-depth analysis of them.

It should be stated, however, that some of these theories have had adverse effects on managers. That is not to say that the theories were necessarily bad or ineffective, but rather the failure could be attributed to managers' overreliance on and/or misuse of them. For example, some managers perceived them as a panacea for all their problems. Many managers saw them as saviors for their deteriorating administrations. They felt that by employing these theories, their failing organizations would be resurrected. Unfortunately, for some organizations, the theories never worked. They did give some organizations a needed boost, but it did not last long. Many managers never understood how to apply them. However, for some organizations that were able to properly apply them, the results had a long-lasting effect (i.e., Motorola).

The point is that management is not only about theories and widgets; it is about people—not just their bodies, but their minds as well. Management, for those who understand it and are interested in properly practicing it, can be easy. It does not have to be complicated. It can be argued that business operations can be summed up in three words: people, product, and profit. And people have to come first. After all, if an organization does not have a good team, it can't do much with the other two.

The surest way to continue the success of a successful organization, other than people, can be summed up in two simple words: trust and entrepreneurship. If a CEO could instill in his or her ongoing and successful organization real trust and a real spirit of entrepreneurship, the success of the organization would practically be assured. When Jack Welch, chairman and CEO of General Electric, was named manager of the year by the National Management Association, he said that at GE "it's sometimes dangerous to call somebody a manager." The term has come to mean someone who "controls rather than facilitates, complicates rather than simplifies, acts more like a governor than an accelerator." He says that's not what we want. "At GE," he continues, "we are trying to develop an effervescent culture that crackles with creativity. We are trying to become an $80 billion global company with the fire and zest, the heart and soul, of a start-up." He has opened communication between employees and bosses, cut the bureaucracy, and refocused GE's businesses.[2]

Mr. Welch states:

> To go with our business strategy, we've got a management system now in place and functioning that supports that strategy—one that is lean, liberating, fast-moving—an organization that facilitates and frees and, above all, understands that the fountainhead of success is the individual, not the system.
>
> This management system, designed to draw out the best in the 222,000 individuals who make up this company, is drawing it out. We're a long way from having those levers of responsibility in front of every workstation and desk in this company, but that is our ultimate objective. We know where competitiveness comes from. It comes from people—but only from people who are free to dream, to risk, free to act.
>
> Liberating those people, every one of them, is the great challenge we've been grappling with all over this company. And from what we've seen of the ocean of talent, initiative, and creativity that is unleashed when we have the self-confidence to turn it loose, we are convinced our company is more than a match for anything the world can throw at us.[3]

CEOs cannot afford to act in a vacuum. In order to be successful, they need the cooperation and creativity of all the employees in the organization. They don't need carbon copies or rubber stamps, although they do need loyalty. In the end, the CEO has to represent the unified voice of the company. The CEO has to focus on where he or she wants to take the company.

To again quote Jack Welch:

> We have to get faster if we are to win in a world where nothing is predictable except the increasingly rapid pace of change.

The process of getting through function after function can be so time consuming and complex that it can force the organization to focus on itself, on its own inner workings, and distract it from its real mission: serving customers.

Give people the chance to make a contribution to winning, let them gain the self-confidence that comes from knowing their role in it, and before long they abandon the paraphernalia of status and bureaucracy. They simply don't need it any more.

Self-confidence is the fuel of productivity and creativity, decisiveness and speed.[4]

The survival skills of the CEOs of the future will of necessity be somewhat different than the skills required of the CEOs of the past. A number of years ago, Yogi Berra foresaw the changing future and predicted what would happen when he said: "The future ain't what it used to be." The authors of an article entitled "The Leader's New Work" state:

It is simply no longer possible for anyone to "figure it all out at the top." The old model, "the top thinks and the local acts," must now give way to integrating thinking and acting at all levels. While the challenge is great, so is the potential payoff. "The person who figures out how to harness the collective genius of the people in his or her organization," according to former Citibank CEO Walter Wriston, "is going to blow the competition away."[5]

Mission Possible

A leader needs to take command to accomplish the mission of the organization. Preferably, the mission should be in congruence with the leader's personal mission or goal. When that happens, it is generally a win–win situation.

Peter Drucker writes that the Japanese recognize that there are really two demands of leadership:

One is to accept that rank does not confer privileges; it entails responsibilities. The other is to acknowledge that leaders in an organization need to impose on themselves that congruence between deeds and words, between behavior and professed beliefs and values, that which we call "personal integrity."[6]

CEOs can begin their road to "greatness" by defining the limits of their organizations and truly adopting a philosophy of respect for the individual.

They must, as Mark Shepherd of Texas Instruments was quoted as saying in *In Search of Excellence,* embrace a philosophy where "Every worker [is] seen as a source of ideas, not just acting as a pair of hands."[7] Mary Kay Ash put it well when she said, "Everyone has an invisible sign hanging from his neck saying 'Make Me Feel Important!' Never forget this message when working with people."

Leaders need to expand opportunities for their companies. Even in the midst of crisis, opportunities exist. Sometimes opportunities are created in chaos. We have to pay a high price for certainty. It is important, however, while expanding opportunities, that bureaucracy does not expand proportionally. Sometimes organizations are saved from expanding bureaucracy because of its inefficiency. Leaders have to learn how to really share power as well as know when they need to intervene. They often should be more afraid of what they take on and less of what they delegate. Leaders have to be honest and realistic about their mistakes. Mistakes do happen; that's a given, and it is understandable and tolerated. What is not understandable and tolerated is compounding a mistake. Robert W. Haack, former president of the New York Stock Exchange, said, "The public may be willing to forgive us for mistakes in judgement, but it will not forgive us for mistakes in motive." Leaders have to be strong enough and confident enough to admit their mistakes and try to remedy the situation. As Donald Burr said about People Express, "It was bad enough that we made a bad business mistake but the worst part was that when we realized it we didn't want to admit it so we just kept compounding it."

Leaders should not be impervious to the idea of radical redesign, even starting from scratch if that is what needs to be done. It may be somewhat embarrassing or may look bad at the outset, but in the long term, following a new course of action when necessary will serve them well. If CEOs don't voluntarily adopt such a policy, their boards should see that they do. The rubber-stamp board must become a thing of the past. Neither the boards or CEOs should resist modern governance. Directors need to do more than just minimize the possibility of being sued. CEOs must face reality as it exists, even when doing so is uncomfortable, and they must act properly, even when doing so is not popular at the moment. If they cannot implement change, if change is necessary, they must manage the situation accordingly. Change often has to take place before it becomes necessary. Changes in organizations often do not occur incrementally but rather occur in quantum leaps. Even though some leaders may associate risk with such changes, they have to move forward. If they happen to be wrong, they should minimize their losses and proceed accordingly.

Leaders must realize that their strength and power in the organization depend primarily on their vision. Commenting on vision, one CEO said, "We don't have any visionaries in our organization—not even one person." That's tragic! For the vision to be effective, the CEO must be sure that every employee is aware of it. After all, the organization cannot be something that its employees are not. The CEO can't spend his or her time putting out little fires—that's too myopic and amounts to micromanaging. It is important that the CEO clearly communicate the vision for the company. In addition, if the CEO institutes an open-door policy, where employees at all levels have access to each other and can even question policy decisions, the organization will be much better for it. This would permit employees to analyze the vision, which would then be better articulated and better implemented.

Organizations with vision excel, whereas shortsighted ones stagnate and lose direction. To excel, it is important that the work force be well educated, which doesn't occur without the support of the CEO. Many organizations realize how vital a well-educated work force is to their business; unfortunately, others do not. The days of the unskilled, uneducated worker in industrial America are gone. Today's work force is better educated and multiskilled. An important task of the leader is to help employees reach their true potential. The modern leader has to be oriented more toward the participation and empowerment model than the autocratic and militaristic model. It should be noted that empowerment must be accompanied by trust throughout the organization. After all, the leader leads not for himself but for the organization. Leadership must be spread not only up but down the organization. If we want to reduce power at the top, we must be willing to delegate more responsibility to the lower levels of the organization.

It is important that CEOs realize that their actions are monitored and scrutinized. As Peter Drucker states:

> "The higher up the monkey goes, the more of his behind he shows" runs an English schoolboy jingle. What executives do, what they believe and value, what they reward and whom, are watched, seen, and minutely interpreted by the whole organization. And nothing is noticed more quickly—and considered more significant—than a discrepancy between what executives preach and what they expect their associates to practice.[8]

A CEO must not let his or her personal goals and ambitions in the short-term force him or her to make decisions that are inconsistent with the company's mission or the best interest of the organization. It is not enough for the CEO to do his or her best; the CEO must do what is necessary for the organization. Furthermore, it is not enough for an incompetent CEO to do his or her best; the standard of performance for the CEO is excellence. If the CEO cannot provide what is necessary for the organization, then he or she is duty bound to get others to help provide what is necessary. In some instances, that may mean stepping aside and letting others guide the organization in achieving its mission. As Howard Head (founder and CEO of Head Ski Company, Inc.) said, "Sometimes you may have to re-engineer yourself out of your CEO job." Employees must be properly prepared for their jobs, and that, of course, means that they must have a clear vision of the company. The present way of conducting business in some organizations is "ready, aim, fire"; it must be replaced with "be prepared, aim at the right place, fire."

It is troubling that only 33% of Americans believe that corporate executives demonstrate "excellent or good" ethical and moral conduct. Character and integrity must be the cornerstone of every organization. There are no compelling reasons why CEOs cannot improve in that department. They need to pay attention to their inner voice. But they need to be careful not to confuse the right thing to do with rationalization. They need to lead with both their heart and their brain. Unfortunately, on occasion, doing the right thing may not be the popular thing, but how does one justify doing the wrong thing? To put it in Mahatma Gandhi's words: "In a matter of conscience there is no room for democracy." There is a pressing need for all stakeholders to maintain the highest standards of honesty, integrity, and ethics in all aspects of the business. Greed should not be considered acceptable conduct, and CEOs should not be tempted to "take all they can get." They should also avoid the temptation of setting people up to fail—intentionally or otherwise. CEOs must do and be their best in all their actions. Nothing less should be tolerated. One manager, referring to his previous CEO, said that during the man's tenure with the company, he was called many different names, but the manager couldn't recall anyone accusing the CEO of being a gentleman. What a wasted opportunity! Creating trust is a very important part of the CEO's job.

To summarize, the CEO must first establish and convey the vision of the organization, then continuously modify the strategy and establish the proper structure, and finally organize the proper resources to achieve the mission in an ethical and decisive manner. Where success exists, the CEO must be careful not to assume that success will guarantee continued success. In commenting on whether IBM was a victim of its own success, the author of an article entitled "The Decline and Rise of IBM" states: "The answer is certainly yes.

Intoxicated with good fortune, the company over-reached in the 1980s and paid a bitter price in the 1990s."[9] In discussing whether IBM was the victim of a corporate culture that pushed the wrong type of executive to the top, the same author states: "Yes. IBM chief executives were too inbred, too steeped in the arrogance of success, and too certain of their own judgment in a time of challenge. IBM's culture contributed greatly to each shortcoming. Most of these failures were avoidable. Because IBM's difficulties were largely the result of executive error, other large firms can hope that, with the right leaders, they can remain successful as they grow."[10]

Notes

1. William Ouchi, *Theory Z: How American Business Can Meet the Japanese Challenge* (New York: Addison-Wesley, 1981).
2. Mindy Fetterman, "Cover Story: 'CEO of Year' Will Focus on Soft Stuff," *USA Today*, July 15, 1991, B, 1:3.
3. Jack Welch, "Managing for the Nineties," address at GE Annual Meeting, Waukesha, WI, April 27, 1988.
4. Jack F. Welch, Jr., "In Pursuit of Speed," address presented at the General Electric Annual Meeting of Share Owners, Decatur, AL, April 24, 1991.
5. Peter Senge, "The Leader's New Work: Building Learning Organizations," *Sloan Management Review*, Volume 32, Number 1, Fall 1990, pp. 7–18.
6. Peter F. Drucker, *Managing for the Future: The 1990s and Beyond* (New York: Truman Talley Books/Dutton, 1992), pp. 116–17.
7. Thomas J. Peters and Robert H. Waterman, Jr., *In Search of Excellence: Lessons from America's Best-Run Companies* (New York: Harper & Row, 1982), p. 15.
8. Drucker (note 6), p. 116.
9. D. Quinn Mills, "The Decline and Rise of IBM," *Sloan Management Review*, Summer 1996, p. 81.
10. Ibid.

CHAPTER 14

The Professional Manager:
The Search for the "Ideal" Manager

A leader knows what's best to do; a manager knows merely how to do it.
—Ken Adelman

The United States should go into space, not because it is easy but because it is hard.
—John F. Kennedy

The Actual is Limited...The Possible is Immense.
—The Lincoln Electric Company's Motto

The wicked leader is he who the people despise. The good leader is he who the people revere. The great leader is he who the people say, "We did it ourselves."
—Lao Tsu

The best executive is the one who has sense enough to pick good men to do what he wants done, and the self-restraint to keep from meddling while they do it.
—Theodore Roosevelt

I must follow the people. Am I not their leader?
—Benjamin Disraeli

All workers must manage...All managers must work.
—James F. Lincoln

You don't lead people by hitting them over the head; that's assault, that's not leadership.
—Dwight Eisenhower

The ultimate measure of a man is not where he stands in moments of comfort and convenience, but where he stands at times of challenge and controversy.
—Martin Luther King

The preceding chapters presented the panel's responses and comments on the present status of managerial competence in corporate America. They also provided an analysis of the seven fatal managerial sins that result in the downfall of chieftains and even included advice for the "sinners." Now it is time to take a look at an "ideal" CEO who possesses the values and attributes that corporate America needs to lead its organizations. This chapter focuses on one of those ideal managers who has been leading (retired May 1997 as CEO and has assumed the title chairman emeritus) one of America's corporations. It should be noted that the purpose here is not to identify the "perfect" or "best" leader in the United States, but rather to present an "ideal" leader.

It may be difficult to define or describe an "ideal" leader, but if you were to meet one, you would readily recognize him or her. Working with a mediocre leader after having worked with an ideal leader can be discouraging, perhaps even unbearable.

A Hero, A Hall-of-Famer, A Breed Apart, or an Employee with a "Real" Commitment—A Visionary

"The first responsibility of a leader," writes retired Herman Miller CEO Max DePree, "is to define reality." Leader as teacher does not mean leader as authoritarian expert whose job is to teach people the "correct" view of reality. Rather, it is about helping everyone in the organization, oneself included, to gain a more insightful view of reality. This is in line with a popular emerging view of leaders as coaches, guides, or facilitators. In a learning organization, this teaching role is developed further by virtue of explicit attention to people's mental models and by the influence of the system's perspective.[1] Such leaders are ordinary people with a true commitment. They are not leaders with a capital "L," but people of sincerity, honesty, and vision.

It has been said that leaders are individuals who do the right thing, and managers are people who do things right. While both roles are important, they differ substantially. How often do we hear of leaders in high positions doing the wrong things very well? Some of them seem to be convinced that they are doing the right thing for their organizations. Anais Nin, a French-born American author on surrealism and psychoanalytic theory, said, "We don't see things as they are, we see them as we are." They try to justify such a conclusion by pointing to the results—the ends—and believe that if the ends are good, then both the ends and the means are noble.

What we need are leaders who are visionaries, who can establish and continuously modify the strategy. We read in Matthew 15:14, "If the blind lead the blind, both shall fall into the ditch." But sight alone is not sufficient; there must also be vision. We need leaders who lead with integrity and trust, who can accomplish the mission of the organization in an ethical manner. We need leaders who understand that mistakes are inevitable. "Punishing failure," says Jack Welch, "assumes that no one dares." Our organizations need leaders who listen to their constituents rather than muzzle them—leaders who encourage their employees to speak out when they see injustices or have something to say that matters. Martin Luther King said, "Our lives begin to end the day we are silent about things that matter." Only mediocrity, says Laurence J. Peter, co-author of *The Peter Principle*, rises to the top in a system that won't tolerate wavemaking. We need leaders who do not encourage their employees to be robots or to agree regardless of whether the leader is right or wrong. Leaders should encourage their employees to be more than yes-men. Employees should feel free to say what is right for the organization rather than what they think the boss wants to hear. The latter brings to mind the following passage from *Hamlet,* act III, scene 2:

> *Hamlet*: Do you see yonder cloud that's almost in the shape of a camel?
> *Polonius*: By the mass, and 'tis like a camel, indeed.
> *Hamlet*: Methinks it is like a weasel.
> *Polonius*: It is backed like a weasel.
> *Hamlet*: Or like a whale?
> *Polonius*: Very like a whale.[2]

Leaders should be careful not to encourage their employees to follow Polonius's thinking when they are asked for their opinion.

We need leaders who are able to separate good advice from bad, who are firm yet compassionate, and who can effectively delegate and empower others and yet are not afraid to decide and to take the necessary risks associated with making decisions. Our organizations need leaders who lead by reason rather than by force and intimidation, who are able to draw—to pull—the best out of their people, and who can create an environment that is conducive to drawing the best out of people. To illustrate that point, General Eisenhower would place a piece of string on a table and say, "Pull it and it will follow wherever you wish. Push it and it will go nowhere at all." That's how he believed people should be led. Pull—don't push. We need leaders who perceive their employees as an investment rather than an expense.

Our organizations need leaders whose focus is not limited to the short term but includes the long term, whose focus is not limited to the bottom line but includes other organizational matters, and who are truly interested in managing their organizations rather than their careers. They must focus on giving instead of just receiving. Winston Churchill put it well when he said, "We make a living by what we get; we make a life by what we give." We need leaders who, to paraphrase Will Rogers, know what they are doing, love what they are doing, and believe in what they are doing. We need leaders who strive for excellence by overcoming obstacles. We need leaders who know when their time is up in an organization and gracefully step aside. Abraham Ribicoff expressed it well when he said, "There is a time to stay and a time to go. You tip your hat when you're on top, and say goodbye. There's no greater tragedy for a person of ability, character and prestige than to try to stay that one extra term. You forget that you don't have a lock on anything forever…Once you are out of office, don't try to second guess. Be an observer, not a participant. Forget the power that you had. Be available for advice and friendship, but don't try to run the show any more."

We need leaders who do not have to be forced into being accountable but who sincerely believe that accountability is their responsibility—who genuinely believe that they are accountable to all the stakeholders. We need leaders who believe in the philosophy of John Deere, founder of John Deere Company: "I will never put my name on any implement that does not have in it the best that is in me." We need leaders who autograph their work with excellence because their work is a reflection of themselves. We need leaders who have a spiritual side, believe in words such as caring, compassion, sympathy, and service. We need leaders who are humanistic and whose humanistic qualities are part of their leadership style. We need leaders who believe that the wealth of the organization should be proportionately shared by those who helped create it. We need leaders who are fair. And fair doesn't mean what Henry Jordan said: "He's fair. He treats us all the same—like dogs."

In summary, the ideal manager should give his or her employees a voice in decisions, an opportunity for development, and rewards which are commensurate with performance. The ideal manager should consult with his or her employees, inform them of what is going on, listen to what they are saying, understand and try to help them with their needs, and be conscious of their feelings and frustrations.

Is that demanding too much? Not really—anything less should be unacceptable. Do such leaders exist, and can they be found in our organizations? The answer is yes—they are there. Perhaps not as many as we want, but they are present. Let's focus on one of them.

A Glimpse of One of America's "Ideal" Managers

What makes this "ideal" manager tick. Is he a hero, a hall-of-famer, a Nobel laureate, a breed apart, or just a "plain" employee with a real commitment—a visionary? The company he headed for a number of years until May 1997 has been written up as a case study, featuring its unique incentive management system. The case has been used in many graduate business schools since 1947. Many have studied the case as students and later taught it to others. The company is the Lincoln Electric Company.

The Lincoln Electric Company was founded by John C. Lincoln in 1895 as a manufacturer of electrical motors and soon thereafter became a giant in the emerging field of arc welding. "Lincoln believed strongly," says Richard S. Sabo, director of Lincoln Electric's corporate communications and industrial relations and assistant to the CEO, "in the natural abilities of each individual and the effectiveness of competition. He founded his new Lincoln Electric Company with the Golden Rule as its guiding principle. That a company built on this philosophy has survived and prospered for 100 years is a testimony to Lincoln's vision and the strength of the creed behind the corporation. Just as remarkable is the firm's unique management program that links productivity with pay and has enabled the company to operate without a layoff in the 45 years since the program was introduced."[3]

During its 102 years of operation Lincoln Electric has had only six CEOs. The present chairman emeritus and former chairman of the board and CEO is Donald F. Hastings, one of America's "ideal" managers. Let's see why he has earned such a designation. What qualities does he possess?

"As a young man," says Donald Hastings, "I had the opportunity to hear James F. Lincoln talk about the company his older brother had founded. He talked about employees being paid according to their actual contribution to the company's profits. He talked about a working environment designed to encourage individual achievement. He talked about responsibility, accountability and job security. Everything he said appealed to me. Shortly after I heard Mr. Lincoln speak, I went to work for the Lincoln Electric Company.

"Starting in an entry-level sales position, I discovered a work place in which the top management set an example of consistently ethical behavior. This is essential to corporate responsibility. If the people at the top are anything less than truthful, cynicism will infect the organization, gradually poisoning it, and ultimately, resulting in its demise."[4]

With a degree in economics from Pomona College in California and an MBA from Harvard and a career spent largely in sales and marketing, he is the first of the company's six CEOs not to come from an engineering background. He has been a member of Lincoln's board of directors since 1980, was appointed president in 1987, and became chairman of the board and chief executive officer in 1992.

"At work," says Frederick W. Mackenbach, Lincoln's president and COO, "Mr. Hastings is a master motivator with a distinctive style...never criticizes, always optimistic, sees only the good in people, and inherently addresses all problems as opportunities. His goal has been to make Lincoln an enjoyable place to work while creating a quality and customer-focus throughout the corporation. He has accomplished these objectives. The dynamic and energetic spirit at Lincoln is all-encompassing, and Don is the driving force behind it."[5]

The company's philosophy had been articulated many years ago and has been followed since. "When John Lincoln's younger brother James became president in 1913, the company's reputation evolved again. James exhibited a near-religious zeal (their father had been a Congregationalist minister) for relating productivity to profitability. And then in 1948, Lincoln workers were guaranteed—after three years 'apprenticeship'—lifetime employment, with payment on a piecework basis, and a share of the company's profits at the end of the year. [That policy continues. At the end of 1994, the highest paid plant worker at Lincoln Electric earned $117,000. The plant average was $55,000.] James Lincoln found his portrait on many magazine covers, and his corporate descendants have appeared on TV shows such as CBS' '60 Minutes.'"[6] The portrayal of Lincoln Electric and Mr. Hastings on "60 Minutes" was very positive. It showed how a company located in the Rust Belt could not only survive but indeed prosper, if properly managed, at the same time other companies were failing right and left.

It has been said that a professional does what he says he will do when he says he will do it and does it in a proper manner. Mr. Hastings fits the definition well. Employees know where they stand with him and with the organization. There are no surprises. What you are promised is what you get. No promises made that are not kept. Compare that with other companies that promise employees much but employees end up getting little. "He respects and treats employees as 'family,'" says Paul Beddia, Vice President, Government & Community Relations. "He is considerate, patient, sympathetic, understanding and able to forgive." Adds Diane Fleming, Systems/Methods Analyst, "He definitely perceives employees as an investment. He will offer you as many challenges and opportunities as you want in an effort to help you grow."*

---

* This employee interview, as well as several other employee interviews that follow, were conducted prior to Mr. Hastings' retirement as CEO and chairman of the board in May 1997.

Regarding responsibility, Mr. Hastings says, "At every level of the Lincoln organization, employees take individual responsibility for their jobs. Every worker is a manager, and every manager is a worker. In self-management, we find the true meaning of efficiency, because nothing increases overhead as quickly and non-productively as extra layers of management. We believe that the ability to be self-managing is latent in all human beings. In developing that potential, Lincoln Electric has found the following practices indispensable:

- individual accountability for quality;
- individual accountability for output;
- wages and bonuses tied directly to quality and output;
- exact staffing of departments to cut absenteeism and emphasize the importance of each employee's job; and
- maintaining the fewest possible layers of management."[7]

Trust, integrity, and character head the list of Mr. Hastings' characteristics for managing. "When I came to Lincoln Electric—42 years ago—as a sales trainee," he says, "top management was consumed by its commitment to ethical behavior. They didn't believe that commitment was inconsistent with business success. They believed—and we believe—that it is essential to business success."[8] Commenting on this, Ms. Fleming states, "Mr. Hastings has an extremely high degree of trust and integrity. He has an excellent character when it comes to dealing with business, his employees, etc."

When asked why, if the Lincoln method is so successful, it is not more widely imitated, Mr. Hastings puts it this way: "Basically I think it's a lack of trust; workers who don't believe the company will live up to its promises, and companies who believe the workers will betray them. Many managements wouldn't want to live in the glass bowl atmosphere we have here. And another thing they might not like is the lack of executive perks. There are no country club memberships or special benefits in our system. I get the same benefits as the newest plant worker on the floor."[9]

Mr. Hastings writes that he had been chairman and chief executive officer of the Lincoln Electric Company for exactly twenty-five minutes when he received a phone call telling him that losses in the company's European operations were much worse than previously reported. In fact, they would force the company to declare in 1992 the first annual loss in its history. "Worse yet," he says, "if the situation was not addressed immediately, unprofitable overseas production facilities—which had grown by that time to 21 plants in 16 countries—could actually sink the entire company. It has taken us close to three years to turn the situation around. During that period I have had to rely time and time again on the reservoir of trust that our management built up with employees over the years."[10]

During 1992 and 1993, says Hastings, "there was pressure for us to consider sharply curtailing our famous annual bonus. I felt very strongly that such a move could be fatal to the previous 'reservoir of trust' that existed between employees and management. And frankly, I did not want to preside over a Lincoln Electric Company in which employees have lost faith. The parent firm was profitable, and our U.S. employees had created those profits. I believed they were entitled to benefit from their dedication and hard work."

"On the other hand, due to our disastrous result in Europe, we had to take the unprecedented step of borrowing the money to pay the bonus—$44 million in 1992, and $55 million in 1993. It seemed to me that the only way out of this crisis would be to sell our way out. By concentrating on the top line, we could improve our bottom line."[11] The successful result was that in 1995, the company's centennial year, it broke the billion-dollar barrier in sales, dramatically increased its profits, and launched a public offering that significantly reduced its debts and provided capital for future expansion.

What does that say about Hastings' commitment and vision? Was it a proper move? How many companies would have taken such a risk? How many CEOs would not only refuse to pay a bonus but would instead lay off some employees to make the bottom line look better? When asked whether Mr. Hastings is a visionary, Mr. Beddia said, "Yes! Both short and long term…but he can change priorities based on opportunities and can be amazingly proactive in a reactive sort of way." "He has excellent instinct and feel for the market place and how the company should compete in the market," says Richard J. Seif, Lincoln's Vice President–Marketing.

When it was fashionable for CEOs to continue getting raises regardless of company earnings, Hastings didn't follow the trend (i.e., several years ago he ended up making less than the previous year). His salary is very modest for a Fortune 500 CEO. He could have taken healthy raises instead of paying a bonus to the rest of the organization. But he didn't. Obviously, by doing so he made a bold statement. He practiced what he preached—and his message was loud and clear. Rewards follow performance. He has been described as "…a down to earth focused CEO, leading a company that has a clearly delineated mission, focuses on its core competencies, provides a quality product, rewards his employees and enriches his shareholders."

He is convinced that nice guys can and often do finish first. There is no reason why they shouldn't. He not only follows that philosophy but preaches it and instills it in all his employees. He walks the talk. Says Karen Robinson, an employee at Lincoln Electric, "Mr. Hastings is available to employees whenever they need him. When the bonus was not as good, a couple years ago, he didn't hide from the employees, he didn't go out to play golf, rather he sat for hours in the cafeteria meeting with employees to answer questions and to help them with their concerns. He could have sent someone else to meet with the employees but he didn't. He was there when they needed him. He is good to tell you when you do a good job and when needed gives constructive criticism in private." Adds Joe Sirko, an employee of the company for over forty-five years and whose wife also works there, "Mr. Hastings has always been there for us when we needed him and we've been there for him. He is one of us. I feel comfortable to walk into his office without an appointment—and I feel welcomed."

Determined to reverse the impact of the economic slowdown on his company in Europe, Mr. Hastings rented a combined office and apartment in Sunningdale, England, and spent half his time in Europe and half in the United States. His reaction to that was: "Well there was a lot of jet-lag but a CEO command post was what was needed in Europe at the time." When duty calls, the leader must respond. The move paid off.

It was obvious from talking to his employees that Mr. Hastings is a leader who leads from both the head and the heart. It was equally obvious that his humanistic approach, his warm personality, his sincerity, his concern for all the stakeholders, and his dedication to his job and family have made him a leader who has "earned" respect.

I heard him speak, from the heart, to an auditorium full of MBAs and businesspeople. He presented a dynamic message about American business and impressed the audience with his candid remarks. And I witnessed his leadership ability when I recently visited his plant in Cleveland. The day I arrived, he was meeting with his board of directors, yet he took time to join me for lunch. Later on that afternoon, when I met with him in his office, I felt as though I had known him for years. His friendliness, his confidence, his personality, and his dedication to his company and his employees were very apparent. The qualities of a true leader were on display. It was obvious that he leads by reason, not by force. It was also obvious that he not only knew what he was doing but loved what he was doing.

His numerous awards and citations and his involvement in many organizations provide more evidence of the confidence others have in him. He gives unselfishly of his time to benefit others. In studying his career with Lincoln, it became apparent that he traveled and stayed on the road to "goodness" when it may have been fashionable to take a shortcut by committing one or more of the seven fatal sins. His focus has been on excellence, not mediocrity.

He defends the best of the business community but at the same time is not afraid to speak out against what he sees as abuses and injustices in the system. For example, he has been critical of what he considers unjust and poorly decided layoffs. Hastings' remarks at a recent CEO forum illustrate that point, as well as his leadership style and philosophy:

> Some months ago, business author Tom Peters referred to America's overly cautious corporate leaders as "wimps." Nowadays, however, one news magazine describes some of our nation's cost-cutting executives as "corporate killers." The reference is to top managers who have dropped the downsizing "bomb," annihilating hundreds of thousands of jobs: for example, 11,000 at Scott Paper, 15,000 at Delta Airline, 17,000 at GTE, 40,000 at AT&T, 50,000 at Sears, 60,000 at IBM, and 74,000 at GM. Based on my 42-year experience at the Lincoln Electric Company, I believe massive layoffs generally are a sign of catastrophic failure on the part of management.
>
> When past and present management miscalculations have led a company into severe financial troubles, it's not fair to make workers pay with their jobs for the mistakes of others. In some cases, it appears that corporations which engage in mass layoffs suffer less from having "too many people" than from having too few managers who know how to lead workers to generate higher levels of productivity and profitability. Senior executives at such corporations are reminiscent of the unfortunate military commander who announced that he "had to destroy the village in order to save it."
>
> During the past decade, Lincoln Electric and its employees have watched in amazement as millions of people have lost jobs that once seemed secure, as many of the remaining workers' wages have been squeezed, and as Wall Street has saluted the downsizers by bidding up their stocks. But at Lincoln, we've been doing a lot more than watching. In 1995, our company's centennial year, we broke through the $1 billion barrier in sales; we dramatically increased our profits; and we launched a public stock offering that significantly reduced our debt and provided capital for future expansion.
>
> Expansion: that's an unfamiliar word at too many of today's businesses. But in the past year, Lincoln significantly expanded our

worldwide manufacturing capacity; opened a new electric motor facility in Ohio; and added about 800 jobs to meet the growing demand for our arc-welding products and electric motors. We're especially proud that 1995 marked Lincoln's 48th consecutive year of operating without laying off a single employee because of lack of work. In fact, that last such layoff at Lincoln occurred in the same year as the Truman-Dewey race for the U.S. presidency.

At Lincoln Electric, we may be out of step with some contemporary management fashions. But we believe that those who seek to justify mass downsizing as essential to competitiveness are out of touch with economic realities and sound business practices. Our approach reflects our business heritage that traces back to two extraordinary men: John Lincoln, our founder, and his brother, James F. When John founded the company with his name, he did so with a small amount of cash ($200), but a great faith in a new technology, electricity, and the motors it would power.

In the case of James F. Lincoln, he had a philosophy of management that was ahead of his time...and apparently still ahead of our time. He didn't see Lincoln employees as faceless "hired hands." Instead, he saw them as individuals who would seize the opportunity to build better lives for themselves and their families. To that end, James F. proposed a novel idea: that employees' jobs should reward them not for their status in life or their seniority, but for the results they produced. In a company based on those principles, Jim Lincoln believed, employees would work efficiently and enthusiastically. Moreover, the company would prosper because the employees' productivity and dedication would result in customer satisfaction.

Over the years, the Lincoln brothers' philosophy has embedded itself in our company's culture in an approach we call the Incentive Management System, which rests on the following principles:

■ Guaranteed continuous employment, which ensures that employees with three or more years of service will be able to work no less than 75 percent of the standard 40-hour week.
■ Pay based on strict measurements of performance, so that the more productive workers are, the higher their pay.
■ Payment of an annual bonus based on the company's profits. For, as James F. Lincoln said, "There will never be enthusiasm for greater efficiency if the resulting profits are not properly distributed."

This system works extremely well. Currently, Lincoln's factory employees are much more productive than their U.S. counterparts in comparable businesses. At the same time, their total compensation is almost double the average for U.S. manufacturing.

Perhaps the greatest beneficiaries of our employees' productivity are our customers, who receive high quality products at reasonable prices. The fruits of our employees' efforts also benefit our shareholders, including most of our employees, who collectively own a large portion of Lincoln's common stock.

One more point: unlike some companies, we don't see every employee with gray hair as a potential candidate for the kind of "early retirement" that's actually no more than a glorified layoff. Instead, we place a high value on the experience that comes with age. Currently one third of our employees have more than 20 years of service, and 34 employees have served more than 50 years.

Admittedly, some critics have questioned whether Lincoln's approach would work as well in difficult times as it obviously does in good times. We received an answer to that question earlier in 1993 when the European recession led to heavy losses in our overseas operations. Then, as a new CEO, I came under heavy pressure to cut back sharply on employee benefits. I resisted that pressure, because I thought it would be a breach of faith to our loyal, dedicated employees. Instead, we challenged our production people to find and eliminate every bottleneck. In addition, we sent our sales people on a marketing blitz. And, in our hour of need, our employees were there for us. For example, key manufacturing people voluntarily deferred 614 weeks of vacation, and worked weekends and holidays. As a result of all these initiatives, we increased our domestic revenues to record levels, and we had a positive turnaround of our earnings totaling $86 million.

People from other companies and from the academic world often come to Lincoln to study our Incentive Management System. At times, we believe they may concentrate too much on the "management" and too little on the real key, "incentive."

It's impossible to overstate the role of incentives in creating a dedicated, effective, productive work force. After all, an economy, a company, and a work force do not operate in a vacuum. As the Lincoln brothers knew, the carrot, the incentive, is a mightier weapon than the stick.

The Lincoln approach, like the free enterprise system, does not ensure that all "boats," or all employees, will float. But it does recognize that the rewards of good performance must not go only to the privileged few, but to the deserving many.

What the apostles of downsizing sometimes forget is that business is not an island unto itself. Clearly, companies must remain competitive and profitable. But the way to do that is through encouraging productivity and ingenuity, not through terrorizing and demoralizing employees and devastating communities. It's a matter of common sense: we cannot have healthy businesses within the context of disrupted families and a decaying society.

Admittedly, Lincoln Electric stakes no claim to perfection. We make our share of mistakes and, when we do, our employees are outspoken enough to bring them to our attention. However, there is no disagreement at Lincoln over the fundamental need in business to regard our employees as precious assets. If they adhere to that principle, businesses can avoid the trauma of major downsizings. They can do so by concentrating their energies on making employees more productive, more ingenious, and more flexible. If businesses take that approach, then, as Lincoln Electric and other companies have demonstrated, corporate America can produce the kind of prosperity that creates jobs and energizes our economy.[12]

To highlight Mr. Hastings' decision skills, Mr. Beddia states, "He has an unusual quality of deciding, marked by determination and firmness…extremely thorough in listening and in obtaining pertinent details." Concerning his focus, Mr. Beddia explains, "He is focused on both the top line *and* the bottom line, and his goal far exceeds survival…but includes growth and prosperity for employees and shareholders."

With his confidence in his work, his integrity, and his commitment to the mission of the company and to all the stakeholders, one would expect him to be very accountable to all stakeholders. And that he is. Says Ms. Fleming, "He is very accountable to *all* the stakeholders from the Board down to the employees and community."

When the question is asked where all the good leaders are, we can answer by saying that there are many around, starting with Mr. Donald Hastings.

Excellence, not mediocrity, in managing should be the motto and the commitment of our CEOs. Unquestionably, many of our leaders have what it takes; they have the necessary ingredients to achieve the desired goal—to practice management as true professionals. And many of them have been able to put into practice what they know and have done well; they are great leaders—indeed, they are "business giants"! Many of them have embraced the concept that it takes the joined efforts of all the employees of an organization to have a successful company. What we still need is a clearer commitment to excellence and the application of leadership qualities by the rest of those who head our organizations. We can't put it off any longer; after all, there is no speed limit in the pursuit of excellence—in the pursuit of happiness—for all corporate stakeholders. Nothing less should be acceptable. We have done well; however, there is no compelling reason why we can't do even better! All the necessary tools are there, and with the proper commitment we can lead our organizations to a point even beyond excellence.

Notes

1. Max DePree, *Leadership Is an Art* (New York: Doubleday, 1989).
2. William Shakespeare, *Hamlet, Prince of Denmark, The Complete Works of William Shakespeare* (Cleveland/New York: The World Syndicate Publishing Company [Undated]), Act III, Scene 2, p. 925.
3. Richard Sabo, "The Lincoln Electric Company Celebrates 100 Years of History," *The Case and Welding Distributor,* March/April 1995, p. 1.
4. Donald F. Hastings, A Reservoir of Trust, The Charles E. Spohr Chair in Managerial and Corporate Ethics (Baldwin Wallace College, Berea, OH), 1995, p. 5.
5. Introduction of Mr. Donald F. Hastings on June 7, 1995, reported in a pamphlet on the Lincoln Electric Company and Donald F. Hastings, p. 5.
6. William Troy, "Facing the Leopard," reprinted from the November 1995 issue of Cleveland Magazine's Inside Business, November 1995, p. 5.
7. Sabo (note 3), p. 10.
8. Hastings (note 4), p. 11.
9. Hastings (note 5), p. 19.
10. Hastings (note 4), pp. 6–7.
11. Sabo (note 3), pp. 7–8.
12. Donald F. Hastings, remarks at a CEO forum, unpublished paper.

APPENDIX 1

The Survey Sent to Panel Members

Rating Managerial Performance Survey

Part I

Note: As used in this survey the word "manager" refers to chief executive officers as well as senior-level executives.

Circle DS if you *disagree strongly* with a statement.
Circle D   if you *disagree* with a statement.
Circle N   if you *neither agree nor disagree* with a statement.
Circle A   if you *agree* with a statement.
Circle AS if you *agree strongly* with a statement.

DS D N A AS 1. Generally, managers are more interested in managing their careers than in managing their organizations.

DS D N A AS 2. "Managing for survival" is the norm today in corporate America.

DS D N A AS 3. Generally, managers are interested in and focus on the "simplistic fix."

DS D N A AS 4. "Indecisiveness" (unclear on when and who decides) is a trait of many managers.

DS D N A AS 5. Managers today, generally, have a "fuzzy vision" regarding their organizations' future.

DS D N A AS 6. Generally, there is a lack of "real" accountability by chief executive officers.

DS   D   N   A   AS   7. The actions of managers are being well monitored.

DS   D   N   A   AS   8. The focus of managers is on "downsizing" rather than "rightsizing."

DS   D   N   A   AS   9. Corporate restructuring today is *generally* problem driven rather than vision led.

DS   D   N   A   AS   10. When it comes to managing change, managers generally do an "excellent" job.

DS   D   N   A   AS   11. Generally, employee performance appraisals are used more for formality rather than for a meaningful and constructive purpose.

DS   D   N   A   AS   12. Managers possess less loyalty and integrity to their organizations than they should.

DS   D   N   A   AS   13. There is lack of trust between employees and managers.

DS   D   N   A   AS   14. Managers do an excellent job in placing (matching) employees in the right job (doing the right tasks) in the right organizations.

DS   D   N   A   AS   15. There has been a decline in the last twenty (20) years in managerial ethics.

DS   D   N   A   AS   16. Managers, in general, perceive their employees as an expense to the organization rather than as an investment.

DS   D   N   A   AS   17. American organizations are being managed by the "best" and the "brightest."

DS   D   N   A   AS   18. The word to describe managerial performance is "excellent."

DS   D   N   A   AS   19. The word to describe managerial performance is "mediocre."

DS   D   N   A   AS   20. The relation of managerial compensation packages to the compensation for the rest of the employees in the organization can be described as "equitable."

DS D N A AS 21. The wealth of the organization should be *proportionately* shared and enjoyed by those who have helped make it happen.

DS D N A AS 22. In actuality, "golden parachutes" are generally designed for the benefit of managers rather than for their organizations.

DS D N A AS 23. There should be a "cap" on managers' compensation.

DS D N A AS 24. Across-the-board salary increases may be easy to administer but are *less effective* than individualized increases.

DS D N A AS 25. I would favor "quarterly" raises for employees (similar to the way quarterly dividends are paid) instead of the traditional yearly raises.

DS D N A AS 26. Early "optional" retirement, as presently administered in corporate America, is sound.

DS D N A AS 27. Overall, early retirement benefits the organization rather than the employees.

DS D N A AS 28. Sabbaticals for managers should be a part of corporate policy.

DS D N A AS 29. Limiting the term in office for managers is a sound business strategy.

DS D N A AS 30. U.S. organizations are governed by strong and effective boards of directors.

DS D N A AS 31. In "reality," corporate boards of directors are "rubber stamps" for presidents and/or chief executive officers of organizations.

DS D N A AS 32. Corporations should be required to have a "public director" (to be selected by some group other than the stockholders) on their boards.

DS D N A AS 33. Chief executive officers should be required to hold annual "press conferences."

DS D N A AS 34. Organizations would function better if they stopped referring to their employees as either "labor" or "management," but instead refer to all of them by one name, i.e., "associates."

DS D N A AS 35. Organizations are doing a good job in managing management–labor disputes.

DS D N A AS 36. The *ultimate* responsibility to settle labor–management disputes lies with management.

DS D N A AS 37. Generally, whatever recommendation management makes, the board of directors approves.

DS D N A AS 38. The main factor in determining whether the organization is "winning" is whether it is making a profit for the shareholders.

DS D N A AS 39. Most companies fail because of poor management.

DS D N A AS 40. Most managers generally see the bottom line as proof of success.

DS D N A AS 41. There are employees who are promoted to managerial positions not because they possess the proper qualifications, but rather for political or personal reasons.

DS D N A AS 42. There are instances in organizations where "managerial malpractice" may be a proper legal remedy/cause.

DS D N A AS 43. Managers today, in general, adopt the philosophy, "If it ain't broke, don't fix it!"

DS D N A AS 44. Lack of ownership has affected the degree of commitment to the operation of the organization.

DS D N A AS 45. Lack of ownership has affected managerial performance.

DS D N A AS 46. Chief executive officers have too much power.

DS   D   N   A   AS   47. Managers today tend to take fewer risks than they have in the past.

DS   D   N   A   AS   48. It is the duty of managers to develop their subordinates to their potential.

DS   D   N   A   AS   49. The word to describe the overall management climate in corporate America is "mediocre."

DS   D   N   A   AS   50. The word to describe the overall management climate in corporate America is "excellent."

Comments:
Please feel free to comment on any of the above statements.

Part II

Please comment briefly on the following statements:

1. The main weakness of most managers today is: _____

2. The greatest strength of most managers is: _____

3. How do you react to and interpret the term "managerial malpractice"?

4. What are the characteristics of the "ideal manager"? _____

5. Overall, how would you rate the performance of U.S. managers? _____

6. Generally, do you feel that managers' compensation packages are out of line? _____

7. Should a manager's compensation package have a direct relation to the average wage earned by other employees (e.g., X times the average wage of the lowest paid employee in the organization)? _____

8. What are the obstacles to effective management? _____

   _____

   Can they be eliminated? If yes, how? _____

   _____

9. Please list acts, attitudes, and behavior of practicing managers which you feel are fatal managerial sins. (If possible, list them in descending order—#1 being the most deadly.)

   *NOTE—**Fatal managerial sin**,* as used herein, is managerial conduct which, in the *long run,* severely impacts adversely both the manager and the organization.

   1. _____

   2. _____

   3. _____

   4. _____

   5. _____

   6. _____

   7. _____

   8. _____

10. Do you feel managers today, in general, are *more* concerned with managing their careers than managing their organizations? _____

    _____

11. How would you describe the overall management climate in corporate America? _____

    _____

12. Do you feel that delegation is *effectively* used in organizations? _____

    _____

13. Who do you believe is the best manager in the U.S. today?
    Name: _____   Organization: _____
    Why? _____

    _____

14. Do you feel the following traits or conduct affect adversely (harm) the organization? Please rank them from 1 to 7, with one (1) being the *most harmful.* If *not harmful*, indicate by placing *NH.*

Character flaw—erosion of trust and integrity   _____

Interested more in managing own career than the organization   _____

Short-term scare—"managing for survival"   _____

Indecisiveness   _____

Fuzzy vision—"blurred focus"   _____

Perceiving employees as an expense rather than an investment   _____

Lack of "real" accountability   _____

15. Any written comments regarding _managerial performance,_ in general, would be greatly appreciated.

      _____

      _____

      _____

Important Note—Unless you sign this form giving permission to use your name with the statements you made, any statements used _would not be identified with you._ By signing this form, you authorize me to use all or part of the statement(s), and I may identify you with the statement.

Optional

Name: _____

      (please sign)

      _____

      (please type or print)

Title: _____

Address: _____

City: _____ State: _____ Zip: _____

Organization: _____

Telephone: (office) _____ Date: _____

THANK YOU VERY MUCH FOR YOUR HELP.

APPENDIX 2

Sample Provision for Compensation of Directors*

Upon election of the nominees proposed herein, the Board of Directors will consist of twelve members, of whom one is a salaried employee of the Company. Directors who are salaried employees receive no additional compensation for their service as directors. Directors who are not salaried employees of the Company ("non-employee directors") are paid a retainer of $30,000 per year and fee of $1,000 for each meeting of the Board of Directors and each meeting of any committee of the Board of Directors attended, together with the expenses of attendance. The chairman of each committee receives an additional annual stipend of $5,000.

Non-employee directors are eligible to receive stock options and restricted stock pursuant to the 1987 Stock Option Plan. In April of 1995, an option for 2,000 shares of Common Stock and an award of 200 shares of restricted stock were granted to each non-employee director under the 1987 Stock Option Plan. The Board of Directors also has adopted a pension plan for non-employee directors. Under the directors' pension plan, all non-employee directors who are 70 years of age and who have served as directors for five years are eligible to retire and be paid retirement income equal to the annual retainer paid to them as directors at the time of their retirement. Fifty percent of the annual pension amount payable to a retired director shall be paid to a retired director's spouse who survives him or her.

On an annual basis, each non-employee director is eligible to participate in the Directors' Deferred Compensation Plan which allows the deferral of fifty percent or more of the annual compensation (excluding expense reim-

---

* Used with permission from Caterpillar, Inc.'s Notice and Proxy Statement, March 1, 1996.

251

bursement) payable as a result of services performed on behalf of the Company. Ms. Affinito and Messrs. Fondahl, Goode, Gorter, Junkins and Yeutter have elected to defer their compensation for 1996. Directors participating in the Plan may elect to have the deferred compensation invested in an interest-bearing account, a share equivalent account representing the Company's Common Stock, or a combination of the two. The interest-bearing account accrues interest at the applicable prime rate. Deferred compensation in the share equivalent account is treated as though it were invested in Common Stock. If a participant makes a share election, dividend equivalents accrue to a participant's account quarterly, and each account is adjusted to reflect share ownership changes results from events such as a stock split. Participants have no voting rights with respect to the share equivalent account. All distributions from accounts are made in cash.

All directors of the Company participate in the Directors' Charitable Award Program ("Program"). The maximum amount of award payable with respect to each participant under the Program is $1 million and is based upon the director's length of service. A director continues to be eligible to participate in the Program after he or she terminates Board service. Payments under the Program are made in 10 annual installments and commence at the death of a director. The first five installments are paid to charities designated by the director and the last five installments are paid to the Company's Charitable Foundation ("Foundation"). The program is financed through the purchase of life insurance policies. Directors derive no financial benefit from this Program since all charitable deductions accrue solely to the Company. The purpose of the program is to acknowledge the service of the Company's directors, recognize the interest of the Company and its directors in supporting worthy educational institutions and charitable organizations, provide an additional means of support to the Foundation, and enhance the Company's director benefit program so that the Company is able to continue to attract and retain directors of the highest caliber.

This past year, the Company's Board of Directors received special recognition by being named one of the top five boards in the nation by *Chief Executive* magazine (November 1995 issue). The Company would like to take this opportunity to congratulate the Board of Directors on receiving that well-deserved honor.

Index